Cambridge Studies in Oral and Literate Culture   2

FOR THE SAKE OF SIMPLE FOLK

Cambridge Studies in Oral and Literate Culture

Edited by Peter Burke and Ruth Finnegan

This series is designed to address the question of the significance of literacy in human societies; it will assess its importance for political, economic, social and cultural development, and examine how what we take to be the common functions of writing are carried out in oral cultures.

The series will be inter-disciplinary, but with particular emphasis on social anthropology and social history, and will encourage cross-fertilization between these disciplines; it will also be of interest to readers in allied fields, such as sociology, folklore and literature. Although it will include some monographs, the focus of the series will be on theoretical and comparative aspects rather than detailed description, and the books will be presented in a form accessible to non-specialist readers interested in the general subject of literacy and orality.

Books in the series
1 Nigel Philipps: *'Sijobang': Sung Narrative Poetry of West Sumatra*
2 R.W. Scribner: *For the Sake of Simple Folk: Popular Propaganda for the German Reformation*

FOR THE SAKE OF SIMPLE FOLK

Popular Propaganda for the German Reformation

R.W. SCRIBNER

Lecturer in History
University of Cambridge

CAMBRIDGE UNIVERSITY PRESS

CAMBRIDGE
LONDON   NEW YORK   NEW ROCHELLE
MELBOURNE   SYDNEY

Published by the Press Syndicate of the University of Cambridge
The Pitt Building, Trumpington Street, Cambridge CB2 1RP
32 East 57th Street, New York, NY 10022, USA
296 Beaconsfield Parade, Middle Park, Melbourne 3206, Australia

First published 1981

Printed in Great Britain at the University Press, Cambridge

Library of Congress catalogue card number: 81-7710

British Library Cataloguing in Publication Data
Scribner, R.W.
For the sake of simple folk: popular
propaganda for the German Reformation.
– (Cambridge studies in oral and literate
culture; 2)
1. Reformation – Germany 2. Propaganda
I. Title
274.3′06   BR305.2
ISBN 0 521 24192 8

CONTENTS

PREFACE

This book was begun several years ago as a diversion while working on broader themes of the social history of the German Reformation. Subsequently, it has grown far beyond the original conception of a short essay on visual evidence and how it might be of use to the historian. Many of its approaches look less innovatory now than they seemed then, with the growing interest of the last few years in popular belief and culture, and especially in carnival. Often the historian feels like a lonely swimmer striking out for a distant shore, when he or she is really only being carried by the tide, and arrives to find many other swimmers on the same beach. I hope, however, that the work retains something of its first intention: to present a new approach to the analysis of popular mentalities, and to show that there is much work to be done in a neglected area of research.

The approach was also intended to be interdisciplinary, drawing on a range of subjects strange to a mere historian, such as art history, folklore, sociology and semiology. There is always a danger that a do-it-yourself enthusiast who takes up a craftsman's tools will produce a botched job. Here I must crave the good-humoured indulgence of the specialists whose disciplines I have tried to apply to an essentially historical study. I am aware also of the fragmentary nature of the book, that a good many questions have been put to one side, or reserved for examination in broader contexts. To this extent, it still retains its character as a diversion, and many of its unresolved questions more rightly find a place in a systematic investigation of the social history of the German Reformation.

There are many acknowledgements to be made for advice and assistance received in the course of producing this book. Much of the groundwork was laid while I was a fellow of the Alexander von Humboldt Stiftung in Heidelberg. The cost of assembling the photographs was greatly assisted by a very generous grant from the British Academy. I would like to express my gratitude to both of these bodies. The Department of Historical and Literary Studies, Portsmouth Polytechnic, helped in numerous ways to facilitate research, and I owe a special debt for her help and interest to Sandra Taylor of the Portsmouth Polytechnic Department of Fine Art. I should like to thank for her assistance Dr Elisabeth Bliembach of the Berlin Staatsbibliothek.

I owe thanks to many others. Jack McManners and Roslyn Pesman first aroused my interest in art as historical evidence. Bruce Mansfield has given unflagging support over many years of friendship. To Geoff Dickens I owe more than I can express here for encouragement and support, not least for his conviction several years ago that the social history of the Reformation was worth more attention than historians were then willing to concede. Characteristically, we became less supervisor and doctorand and more comrades in arms, assisted by our shared liking for atrocious puns. Peter Burke has been an unfailing source of fresh ideas and enthusiasm, and this book owes a great deal to many hours of discussion, mostly in pubs, we have had on its themes. Useful suggestions were made by Gerhard Benecke, Pat Collinson, Marion O'Connor, Keith Moxey and Alison Stewart. The final version has benefited greatly from Lyndal Roper's sharp mind and rigorous sense of style. Most importantly, Robyn Dasey brought a keen interest and patient encouragement from beginning to end. I hope that all these who have shared in the making of this book will forgive me if I have not always followed their advice. The work is the better for their help, and they should not be held responsible for any of its inadequacies.

In order to keep the book within economic limits, I have adopted the author-date system for modern bibliographical references, and retained the traditional style for sixteenth-century works. Where publisher, place and date are given in square brackets, the attribution is uncertain; firm information on these is given in round brackets. For little-known sixteenth-century works I have cited a location wherever possible, also where the variation of editions is worthy of note. Wherever possible I have given English titles in the text, and retained the originals in the notes. I have used English versions of proper names where these have become common English usage, as with Frederick the Wise; otherwise, German names have been used throughout.

Because of its attempt to combine print and picture, this has been a difficult book to produce. I would specially like to thank Sue Allen-Mills and Chris Lyall Grant for their patient cooperation throughout. Restrictions imposed by format and the need for economy in production have meant that illustrations could not always be reproduced in the size an author might have wished. In some cases, the original printed text of a broadsheet has been omitted from an illustration, although it is closely summarised in the analysis. I must beg the reader's understanding in this, while complimenting Cambridge University Press on the high quality of reproduction they have achieved in small format.

ACKNOWLEDGEMENTS

Photographs used in this work were supplied as follows:

The Warburg Institute: ills. 1, 3, 4, 10, 21–2, 27–8, 30, 39, 49, 57–61, 64, 70–2, 75, 84–5, 100, 115–26, 132, 146, 158, 163, 165–7, 170, 181, 185.

The British Library: ills. 6, 8, 9, 11, 13–14, 16, 25, 34, 43–4, 50, 52, 68–9, 76, 81–2, 90, 92, 94, 97–9, 101, 105–6, 108–14, 127, 136–7, 141–4, 148, 153, 157, 159, 161, 172–3, 188–94.

The British Museum: ills. 32–3, 77, 107, 150–2, 171.

Germanisches Nationalmuseum Nuremberg: ills. 2, 5, 17, 31, 38, 46, 48, 51, 55, 66–7, 73, 80, 168.

Staatliche Museen, Berlin-Dahlem, Kupferstichkabinett: ills. 19, 29, 40, 53, 62, 65, 78–9, 87, 93, 104, 128, 149, 176, 182.

Staatsbibliothek Berlin, Handschriftenabteilung: ills. 24, 35, 37, 63, 129–30, 145, 160, 175, 177, 179, 187.

Foto Marburg: ills. 45, 47, 102–3, 183–4.

Zentralbibliothek Zurich: ills. 23, 83, 96, 135, 174.

Universitätsbibliothek Göttingen: ills. 41, 164, 169.

Graphische Sammlung Albertina, Vienna: ills. 26, 91, 180.

Schlossmuseum Coburg: ill. 36.

Universitätsbibliothek Erlangen-Nürnberg: ill. 89.

Staatliche Graphische Sammlung, Munich: ill. 86.

Kupferstichsammlung, Alte Pinakothek, Munich: ill. 134.

The author expresses his gratitude for permission to publish. All other photographs from the author's private collection.

ABBREVIATIONS

Albertina	Graphische Sammlung Albertina, Vienna.
BL	British Library.
BM	British Museum.
Berlin	Staatsbibliothek, Preussischer Kulturbesitz, Berlin, Handschriftenabteilung.
Dahlem	Staatliche Museen, Preussischer Kulturbesitz, Berlin-Dahlem, Kupferstichkabinett.
GNM	Germanisches Nationalmuseum, Nuremberg.
STC	*Short-title Catalogue of Books Printed in the German-speaking Countries . . . from 1455 to 1600 now in the British Museum*, 1962, London.
UB	Universitätsbibliothek.
WA	*D. Martin Luthers Werke. Kritische Gesamtausgabe*, 1883–1978, Weimar.
Wickiana	Graphische Sammlung Wickiana, Staatsbibliothek Zurich.
Zurich	Staatsbibliothek Zurich.

I thought it good to put the old Passional with the little prayer book, above all for the sake of children and simple folk, who are more easily moved by pictures and images to recall divine history than through mere words or doctrines.

Luther, Passional (1522)

1

PRINTING, PRINTS AND PROPAGANDA

This book is a study of visual propaganda, and of its role in the dissemination of the evangelical movement during the first half-century of the Reformation in Germany. A good deal has been written about the importance of printed propaganda for the spread of the Reformation, and the contribution of visual propaganda to this process has often been recognised, but it has been the subject of no thorough or systematic investigation.[1] This study attempts to plug that gap, but it also seeks to go further, and to examine how the Reformation may have impinged on the broadest masses of the people in sixteenth-century Germany. This is the sense in which the term 'popular' is used in the title, rather than the other meaning 'most acclaimed' or 'most sought after'. Its argument is that through a study of visual propaganda we may gain a wider understanding of how the Reformation appealed to common folk than by concentrating attention more narrowly on printed propaganda alone.

Such a claim may seem surprising, for the importance of printing for the rapid spread of Reformation ideas was recognised in the sixteenth century and has become a commonplace of modern historiography. As Elizabeth Eisenstein has pointed out, printing laid many of the foundations on which the movement of religious reform was able to build, from vernacular bibles and books of popular devotion, to clerical education and theological scholarship. Moreover, from the very beginning of Luther's revolt against the Church, the new religious ideas were made available to a reading public almost as soon as they were written. An important part of this process was the conscious use of printed propaganda addressed to a mass audience, to the entire German people. Indeed, it was one of the great successes of such propaganda that it presented the new belief as a popular movement with a mass base.[2]

There is a danger of being beguiled by the very skill of Reformation propaganda into accepting its own claims at face value. The role played by printing is undeniable, but over-concentration on the printed word may seriously distort our understanding of how Reformation ideas spread among the population at large. Printed propaganda was addressed to the entire German people, but few of them were able to read it, for the Reformation emerged in a society with limited literacy. It is not possible to measure literacy in early sixteenth-century Germany with any accuracy, but it was certainly restricted both geographically and socially. It was more concentrated in towns and in the more culturally advanced south-west. The presence of schools is only a crude indicator, but in Wurttemberg there were as many as eighty-nine schools by

1

the 1520s, and at least half of the towns boasted a school. By contrast, there was no more than a handful of schools in Saxony by the late 1520s, all of them urban.[3]

Literacy was also highly socially stratified. Late-medieval society has been characterised as oligo-literate, where reading ability was a mark of social stratification, distinguishing between 'clerks' and common folk.[4] As Rolf Engelsing observes, a high proportion of the German reading public at the end of the fifteenth century must have been clergymen.[5] There was a strong impulse towards 'pragmatic literacy', literacy as a tool of trade, especially among craftsmen and merchants, but this was a long way from popular literacy, from 'the use of writing as an autonomous mode of communication by the majority of members of a society'.[6] Printing created the potential for mass literacy, but it was a long time before it lost its sense of novelty and became commonplace among the broader social classes. Engelsing estimates that literacy may have been between ten and thirty per cent in the towns, but nationally it was probably no higher than five per cent.[7] In the period with which this book deals, access to the printed word was probably restricted to a small, if growing, educational elite.

It is important, of course, to distinguish between literacy as ability to write and as ability to read. Indeed, it could be argued that Reformation ideas aided the spread of reading ability as much as printing assisted their dissemination. As Engelsing points out, a time of high ideological interest, such as the Reformation, the French Revolution or the age of Social Democracy, creates a demand for knowledge which increases reading (and writing) ability. At the beginning of the sixteenth century there were only about forty editions of works in German produced each year, yet in 1519 alone there were 111 new titles on the market. In 1523 there were 498 titles, and one-third of these came from Luther himself. Taking the works of Luther and his opponents as a whole, a total of 418 of the 1523 titles were evoked by the Reformation.[8]

The scale and impact of this sudden leap forward can only be understood by bearing in mind that the Reformation emerged in a society still heavily dependent on oral communication. Because the Reformation produced a religion of literate bible-reading laymen, and Luther made such an important contribution to German literature, we can too readily assume that the religious revival took root primarily by literate means. Yet Luther was as much a man of the spoken as of the printed word, to which his innumerable sermons bear witness, and the Reformation itself was predominantly a preaching revival. Printing was, in fact, an addition to, not a replacement for, oral communication. Indeed, it was as likely as not that most people would have experienced the printed word only indirectly, by having it read aloud to them.[9]

This changes considerably the question of how to understand the nature and impact of Reformation propaganda. Marshall McLuhan pointed out that one should not look only at 'pure' modes of communication, such as print or the spoken word, but also at what he called 'hybridisation of media'.[10] Purely oral society may be envisaged as a series of face-to-face conversations. Literate society provides alternative means of transmission in reading and writing, but it also creates the possibility of hybrid forms, such as reading aloud, or lecturing on or from a text. The process of transmission involved here is more complex than that of the 'pure' medium. Reading can also be 'hybridised' in the same way: one may read the linear products of alphabetic writing, but one can also read non-alphabetic signs, which may be arranged non-lineally. This is the advantage of visual images – they can be read in any direction.[11] Even when alphabetic writing is incorporated into visual images, it need not be confined to a horizontal axis, but may appear scattered at every angle throughout the work. This occurs frequently in Reformation broadsheets, and shows that this kind of non-linear reading was far from expunged by the effects of print (see examples in ills. 27–9, pp. 38–41).

To assess the importance of various forms of communication in spreading Reformation ideas, we must be aware of the entire range of what was available to and used by the broadest masses of the people at the beginning of the sixteenth century. Engelsing attempts to do this with a useful definition of 'reading ability' in Germany at the time. He suggests that this should be understood in terms of three basic modes: reading, in our accepted, narrow usage; listening; and looking. In early popular books, listening was given equal weight with looking and reading, for reading aloud seems then to have been the custom. Looking was given at least as much weight as reading. Sebastian Brant, for example, aimed his work at three kinds of reader: those who would read him in German, in Latin, and those who would read the woodcuts richly supplied throughout. Only gradually, during the course of the sixteenth century, was there an advance of reading in the narrow sense. This, Engelsing argues, was a result of ideology and propaganda, which offered greater entice-ment to reading than just to looking.[12] For those with little or no reading ability in the narrow sense, listening or looking would have been the major means of acquiring their knowledge of the Reformation. Concentration on the printed word alone thus offers only limited access to the process by which the new movement was spread to the people. We must, rather, see print in relation to oral and visual forms of communication.

One of the most important defining characteristics of late-medieval popular culture was that it was intensely visual. Let us consider the nature of this visual sense. In the realm of popular belief there was a strong desire for the mysteries of religion to be made visible. So Christ the Lord of the world, the Kyrios, the victorious Saviour, was replaced in popular devotion by the infant Jesus in the crib, by Christ the good shepherd or by Christ suffering and dying on the cross.[13] More striking was the attempt to represent theo-logical notions, such as the incarnation, in the crudest visual terms, as with statues of the Madonna whose stomach could be opened to reveal the Trinity inside.[14]

Seeing was an important part of devotion, in what has been called the 'salvific display' (*heilbringende Schau*).[15] A.L. Meyer has indicated three ways of 'seeing' common to late-medieval belief. One was 'mystical seeing', a desire to see through mystical piety some kind of vision or appearance which gave certainty of salvation. Although this was a form of contemplation or even ecstasy, the desired effect was nonetheless visual. A second was a 'seeing of mysteries', seeing with the bodily eye rather than through an inner vision. Here one wished to have made visible a form of sacred action beyond earthly reality. This led to the desire to see the host displayed at the moment of consecration, or afterwards placed on view in a monstrance. A third kind was a 'purely bodily seeing' which involved a sensual connection with the object. This was a superstitious seeing close to magic, entailing a belief in the efficacy and power of the viewing itself.[16] This kind of seeing was involved in popular devotion to the cloth of Veronica, a commemoration of the true features of Christ. Contemplation of this image 'made present the holy', and by looking one received both spiritual healing and salvation.[17] Similarly, pictures of the saints evoked superstitious reverence: the depiction of the holy personage was thought to make them somehow present.[18] This veered into magic, for example, with the custom of dipping the holy lance, used to pierce the side of Christ, into wine and then piercing illustrations of the heart of Christ with it. The visual representation became holy by contact with the holy lance, and so gave the possessor access to its supernatural power.[19]

Such forms of devotion presupposed a highly developed visual sense, and its importance was fully realised at the time. The Church attempted to channel such *Schaufrömmigkeit* or 'visual piety' into more controlled areas of ecclesiastical devotion by displays of relics. At places of pilgrimage special emphasis was laid both on the visit and on the viewing of specific holy objects. In many bulls of indulgence the *visio* was particularly stressed, and certain pictures were often accorded a status as great as that of relics themselves.[20] Nor surprisingly, this provoked a good deal of debate on the role of images and strong condemnation of 'salvific display'. Nicolaus of Cusa wrote against both the display of the host and the viewing of pictures, while on the other side advocates of images stressed their importance as a means of communication. In fifteenth-century England images were defended against the criticisms of the Lollards as the 'books of the common man'. The tract *Dives and Pauper* justified their use on three grounds: that they brought men to think on Christ's incarnation, life and Passion; that they turned the heart to devotion; and that they served as a book for the unlearned, so that what the clergy could read in books could be read by the layman in imagery and painting.[21]

The development of printing gave an enormous impetus to these visual features of popular culture. Not just, as McLuhan claims, because printing by itself so enormously extended man's visual ability, but because it developed alongside, and in conjunction with, mass pictorial reproduction. Printing made possible the exactly repeatable literary statement, but the print created the exactly repeatable visual statement. It thus fulfilled the same communication function for the illiterate and the semi-literate that printing fulfilled for those able to read in the narrow sense. Indeed, the most effective early forms of printed popular literature were predominantly visual – blockbooks, the *Bilderbogen* or primitive comic strip and the broadsheet.[22] These all relied on the use of the woodcut, in the technology of the time the most durable means of mass pictorial reproduction. Although the woodcut could reach great heights in the hands of masters like Dürer or Cranach, part of its appeal was its simplicity of line, and so the ease with which it could be read. Like homemade gin, it was cheap, crude and effective.

Indeed, we can say with reasonable certainty that well before the invention of printing, the first item of mass circulation was the popular woodcut, dating from the end of the fourteenth century. In its earliest form it seems to have been used as a commemorative illustration of a pilgrimage, a memento of the religious experience which could be taken home and used to recall it. From here it passed into use as an item of popular devotion. Pinned to the wall, showing a depiction of the suffering Christ or of some popular saint, such as St Christopher, it could serve for private meditation and devotion. As we have already seen, it could also acquire the sacral features of the holy personage, and some popular woodcuts were used as talismans and carried in a little bag hung around the neck like a magic charm.[23] Given its cheapness and ease of production, the popular woodcut has far more claims to being the first item of mass communication than the elite form of the printed book.

We have no reliable estimates of the numbers in which the popular woodcut circulated, but we can gauge the the possibilities from sales of that other item of mass production and consumption of the age, the pilgrimage token. A best-selling book would probably find around 20,000 readers in all its editions in the early sixteenth century, but there were claims that as many pilgrimage tokens were sold in a single day. This figure may be suspect as the exaggeration of a chronicler, but we have reliable evidence that in Regensburg in 1519–20 some 10,813 lead tokens and 1799 silver tokens were sold.[24] Given an equal demand for the cheap and popular woodcut, there is no reason why an equally high number should not have been in circulation. It has been claimed that the popular broadsheet appeared in editions of only 350, but in 1522 the authorities in Leipzig seized 1500 copies of a broadsheet attacking Jerome Emser. Moreover the woodcut block was capable of yielding perhaps three or four thousand copies before it began to deteriorate, and woodcut illustrations were often passed from printer to printer. The same illustrations were used by various printers for different editions of the Bible in the 1520s and 1530s.[25] Given that the printed book usually had average editions of around a thousand copies, the popular woodcut was more than its equal as a means of mass communication.

As a mode of mass communication the popular woodcut thus had unrivalled potential, yet we rarely find it used in its 'pure' form. Inevitably, it became 'hybridised' with print to produce the woodcut broadsheet, overcoming thereby one of its major drawbacks as a means of propaganda. Pictorial representation can be a crude and effective means of communication, but it can never escape the danger of ambiguity. The addition of the printed word enabled it to spell out its message unambiguously. It thus served as a meeting point between the illiterate, the semi-literate and the literate. For those unable to read, the message of a popular broadsheet could be read from the visual images alone. More effectively, its printed text could be read out by someone who could read, creating a situation of oral interchange which was probably the most powerful means of spreading the Reformation.[26]

The importance of oral transmission for the dissemination of the evangelical message was fully realised by the writers of Reformation propaganda works. A collection of extracts from popular prophecies published in 1522 contains an injunction to pass the pamphlet on to another reader, and to discuss it with them.[27] Another pamphlet expresses the opinion that if one wishes to know the nature of the Antichrist, one should go to a brother who can read, who could then read out the Epistles of St Paul.[28] That such injunctions were put into practice can be seen from an incident in Nuremberg in 1524, when a clerk named Erasmus Wisperger was arrested for reading one of Karlstadt's works aloud on the marketplace.[29] Even for those who could read, the popular broadsheet made propaganda more persuasive and entertaining. We have an excellent example of the process described in a 1524 pamphlet, *A Dialogue between a Christian and a Jew . . . concerning Christ the Cornerstone.*[30]

A Jew and an evangelical Christian fall into conversation in an inn, and the Jew produces a woodcut he has picked up on his travels. The Christian uses the woodcut to explain to the Jew the main points of evangelical belief as the woodcut depicts them. When they part, the inn servant, who has listened to them with interest, promises to set their conversation down in print, along with the woodcut. The case shows the ideal balance of oral, visual and printed means of communication as it is found during the Reformation. Whether the discussion is fictitious or not is of little relevance; more importantly, the author of the 1524 pamphlet wished to show that Reformation ideas were spread effectively by the spoken word aided by the use of pictures. The obvious intention of the pamphlet was to encourage the reader to do the same in like circumstances.

Whether it occurred by design or oversight, the woodcut was omitted from the published pamphlet, although a picture exists which corresponds to that described (ill. 170, p. 212). Ideally, one would have expected to find it pub-

lished with the printed text as a woodcut broadsheet, but the pamphlet contains thirty-two pages of pure, unrelieved print.[31] This points unequivocally
to the long-term triumph of printing over the print as a major form of mass
communication, a fact of which there could be no doubt by the middle of
the sixteenth century. Not that there was necessarily any great leap forward
in literacy, and so less need to provide information to the unlearned by visual
means. It may simply indicate that publishers now had a sufficiently large
market among a reading public to dispense with the task of combining woodcuts with movable type. No doubt readers were also more accustomed to
absorbing information through print alone. Broadsheets continued to be produced for popular dissemination, and book illustration continued to play a
part in providing technical information and as entertainment. Title illustrations, then as now, enticed potential readers by suggesting the attractiveness
of the printed contents. However, the second half of the sixteenth century
saw a noticeable deterioration in technique, which robbed the woodcut of
much of its simplicity of line and so of its effectiveness. It was gradually
replaced by the engraving as the chief form of pictorial representation.[32]
Meanwhile, it was printing which gained dominance as the chief means of
non-oral communication.

At the beginning of the Reformation this development was yet in the
future, and we must resist the temptation to read history backwards in terms
of the inevitable triumph of the printed word. At the beginning of the Reformation, printing was only one of the chief modes through which the Reformation message was transmitted. If we wish to see how it impinged on the
broadest levels of the population, we must look at the whole spectrum of
communication of the time. Here we are faced with 'pure' modes — print,
oral forms and pictorial forms — and with hybrids of these. We shall refer
frequently to the printed propaganda throughout this study, but it cannot be
taken as normative for propagandist appeals to the 'common man'. It would
be immensely valuable to have access to oral modes of propaganda, and of
course we can see traces of some of these in print, as verbal artifacts — in
printed sermons, ballads, songs, proverbs, sayings, reported conversations.[33]
It would also be useful to trace the role of printing in oral communication, in
reading aloud to an audience or in discussion of printed works. This kind of
study would have its own methodological problems, not least that of sifting
how far the evidence has been affected by being recorded in writing or in
print. This is not a task we can pursue here. We shall attempt to understand
popular propaganda through visual representation and its hybridised forms,
which link images to the printed word, or images to the artifacts of oral modes.

The major sources for popular propaganda in this sense are the woodcut
broadsheet, with or without text, book illustrations, titlepages and illustrated
books. These comprise a major category of evidence usually ignored by historians in their preoccupations with written or printed sources. Where such

visual evidence has been used, it has most frequently been merely to illustrate works of history, rarely with any analysis of its visual content.[34] The survival rate of such evidence is certainly low, for it has often been a victim of its own popularity. A single-sheet broadsheet bought for a few pence is soon discarded, or becomes so tattered in passing from hand to hand that it quickly becomes mere litter. Such items found their way only accidentally into official archives, and were preserved only through the mania for curiosities of some private collector, or for their artistic value.[35]

Pioneering work to make popular broadsheets better known was carried out at the beginning of the nineteenth century by H.A. von Derschau, who published three useful volumes of woodcuts in their original size.[36] It was only in the 1920s, however, that Max Geisberg began to publish an extensive collection of extant sixteenth-century German broadsheets, some of them pulled afresh from original blocks which had survived the passage of time.[37] Geisberg carried his work up to 1550, and began work on a parallel edition of book illustrations which did not progress beyond the first few issues.[38] The broadsheet collection was issued in loose-leaf folios, clearly aimed at the art collector and unmanageable for general study purposes.[39] Only recently has it been edited and rearranged in more accessible form by W.L. Strauss, who then continued the edition up to the end of the sixteenth century. In this second collection Strauss included many items overlooked by Geisberg and corrected some of his errors, although some errors also crept into the Strauss editions.[40] In 1976 the Castle Museum at Gotha also issued a facsimile edition of fifty of its more interesting items.[41] However, these editions do not exhaust the rich resources of materials available for the study of visual propaganda. This study is based on work in several of the major collections of broadsheets, as well as on published editions.[42] To these must be added the extensive pamphlet collections from the Reformation period, especially that in the British Library.[43]

There are two other questions about visual propaganda to be considered here. How are we to approach it as propaganda, and how as visual evidence? Let us examine these in turn. In general, propaganda is a deliberate attempt to influence people's opinions and actions, but by itself it provides access not to what people believed, rather to what the propagandist would have them believe. This axiom is often overlooked in the study of Reformation propaganda, which is analysed as though it provided direct information about the views of its audience.[44] Yet from the propaganda alone we cannot tell how well it was understood, nor how deep an influence it has exerted. It is true that a propagandist cannot aim his message too wide of the major concerns of his audience, and at best he may hope to exploit their fears and anxieties. Most propaganda, therefore, will probably reflect in some way the 'common opinion' of its age. The problem of any analysis is to discern what is genuinely common opinion and what is propagandist fiction. This can only be achieved by close study of the techniques and process of the propaganda.

The task of Reformation propaganda was primarily to spread and win allegiance to the evangelical message. This posed several problems. The message had to be transmitted in clear and easily assimilable form; there was the need to break down old patterns of thought and values; and one had to create powerful symbols of attachment to the new movement. Finally, these had to be integrated into an ordered structure of values and allegiances, into a new 'symbolic universe'.[45] A basic technique of propaganda is pretended discourse. Although it can have little or no genuine dialogue with its audience, it often works on the assumption that it does. In part, this is because it assumes that there is an audience 'out there' on which it is having an effect, and because it must anticipate the response of that audience in order to achieve its maximum effect. One method of creating this 'dialogue' is to contact its audience through images and symbols familiar to both, and then to transform these on the propagandist's terms. By a process of amplification and reinforcement, a gradual shift from one 'symbolic universe' to another is brought about.[46] This process is set out in its ideal form in those pamphlets depicting a dialogue about Reformation ideas. Typical of the genre is one in which a son wins his father to Lutheran belief through reasoned discussion.[47]

We cannot take such works as in any way representative of real discussions about religion, but they do provide a foothold for further analysis. We can say with some certainty what kind of people the propaganda is aimed at, and so the 'symbolic universe' it seeks to transform. For Reformation propaganda this was the broadest mass of the German people, the 'common man', typified sometimes by the peasant, sometimes by the artisan, sometimes by the ordinary citizen. These were all defined by virtue of being 'ordinary folk', so that the common 'symbolic universe' assumed by the propagandist was that of sixteenth-century German popular culture and belief.[48] Our task will be to study the kind of raw material chosen from this area and how it was transformed.

How are we to assess the effectiveness of the propaganda? It is an unfortunate difficulty of the study of sixteenth-century propaganda that we can glean little real quantitative information about its success. We must resist the temptation to measure its effects in terms of numbers of editions of propaganda works. As has been said of the measurement of literacy, a new form of publication, or an increase in the volume of production, may be poor indicators of an overall ability to read or write.[49] Similarly, the number of editions of a particular propaganda work may tell us about its popularity relative to other printed works, but little about its overall impact on the broadest range of the population. We may certainly see its effects in broad cultural traces, such as the acceptance of certain words or phrases into common usage. By this test, for example, we can point to the undoubted failure of Thomas Murner's anti-Lutheran propaganda. For all its wit and skill, it has left few cultural traces, and not one word or work of Murner's has passed into the German linguistic heritage.[50]

The only reliable test is to study the impact of propaganda on behaviour, a task which falls well beyond the scope of this book. However, we can attempt to assess how far the propaganda has been successful in transforming the various images and symbols from which it seeks to construct its 'symbolic universe'. This is a means of testing the structural effectiveness of propaganda, to see what new frameworks of values it has created, and how well these conform to its stated intentions. This will be a question we shall pursue throughout this study, and to which we shall return in more detail in the final chapter.

How are we to analyse our material as visual evidence? It would be possible to approach it in terms of the artists and publishers, but these will receive only marginal attention throughout the following discussion. In part, this is because so many of the broadsheets are anonymous and can be dated only approximately. There are also many thorny and unresolved questions about the role of the artist, the woodcutter, the publisher and the author of any printed text in the overall production.[51] To deal adequately with such questions requires a separate study, or even a series of studies, such as that by Zschelletzschky on the brothers Behem and Georg Pencz.[52] Our purpose here is different, to analyse the structure of visual propaganda in and through its images and symbols, to see how it appealed to popular mentalities in the sixteenth century. To this end we shall use some of the concepts and methods of iconography and of semiology.

Iconography is concerned with the description and classification of images, and leads to the more specific study of iconology, the study of the function of images in allegory and symbolism.[53] Semiology is concerned with the study of signs, whatever their nature – whether images, words, gestures or visual conventions such as traffic signs. It regards the sign as constituted by two basic elements, the signifier and the signified. Among traffic signs, for example, a red light can be broken down into the colour red (signifier) and the command 'Halt!' (signified). Or to use an example from the period under discussion, a triple tiara (signifier) signifies the pope (signified) among the system of signs denoting Church offices. Both signifier and signified together form the sign, which thus refers to a relationship between the two elements. Like structuralism, with which it has close kinship, semiology is thus concerned with the latent significance embodied in structural relationships.[54]

Systems of signs can be described as codes, with the implication that knowledge of the code enables the reader of any number or combination of signs to decipher the message they transmit. Sign systems can also be described in terms of 'language' and 'speech'. Language is the set of conventions necessary for communication, speech the actual practice of language. Thus, there could be a 'language' of heraldry, of colours or of attributes of the saints. In such cases, the 'speech' would be the actual use made of these possibilities in any given context. Signs may thus be described in two ways, in terms of actual or of potential relationships. Semiologists describe the former as a syntagma, the latter as a paradigm. In any combination of signs, all those present in it go to make up the syntagma, whereas the paradigm consists of the range of potential images which might have been chosen.[55]

We can illustrate this through the example of a depiction of St George and the dragon by Hans Burgkmair (ill. 1). St George is represented on horseback inside a courtyard or courtly building. His armour and that of his horse have the elaborate decoration of the court pageant. He holds a broken lance, the other half of which has pierced the dragon lying dead under the horse's hooves. A princess holding a lamb on a lead kneels before him, and a Latin inscription identifies him as St George, the Christian knight. This composition constitutes a syntagma with a definite number of specific signs. In this case the paradigm is constituted by the many different ways in which St George might have been depicted.[56] Iconography uses somewhat different terminology to refer to much the same phenomena. Paradigms are similar to what E.H. Gombrich has called 'schemata'. These are conceptual models or formulae on which an artist may draw in depicting particular themes. Gombrich sees the artist as gradually adapting or 'correcting' his schema until it fits the particular subject in hand. Schema and correction thus correspond to paradigm and syntagma.[57] In the following chapters we shall be concerned particularly

1   Hans Burgkmair, *St George*, BM

with what kind of paradigms or schemata were drawn upon by Reformation propaganda, and how these were actually put to use 'in syntagma'. That is, we are interested both in the 'language' of visual propaganda and in its 'speech'. Analytically we shall be examining each example as a 'text' which can be broken down into its component signs and sign systems. However, to avoid overloading the linguistic metaphor and lapsing into jargon, the use of such technical terms will be limited. Schema or paradigm will be used throughout for the potential use of signs, while more descriptive terms such as composition or assembly of signs will be used, along with the term 'text', to refer to the actual use made of such models, the syntagma.

Reflection on the example of Burgkmair's St George also makes clear that any visual text may embody a number of sign systems, involving a number of different 'languages'. It draws, for example, on the sign system of attributes of the saints, and on the system of dress fashions. These sign systems will be referred to as 'codes', although some semiologists have reservations about the conceptual precision of the term. Yveline Baticle, writing about the film poster, points out that an individual image or combination of images could involve several different codes. Some examples are:

code of transmission: related to the physical composition of the image –
    for example, whether a painting, a woodcut, an engraving, a book
    illustration.

morphological code: graphic composition of the image: use of forms, of
    light and dark, of assemblies of lines. For example, important use is
    made in Reformation propaganda of light and dark, and of spatial
    division into antitheses (see chapter 3).

linguistic code: language or the use of language – Latin, German, slang,
    pejoratives, 'low' language.

gestural code: gestures, attitudes signifying moods, states, roles.[58]

In this study we are particularly interested in the kinds of codes which were used to transmit the Reformation message, and in how they were adapted or created for this purpose.

In this way, we shall apply a single method to analyse both visual evidence and propaganda, for in both cases we shall be investigating underlying structural relationships. On this basis, we shall proceed as follows. First, we shall discuss one sign of very great importance for the Reformation, the image of Luther in early evangelical propaganda. The next chapter will examine what system of signs was associated with the opponents of the new religious movement. Here we shall pay particular attention to the structural relationship between the component parts of individual woodcuts, looking at how a 'text' conveyed its message or messages. Taken together, these two chapters explore the 'mechanics' of Reformation visual propaganda, and provide a method of analysis which is taken for granted in later chapters, even though it is not employed subsequently with such rigour. In the following three chapters, we shall examine two large and loosely defined codes of major importance for visual propaganda, popular culture and popular belief, and how they were adapted to transmit the Reformation message. A further chapter will discuss the Reformation's attempt to create signs and codes which imparted its positive theological message. In the final chapter, after a brief glance at Catholic counter-propaganda, we shall attempt to draw some conclusions from the study.

The argument of this chapter can be summed up under three headings. First, Reformation propaganda is useful to our historical understanding of the Reformation only when we study its processes and methods. Second, that we should look at genuinely popular propaganda to understand how Reformation ideas were spread. Third, it will be useful to employ some methods and concepts from iconography and semiology. However, this study is intended to be primarily a contribution to the social and cultural history of the Reformation. Its overall aim is to discover in visual evidence some traces of popular mentalities which have left too little trace in printed or written records.

2

IMAGES OF LUTHER 1519–25

In any discussion of the Reformation, the first name mentioned is invariably that of Luther. The first mass awareness at the beginning of the 1520s that some great religious upheaval was under way was linked to his person. It is, therefore, most important to ask how Luther was depicted or represented during these years. We can trace numerous published Luther portraits from the early 1520s.[1] Allowing for variations and modifications, there were no less than twenty-six different versions. Luther also appears in nineteen illustrations, that is, depictions containing a narrative element or some form of action which includes other figures besides Luther. He features as well in decorative borders of several titlepages, although the overall effect is intended to be more than merely 'decorative': for example, where Luther points to the risen Christ in another part of the border.[2] These depictions can be used to analyse the semiological importance of Luther's image during the decisive early years of the Reformation.

We shall deal first with the portraits. The earliest known representation of Luther dates from 1519 (ill. 2). It appears on the titlepage of a published sermon, which Luther had originally delivered when attending the Leipzig Debate, and was probably produced as a result of widespread interest in the event.[3] Luther is set in a tondo, wearing the beret and gown of a doctor, with a shield containing his heraldic rose. It has little claim to be a likeness, and he is identified only by the inscription in mirror image around the edge as 'Doctor Martin Luther, Augustinian of Wittenberg'. The doctor's cap and gown, and the gesture of the left hand show him to be the disputant at Leipzig, while the Debate is also mentioned in the sermon's title. The tondo form and the mirror-image inscription suggest that it could have been copied from a medal commemorating the Debate.[4]

The second-oldest known portrait is less ambiguous in intent, an engraving by one of Luther's close friends, the Saxon painter Lucas Cranach, showing him as an Augustinian monk with a large tonsure, looking right (ill. 3).[5] A Latin epigram praises Luther with a purely humanist sentiment: 'Lucas' pen portrays the mortal features, Luther himself the eternal image of his spirit.' Here we have a simple combination of a visual sign and a linguistic message. The tonsure and cowl shows that he is a monk, the Latin epigram identifies him as Luther and claims to present an exact depiction, the 'mortal features'. Both the choice of an engraving, rather than the more popular woodcut, and of a Latin inscription suggests that it was aimed at a limited audience. However it may have had a deliberate propagandist purpose, perhaps intended as a reply to the rumour that Luther's likeness had been burned publicly in Rome.[6] If Luther was but a mortal being whose life might easily be snuffed out, his spirit would nonetheless live on. This shows excellently the signifying power of such a simple composition, where the purpose of the whole is far more than the sum of the individual parts. It is an iconic sign, that is, it presents the likeness of Luther; it is an indicative sign, indicating that he is a monk; finally, it is also a symbol of his immortality, thus establishing his ideological significance.[7]

Similar humanist sentiments appear with two other portraits. One is a better-known Cranach engraving dated 1521, showing Luther in a cowl and doctor's beret (ill. 4). The other, also from 1521, shows him as a monk leafing in a book, framed in a niche (ill. 5). Both carry the same connotations as illustration 3, but extend the denotation by identifying him as a doctor and by linking him with the Bible. With slight variations, these are three signs which recur in all depictions of Luther: as monk, as doctor, as man of the Bible. So powerful are these signs that they identify Luther even when any likeness is lacking. Signifier and signified are so fused that any resemblance is unnecessary. The connection can be as oblique as in illustrations 6–7; indeed, as can be seen in some of the examples discussed below, the iconic link was weak as often as it was strong.

2 Titlepage of Luther, *Ein Sermon geprediget tzu Leiptzgk* (W. Stockel, Leipzig, 1519), GNM
3 Lucas Cranach the Elder, *Luther as Monk* (1520)

The basic forms of the Luther portrait are fully established with the early examples. He is shown in a tondo, framed in or before a niche, or else standing against a free background. He may be shown bust or half-length, later full-length, sometimes turned to the left or the right, sometimes directly facing the viewer. The tondo found comparatively little use, appearing only in two book illustrations and two single sheets. The free-standing portrait of the monk was used twenty-nine times in thirteen variations. It appears twice as an engraving, three times as a single-sheet woodcut and twenty-four times in book illustrations. Thirteen of these emanated from Strassburg, four from Augsburg and one from Colmar. The portrait of Luther in the niche was also used twenty-nine times in thirteen variations, including one engraving and five single-sheet woodcuts or broadsheets. The twenty-two which can be traced to their place of publication appeared in twelve editions from Augsburg, five from Strassburg, three from Basel, one from Nuremberg and in one Low German edition. Although based on the likeness supplied by Cranach, the majority of these depictions of Luther as monk were published predominantly in two south German centres, Strassburg and Augsburg.[8]

The three signs identifying Luther as a monk, as a doctor and as a man of the Bible establish a code of recognition for images of Luther, in which they may appear separately or in combination. The most widely used was that of Luther as monk, with or without the Bible, although the Bible appears in over

4   Lucas Cranach the Elder, *Luther in Doctor's Cap* (1521), BM
5   Lucas Cranach the Elder, *Luther as Monk in Niche*, GNM

two-thirds of all Luther portraits or illustrations.[9] Luther in his doctor's cap appears only nine times in the portraits, but this image recurs more frequently in the illustrations to be discussed later. Four of these portraits were engravings, four were book illustrations, one was a single-sheet woodcut.[10] This code of recognition points to an important feature of Luther's early image. Cranach's portraits, with their humanist tributes to Luther's immortality, did not set the tone of the connotations which began to cohere around the figure of Luther. The emphasis, rather, was religious.

This is confirmed by the early pamphlets about Luther. Luther as monk is he who lives a pious Christian life; as doctor he who is a pious teacher; as a man of the Bible he who points to saving doctrine. All three are emphasised in Luther's defence as early as 1520, in a pamphlet which argues that he must instruct the folk by virtue of his office as a monk (*ain ordensmann*), a preacher and a doctor.[11] These features are stressed repeatedly in the pamphlets of 1521–2 dealing with the 'Luther affair'. The Luther portraits thus form part of a powerful and extensive religious sign, based on the most popular image, Luther as monk. However, the portraits go on to develop a more intricate assembly of images around the general notion of Luther as a man of religion.

First, he is shown as inspired by the Holy Spirit (ill. 8). To a woodcut showing him framed in a niche, an extra block has been added above his head,

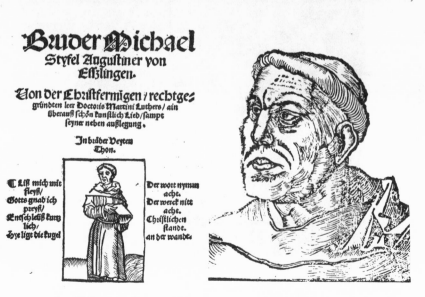

6   Titlepage of M. Stiefel, *Von der Christfermigen . . . leer Doctoris Martin Luthers* (1522), BL
7   Illustration in Eberlin von Günzburg, *History Jacob Propsts* (Colmar, 1521)

containing a dove symbolising the Holy Spirit. This can be dated as 1520 or early 1521, and the sign of the dove was used in five other depictions.[12] The visual connotations attached to Luther here are also echoed in printed pamphlets, which stress that God has enlightened him, inspired him or chosen him to speak out against falsehood. The niche alluded to this indirectly, for in the middle ages it was usually a backdrop for Evangelists or significant theologians. The dove, however, is a much more explicit sign to borrow from the medieval iconography of the saints. The dove, as the bearer of divine inspiration, was an attribute given to Church Fathers, in particular to Gregory the Great. The Holy Spirit was said to have dictated St Gregory's works into his ear, and this sign of divine grace elevated him above all other Church teachers. The attribute was sometimes given to other great Fathers of the Church, for example, in Michael Pacher's *Altar of the Church Fathers* in Munich, which shows SS Augustine, Ambrose, Jerome and Gregory, all with the dove of divine inspiration.[13] The connotations were clear enough, and it was only a short step from here to depict Luther as a saint.

A copy of illustration 8 gives Luther both the sign of divine inspiration and the nimbus of sainthood (ill. 9). When it was used in a 1521 report of the proceedings at the Reichstag of Worms, the notion of Luther as a Father of

EFFIGIES DOCTORIS MARTINI LVTHERI
AVGVSTINIANI WITTENBERGÉSIS
ᴏᴏᴀ 1520 ᴏ᙮

8   *Luther as Monk with Dove* (1520?), BM

the Church was underlined by an inscription calling him 'a servant of Jesus Christ and a *restorer of Christian doctrine*' (my emphasis).[14] This was perhaps the most successful single version of a Luther portrait, appearing as a single-sheet woodcut, and in no less than nine different works. Sainthood was also emphasised in a 1523 copy by Daniel Hopfer of Cranach's portrait of Luther in his doctor's cap. By adding a nimbus, the artist gave a new weight to the original inscription, now translated into German (ill. 10). The most extreme development of this theme is found in the titlepage of Luther's edition of the New Testament, published by Hans Hergot in Nuremberg in 1524–6 (ill. 11).[15] Luther is seated in his doctor's cap and gown, writing in his study, with a crucifix before him, and has the nimbus and the dove. Considering the work in which it appeared, the identification as a Father of the Church, or even an Evangelist, could not be more explicit. This depiction extended its influence beyond Germany, appearing as an illustration in a Czech edition of one of Luther's works (ill. 12).[16]

Such depictions reveal a desire to place Luther within the framework of divine history, and to single him out as a chosen tool of the divine plan. This is confirmed in pamphlets about Luther. These see him as raised up by God, or divinely chosen.[17] For others he is a prophet, even a Daniel awakened among the people.[18] A 1520 pamphlet, written by 'the student Laux

9   Hans Baldung Grien, *Luther as Monk with Dove and Nimbus* in BL 3906.f.119
10   Daniel Hopfer, *Luther in Doctor's Cap, with Nimbus* (1523), BM, GNM

Gemigger', names him an apostle, chosen by God as a light for Christendom.[19] A 1523 dialogue extends this thought further, calling him 'an angel, tool or prophet of God', just as John the Baptist was an angel sent to prepare the way of the Lord.[20] Here the term 'angel' is used in a general sense only, to mean a messenger from God, but there was another usage which related Luther to the prophetic literature so prevalent at the time. Thus a pamphlet of 1524 identifies him with the angel in Apocalypse 18.1–2, who is sent from heaven to overthrow the Babylonian whore and to break the cup of abomination from which all the kings and peoples of the earth have drunk.[21]

The apocalyptic note was made more explicit in 1523 by Haug Marschalck, who linked Luther to popular prophecies about the Emperor Frederick III. This eschatological figure was to return from the grave as the renewer of Christendom, who would overthrow Rome, chastise the clergy and recover the holy sepulchre.[22] Marschalck merges many elements of this legend in a semi-allegorical passage about Luther. The holy sepulchre is guarded by monks and clergy, who attempt to prevent Christ's resurrection, but they are overcome by the 'Emperor Frederick', here in the figure of Luther's protector

11   Titlepage to *Das new Testament Deütsch* (H. Hergot, Nuremberg, 1525)
12   Illustration in Czech edition of Luther, *Vom Anbeten des Sakraments* (1523)

Frederick the Wise. The door of the tomb is then opened, and Christ in the form of the Word of God rises again. The three Marys, who come to the grave seeking Christ, the holy Scripture, and who are told to go and proclaim his resurrection, are Luther, Melanchthon and Karlstadt.[23] This is an allegorical rendition of the old prophecy, to which Marschalck explicitly refers, but he has no doubts about the divine and far from allegorical role of Luther. He gives an acronym of Luther's name which not only singles him out as a prophetic figure, but also links him to the widespread literature on the Antichrist:

L   *Lautere Evangelische Lehre* (Proclaimer of evangelical doctrine – pun on *Luther – Lauter*)

U   *Uberflussige gnad des heyligen geists* (abundant grace of the Holy Spirit)

T   *Trewlich diener Christi* (loyal servant of Christ)
     Daz bedeut (that signifies)

H   *Helian* (Elias)

E   *Enoch, welche den Entchrist verraten* (and Enoch, who expose the Antichrist)

R   *Rabi, das er ist meister worden aller schrifft schender* (Rabbi, for he has mastered all defilers of Scripture).[24]

In popular legend, Enoch and Elias were the two prophets sent by God to expose the Antichrist's identity, so that Marschalck has also assimilated Luther to this evocative realm of popular prophecy.[25]

Sanctification of Luther reaches its apogee in a pamphlet published by Melchior Ramminger of Augsburg in 1521, where Luther's trial at Worms is described in terms of Christ's Passion. This pamphlet, which exists in two versions, the other also published in Augsburg in 1521,[26] indicates how important pictorial representations of Luther were thought to be at the time. The parallel between the Passion and Luther's hearing at Worms is kept as close as possible until the crucifixion, where Luther is not executed, but his books are burned instead. However, a Dominican pins up a picture of Luther to be burned, over which is written: 'This is Martin Luther, a teacher of the Gospel.' Here the parallel is once more made exact, for burning in effigy was regarded as a magical means of harming the person represented. To the left and right of Luther are burned (depictions of?) Hutten and Karlstadt, but Luther's picture miraculously refuses to burn, until placed in a container of pitch, which melts into the flames. This book-burning was wholly fictitious, but it has all the truth of incipient myth, and while the further implied parallel, Luther's resurrection, is not referred to in this work it was explicitly drawn in others.

In 1523 Heinrich von Kettenbach published an evangelical version of a prognostic: small popular works issued annually with predictions for the coming year or years. These formed the backbone of popular prophetic literature, and in the manner of the genre, Kettenbach foretold Luther's resurrection, linking him again to the Antichrist literature:

> Luther will be as if buried, and the tonsured ones will guard the grave, but he will rise again afterwards (like Christ), and will alarm the antichristian horde of Gog and Magog, and defeat a great part of it, and will become valued again throughout the world, as Christ's belief was, when he rose again.[27]

These sentiments also found expression in Luther portraiture. A depiction of Luther as monk, shown full-length and carrying the Bible, in the collection of Dahlem, has the inscription around its four sides: 'Luther has suffered under the papacy, and has risen again in the hearts of Christians.'[28]

How are we to interpret these views of Luther? They certainly show an attempt to present him as a figure embodying the religious yearnings of many Germans during 1520–1. They also show that he has been assimilated into a traditional religious framework, creating a hagiography through which he appears as a living saint. The Passion parallel is especially significant here. It cannot be regarded merely as allegory, or as a version of the pious medieval tradition of conforming to the life of Christ.[29] The Reformers themselves took so many pains to point out that exaggeration of this tradition had led to mere humans being placed almost on the same level as the divinity, or at least to attributing to them such exceptional sanctity that they seemed to challenge the role of Christ as sole mediator. The aura of sanctity cast around Luther certainly approached this level. Here visual depictions were both more suggestive and less open to qualification than printed pamphlets. Even the use of simile or allegory could be ignored by many of Luther's supporters, and his glorification taken literally.

In some accounts Luther's journey to Worms was recorded like the legend of a medieval saint. One chronicler recorded how the church timbers began to crack under the weight of those gathered to hear him preach in the Erfurt Augustinian church. Luther is said to have stilled the danger with a word, and the chronicler commented: 'This was the first sign that Luther worked, and his disciples came to him and served him.'[30] In his *History of the Reformation*, written in 1546, Friedrich Myconius, who had been present at Luther's progress through Erfurt, wrote how the Devil had torn down stones from the gables to prevent Luther preaching in nearby Gotha.[31] Such later testimony might be called into question had the papal legate Aleander not reported indignantly about a similar adulation of Luther in Worms. As he stepped down from the cart on his arrival, a priest touched him three times on his garment, and boasted thereafter that he had a relic of the greatest of the saints. One man even argued before a crowd on the marketplace that Luther was without sin, had never erred, and was therefore to be placed above St Augustine.[32]

Portraits of Luther played an important part in this adulation, and Aleander was incensed over their wide distribution in 1521. He mentioned one showing Luther and Hutten side by side as defenders of Christian liberty,[33] but two others correspond to the religious sign discussed above. One showed Luther with the nimbus of sainthood, the single-sheet version of illustration 9; the other was perhaps a version of illustration 11. The former was still circulating in 1522, when the Nuremberg Council prohibited its sale.[34] There was, without doubt, an extension of late-medieval veneration of the saints onto Luther, and it seems that the widespread demand for Luther's portrait was influenced by a desire for the *heilbringende Schau* discussed in the previous chapter. Without doubt, Luther was well on the way to becoming the object of a new cult, what both he and Erasmus called a 'sect' when applied to the followers of medieval saints. The growing usage of the term 'Lutheran' as a partisan label during the years up to 1525 confirms this view.[35]

The pamphleteers, at least, soon tried to correct the impression that adhering to Luther's doctrine meant adhering to a new sect. *A Dialogue between a Father and Son concerning Martin Luther's Teaching* of 1523 is typical. The father is won over by his son to Luther's belief, and avows that he will be a good 'Martinist', but he quickly corrects himself and states that one should be not Martinist but Christian.[36] Another dialogue of 1523 contains a similar admonition to be 'not Lutheran but Christian'.[37] But this was only a marginal modification to the myth developing around Luther's figure. Myth is understood here in Roland Barthes' sense, in which Luther becomes a sign which itself constitutes a signifier in a more elaborate semiological system.[38] We may see this by examining Luther illustrations, where the sign created by the portraits is placed in a narrative context.

One or two of these illustrations contain the simplest narrative action, as in illustration 12, where Luther is greeted by a messenger. Similar is the title-page of a 1524 pamphlet describing the Devil issuing a challenge to Luther. Two versions of this titlepage simply show Luther seated in his study as a messenger from hell enters through the door.[39] Such depictions, however, show a narrative development from illustration 12, for Luther is confronted by an adversary. Indeed, the most common form of narrative shows Luther as protagonist. Its lowest level of polemic is found in the titlepage to a report of Luther's hearing at Worms (ill. 13), where he is denoted by the familiar figure of the monk, but where there are few other connotations. It is more complex in illustration 14, where Luther is present at the burning of his books before the pope, cardinals and clergy. Luther confronts the pope and the clergy in another report of the proceedings at Worms, published in Augsburg in 1521 by Melchior Ramminger (ill. 15). In both cases, the literal truth of the encounter matters less than the fact that the Church authorities are established as Luther's true adversaries. (Luther never confronted the pope, nor were his books burned before the pope and his cardinals.)

It is illuminating that a simple juxtaposition can change the way in which a work can be read. Ramminger had used the same block for another work that same year, to show the pope in league with the Devil (ill. 16). For the Luther illustration, the left half of the block was cut away, and the figure of Luther as monk inset on another half-block in its place: collaboration thus becomes antipathy. This reveals how quickly the Luther image had become a schema which propagandists could adapt to their purposes.

Two paradigms of Luther's adversaries emerge in these illustrations. One is the Devil, the other the pope and the clergy; the two could easily be merged. This occurred in very simple form in a 1521 pamphlet attacking Luther's opponents, by Mattheus Gnidius, where the Devil is shown as a crouching beast dressed in a monk's habit (ill. 17). Luther is depicted full-length, holding the book and facing the reader directly. The arrangement of shapes is very effective here. Luther is a solid, vertical figure, feet spread apart, firmly facing the reader, strongly contrasted with the horizontal, crouching, bestial form of the monk demon which faces sideways. Luther appears firm but placid, the demon angrily breathes fire and tears with its claws at a cowl. The spatial arrangement in which Luther is placed above this figure rounds off these contrasts with the suggestion of Luther's ultimate victory over his adversaries.[40] Two other examples which stress the theme of confrontation, *Luther*

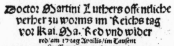

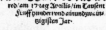

13   Titlepage to *Doctor Martini Luthers offentliche verher zu Worms* (J. Nadler, Augsburg, 1521), BL
14   Titlepage to *Ein unterred des Bapsts und seiner cardinelen* (1524?), BL

as German Hercules and the titlepage of the pamphlet *The Lutheran Strebkatz* (see ills. 23, 43), will be discussed below.

Let us turn our attention to illustrations with more detailed narrative. Luther appears with Hutten and Johann Reuchlin as 'defenders of Christian liberty' in the 1521 titlepage of the *History of the Four Heretic Dominicans of Berne* (ill. 18). The pamphlet describes a notorious case of monastic fraud from the beginning of the sixteenth century, which involved a fake miracle. Luther had no connection with the case, but he is included here, possibly because some of those responsible for the prosecution of the offenders were among Luther's leading opponents. Luther is depicted in his doctor's cap in his role as adversary. He appears in this role in the complex titlepage to a Swiss pamphlet of 1520, *On the Old and New Belief* (see ill. 48), and again in the titlepage of a pamphlet sympathetic to the orthodox viewpoint, *A Game of Bowls*.[41] In all these cases the depiction of Luther is a sign of his opposition to orthodox belief.

Other woodcuts reveal the steady accumulation of layers of connotation around Luther's image. The illustration known as *The Divine Mill* (see ill. 76) takes up the associations with the Bible established by showing Luther with a

15   Titlepage to *Ain anzaigung wie D. Martinus Luther zu Wurms* (M. Ramminger, Augsburg, 1521)
16   Titlepage to *Ain grosser Preiss so der Furst der hellen* (M. Ramminger, Augsburg, 1521), BL

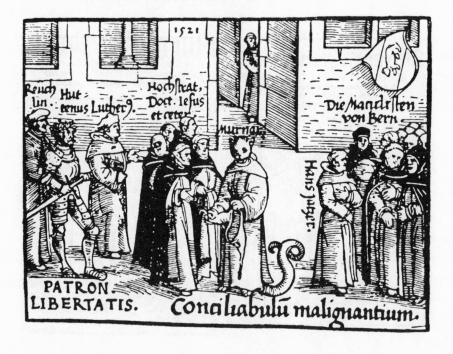

17   Illustration to M. Gnidius, *Dialogi* (1521), GNM
18   Titlepage to *History von den fier ketzren Prediger*
(H. Preuss, Strassburg, 1521)

book. Luther is shown distributing the Bible to the pope and the clergy, who reject it with horror. A fragment of a coloured woodcut (ill. 19) links Luther and Hus as good shepherds. Luther, holding the book, stands beside the crucified Christ in the sheepfold. Hus stands outside, clearly an indication that he is but a forerunner of Luther. A reference in the accompanying text to false shepherds doubtless refers to a lost part of the woodcut, which probably showed the pope and cardinals as ravening wolves. In the works so far discussed, this is the first iconographical reference to Luther's doctrinal emphasis on the crucified Christ as the sole mediator of man's salvation.

The next example (ill. 20) makes many of these references more explicit, although Hus is omitted. Here we see a pope and cardinal as wolves ravaging the flock of Christ, which seeks shelter around the crucifix. Luther, in his doctor's hat, carrying a pen and the Bible, moves towards them with a gesture warding them off. The pen is no doubt a sign of his writings in defence of true Christians. On a small hill in the background, two saints, each carrying a book, and perhaps intended to be Peter and Paul, point to the crucified Christ and the open page of Scripture. In the top right-hand corner, a goat and a wolf stand before a church building. This may allude to the biblical separation of the sheep from the goats at the Last Judgment. It may also imply that those who seek shelter in the old belief are goats, who will fall prey to the wolves when removed from the protection of Christ. The contrast between salvation and damnation is also alluded to by the rays of the sun which suffuse the left-hand side of the woodcut, while the right-hand side, towards which the wolves carry the stolen sheep, is clouded in darkness. The left-hand side is also rich with vegetation, the opposite side desolate and stony.

In the printed text Luther speaks in the first person, stating that the shepherds have become wolves in disguise. He has taught, preached and written about this, even at danger to his own life. Indeed, Luther's vulnerability to attack from the wolves is emphasised iconographically by placing him outside the fold. With this illustration, we can see evangelical propaganda reaching a more subtle and complex level than the near-hagiography of the portraits. It uses a wider range of signs and codes, which will be discussed in detail in a later chapter. Here we must note that it allows the presentation of a more elaborate message about Luther's doctrine.

This can be seen in a 1524 broadsheet, *Luther leads the Faithful from Egyptian Darkness* (ill. 21). Luther in his doctor's cap leads the faithful out of a dark cavern towards the light, where they gather around the saving image of Christ crucified. Above the cave, a throng comprised of the pope, the clergy and Luther's opponents attempt to prevent this. Using the paraphernalia of orthodox belief, they try both to distract the faithful from the crucified Christ and to drown out Luther's words. Inside the cave, the figures of an emperor and a king, representing secular authority, resolutely face away from the light into the darkness, completely disregarding Luther's message. The

19   Master MS, *Luther and Hus with Christ in the Sheepfold*, Dahlem

printed text elaborates on this basic idea. The faithful in the darkness cry out to Luther to pity them, so blinded are they by human laws and teaching that they cannot recognise Christ, who alone is the mediator to God. Luther replies that he has long taught God's Word and opposed false teaching, but his teaching has been condemned and secular rulers have turned their backs on him. He points the right way to God. The faithful respond by praising God for sending the prophet Luther, who has enabled them to recognise Christ. Throughout the rest of the text, the pope and his adherents rage against Luther for his teaching.

In this broadsheet there are several features of Luther's image layered one upon another. He is the prophet who shows men the right way; he is also the teacher of true belief. There is a possible parallel with Christ's harrowing of hell, and traces of Luther as medieval saint, for it is Luther to whom the people appeal to show them the way to God. The visual signs of the latter are the woman kneeling behind Luther in the cave, with her hands clasped in a gesture of supplication or prayer, and the man who grasps Luther's left hand as Luther points to the crucifix with his right. Luther is thus simultaneously teacher (emphasised by his doctor's beret), leader and prophet. He is also the adversary of false belief – it is the pope and his followers who actively oppose Luther and seek to hinder him in his mission. His vulnerability, and by implication his selflessness, are stressed by the allusion to his condem-

20   *Pope and Cardinal as Wolves, with Luther and Christ*

nation by authority. Finally, there is the doctrinal content, the stress on Christ as the sole mediator, which is established to be the purpose of Luther's teaching.

A final example of this kind of narrative illustration comes from the Nuremberg artist, Hans Sebald Behem, with a text from Hans Sachs (ill. 22).[42] Luther confronts those who stand to lose by his proclamation of true doctrine. Wearing his doctor's cap, he leads a group of common folk, largely of humble origin, including a peasant holding a flail on his shoulder. Facing them are a group of the 'godless', those whose material interests are endangered by Luther's attack on Catholic belief and practice. Depicted are the canon, the mass-priest, the painter, the bell-founder and the fisherman. The printed text adds several others: prelates, monks, organists, gold-beaters and manuscript illuminators, woodcarvers, glass-painters, scribes, choristers, candlemakers, parchmenters and, of course, priests' concubines. The leader of the godless points an accusatory finger at Luther and his followers. In reply, Luther points to the open page of Scripture. Behind him, his argument is supported by the peasant with the flail, whose open-palmed gesture indicates his approval of Luther's reference to Scripture. In a circle of clouds, Christ as Lord of the world, with orb and sceptre, sits in judgment over the dispute,

21   *Luther leads the Faithful from Egyptian Darkness* (1524)

Ein neuwer Spruch/ wie die Geystlicheit vnd etlich Handtwercker vber den Luther clagen.

Der geitzig clagt auß falschem müt/
Seit im abget an Eer vnd Güt.
Er zürnet/Dobet/vnde Wůt/
In dürstet nach des grechten plůt.

Die warheit ist Got vnd sein wort/
Das pleibt ewiglich vnuerstort.
Wie ser der Gotloß auch rumort/
Gott bschützt sein diener hie vnd dort.

Der Grecht sagt die Gotlich warheit/
Wie hart man jn veruolgt/verleit.
hofft er in Gott doch alle zeit/
Pleibt bstendig in der grechtigkeit.

Die clag der Gotlossen.

Hör vnser clag du strenger Richter/
Vnd sey vnser zwitracht ein schlichter.
Eb wie die hend selb legen an/
Martin Luther den schedlich man.
Der hatt geschriben vnd gelert/
Vnd schit das gäg Teütsch land verkert.
Mit schmehen/lestern/nach vnd weit
Die Erwirdige Gaistlichait.
Von jren Pfründen/Rent vnd Zinßl/
Vnd verwürfft auch jren Gotz dinst.
Der Vätter gepot/ vnd aufftzen/
hayßt er vmbsust/ vnd menschen gschwätz
helt nichts von Aplaß vnd gestrew/
Die Meß kan auch kainr Seel zu stewr.
All Kirchen Pew/ Zir/ vnd gschmuck/
Veracht er gar/ er ist nit clůck.
Des clagen die Prelaten ser/
Pfaffen/ Münch/ Seationirer.
Glockengiesser vnd Organisten/
Goltschlager vnd Illuministen.
Hädtmaler/ Golschmit vn bildschnitzer
Ratschmit / Glaßmaler/ seydenfixer.
Stainmetzen/ Zimerleüt Schreiner/
Paternoster/ Karten macher.
Die Permenter/ Singer vnd Scheryber/
Fischer/ Zopffman vnd Pfaffen Weyber.
Den allen ist Luther ein bschwer/
Von dir wirt ein Vrtail begert.
Sunst werde wir weitter Appellieren/
Vnd dem Luther die Pfrend rechte schären/
Müß Pürmen/ oder Reuocirn.

Antwort .D. Martini.

O da erkenne aller hertzen/
Hör mein antwort des ist kein schertzen.
Die schertzen faßt ich thůn mich frewen/
Vnd wöllen doch mit Disputirn.
Sonder mich mit wo am schuechen/
Jn klaus wo das ich thů auff suechen.
Jr grossen geyz vnd Simoney/
Jr falsch Gotzdinst vnd Glessnerey.
Jr Bannen/ aufftziz vnd gepot/
Vol aller welt zu schand vnd spott.
Mit deinem wort/ das ich dann leid/
Nun jn abget an gut vnd Eer.
So kunden sy dein wort nit leiden/
Dann mich schelten/hassen vnd neiden.
Wenn ich hett geschriben vnd gelert/
Das sich jr Reich vmb het gemert.
So wer kain besser auff gestanden/
Jn langer zeit in Teütschen Landen.
Die ist auch die vrsach ich sag/
Das gegen mir auch fünt in clag.
Der Handtwercks leüt ein grosse zal/
Den auch abgat in disem wal.
Seyt diß Apgötterey entnimpt/
Also frend vber Reich ergrimt.
Von seht der Baals Tempel knecht/
Den jr jarmarck thůt nimmer recht.
Vnd Demetrius der werckman/
Dem sein handtwerck zu nack wol gan.
Her durch dein wort das ich thů schreiben/
Jr in den soll mich nitt abtreiben.
Bey deinem wort will ich pleiben.

hans Sachs Schuster.

Das Vrteil Christi.

Das mein gricht das ist grecht/
Vil marck vermaint gaistliche gschlecht.
Was schad sellt sand ihem han/
Das jr in die gantz welt sollt gan.
Predigen aller Creatur/
Das Euangeli rein vnd pur.
Darselbig hont jr gar veracht/
Vnd sei numer Gottdurst auff pracht.
Der ich doch kein geheissen hab/
Vnd veruassts in wol gelt vnd gaß.
Mit Vigil/ Jartäg vnd Selmeß/
Den wucher jr ir pawser fresse.
Vnd verspert auch das Himelreich/
Ir seyt den Toten grossen gleich.
Da schlacht zu bot euch mein Propheten/
Die gleich die Pharisäer thaten.
Als veruolge jr die warheit/
Die euch täglichen wirt geseit.
Vnd so jr euch nit pesser werd/
Jr veruainat. Darumb so hort.
Von einertm falschen woluerschert/
Dergleichen jr handtwercks leyt.
Die jr mein wort veracht mit bey/
Von wegen ewers eygen nutz.
Vnd hört doch in den mouw wrdo/
Das jr mit solt seyfftzig fein.
Vnd zeitlich güt/ dadurch den Haybm/
Gb der sůcht das Reich gots mit freuden.
Das zeitlich wirt euch wol zufallen/
Sunst wert jr in der hellen qualen/
Das ist mein vrteil zu euch allen.

awarding the judgment to Luther's group (indicated by the inclination of the sceptre to that side).

In the printed text this scene is described as a dispute largely about simony, the sale of holy things as a form of financial exploitation of the faithful. The text placed in Luther's mouth makes clear that the godless also seek to profit from false belief. Moreover, they refuse to debate the matter, but by means of bans and prohibitions attempt to intimidate Luther from revealing the truth. The true judgment, however, is given by Christ, who condemns false belief and reminds the reader of his command to preach the pure Gospel. Christ's condemnation of those who persecute his prophets again underlines Luther's prophetic image. Luther is a teacher, an adversary of false belief, a proclaimer of true doctrine and one specially favoured by God.

In the Luther portraits we discerned one dominant image, Luther as saint, which constituted a major paradigm for propaganda in Luther's cause. We can now add a second, based on the illustrations. Luther appears as a teacher of true doctrine, an opponent of false belief and the exposer of the unchristian nature of the papal Church. Both paradigms can be directly related to distinct images of Luther. Luther as saint draws largely on the image of Luther the monk; Luther as teacher on that of Luther the doctor.

There was also a third image, which seems to be visually less developed in the propaganda: Luther as nationalist and humanist hero. The early portraits were given a humanist tag about Luther's immortality, following perhaps the Renaissance custom of portraying the great and glorifying the deeds on which their greatness rested. The niche was used in the Renaissance as a backdrop for portraits of famous men. Such forms of representation stressed non-religious, secular values, something far from Luther's purpose. It shows how humanists attempted to assimilate him to classical models, rather than to biblical or devotional images, such as the prophet or the saint. A good example of the type is the illustration *Luther as German Hercules* (ill. 23).[43] Luther is depicted in monastic habit with tonsure, but he has been given the signs of the classical hero Hercules, the lion's pelt and the club. Hanging from a rope through his nose is the pope, and with his club he smites down the cowering figure of Hochstraten. On the ground lie those already dispatched: Aristotle, Aquinas, Occam, Nicolas of Lyra, Peter Lombard (identified by his *Book of Sentences*) and Duns Scotus. Behind Luther, another monk flees in terror from the scene.

The Latin text fills out the classical allusions, to three of the labours of Hercules. Equated with the many-headed hydra are the various figures who represent pagan philosophy and the Scholastics who, like the hydra, grow another head as quickly as one is cut off. They are as wild as savage Cerberus, by which perhaps Hochstraten is intended. Luther is especially praised for his defeat of the triple-bodied Geryon, an allusion to the triple tiara of the pope. This broadsheet was produced in 1522, possibly from humanist circles close

Germanum Alcidem tollentem monstra Lutheru̅
Hostem non horres impia Roma tuum?
Nō me a̅des, nafo ut triplicem fuspenderit unco
Geryonem, & lasset penduli crista caput?
Ecce tibi infa̅: feciat qua̅ mole fophistas,

Ecce cadit male sana cohors, cui cerberus ipse
Cedit, & in fauces fertilis hydra nouas.
Quin ig.tur fortem agnoscis dominumq̃ pa̅ miē,
Tendisti in.las cui femel icta manus?
Erratum, subier.te fatis, sate,iiq̃ r nurga,

23   Hans Holbein the Younger, *Luther as German Hercules* (1523), Zurich

to Erasmus. It attests the narrow confines within which the humanists could regard Luther, and it is not surprising that the image of Luther as classical hero found little broad popular usage.

The other feature of humanist depiction of Luther was his portrayal as national hero. There are overtones of the theme in *Luther as German Hercules*, for it was no doubt modelled on an earlier version of Maximilian as German Hercules.[44] The theme is most evident, however, in depictions pairing Luther and Hutten as defenders of truth and Christian liberty. Aleander recorded his annoyance at the rapid sale of such a picture in Worms in 1521.[45] Two such depictions are known. One shows both figures half-length (ill. 24). Hutten is clad in armour and crowned with the wreath of the poet laureate, his sword half-drawn from the scabbard. Luther is shown as a monk holding the book, facing right, before a niche. The text in Latin emphasises Luther's divine mission, but in humanist terms: if he is defeated by papal error, the anger of the gods will be aroused. In like fashion, Hutten's inscription invokes the gods, promising to restore Germany's golden liberties.

Another version shows Luther and Hutten full-length, the Luther depiction being that used for the Gnidius dialogue (see ill. 17). It found its most effective use in the titlepage to Hutten's *Dialogues*, which appeared in Strassburg in 1521 (ill. 25). The figures are used almost as title decorations, placed to left and right of the printed title. Both figures have Latin inscriptions. Luther's reads: 'I sing the truth'; Hutten's: 'We shall conquer, we shall con-

CHRISTIANAE LIBERTATIS

PROPVGNATORIBVS.

M. LVTHERO.

VL. AB HVTTE.

Numina cœleſtem nobis peperere Lutherum,
Noſtra diu maius ſœcla uidere nihil.
Quem ſi Pontificum crudelis deprimit error,
Non fine iratos impia ſciri Deos.

Si qua fides Superis,potitur ſi limine Diuum
Iuppiter,aut ſpes eſt ſi qua relicta pijs.
Hac dextra oppreſſis reparabitur aurea quondam
Libertas.Neſcis?Alea iacta diu eſt.

24   *Luther and Hutten as Defenders of Christian Liberty*, Berlin

quer!' Hutten's comment refers to the scene below, where armed knights and mercenaries drive off the pope and a crowd of Catholic clergy, alluding to Hutten's solution to Germany's problems, an anticlerical war. The text above this scene also expresses Hutten's sentiments: 'I hate the church of the wicked.' At the top of the page, God the Father holds an arrow poised to throw at the retreating clergy, and David, identified by his harp, holds an inscription from Psalm 92.4: 'Arise, O judge of the earth, render to the proud their deserts.'

This titlepage portrays Luther and Hutten as proclaimers of divine wrath against the Roman Church. Luther has been assimilated to Hutten's programme, but the image of Luther on which the work draws is still that of the religious man who speaks the truth. This shows the strength of the paradigms of Luther as saint and Luther as teacher of true belief. In visual propaganda, the image of Luther as nationalist or humanist hero is usually subordinate to either or both of these, and the paradigm of Luther as humanist hero did not achieve any comparable popularity.[46]

How are we to understand the use made by Reformation propaganda of

25   Titlepage to Hutten, *Gesprach büchlin* (J. Schott, Strassburg, 1522), BL

these paradigms? It is the function of the early portraits of Luther that they invest him with a kind of Weberian charisma, with an extraordinary quality by which he is set apart from other men.[47] Continual emphasis on his office as monk, and so a man of religion, and on his personal piety designates him as someone especially close to God. It was natural to present him as a saint, acting within the context of divine history. This propaganda image invested him with a special form of authority, identifying him as a prophet – in Weber's terms, 'a purely individual bearer of charisma, who by virtue of his mission proclaims a religious doctrine or divine commandment'.[48] In this way he could be seen to break legitimately with the established order in the Church. By invoking a source of authority outside and above it, opposition to the Church is morally legitimate.[49] The logic goes a step further. Those opposed to Luther are also opposed to the source of his message, and since this is of divine origin, they oppose God and are in league with the Devil. We shall see in the following chapter how this theme was developed.

Finally, it is necessary to be aware that we are describing not the real-life, historical Luther, but the Luther of the propaganda works. These sought to construct an ideological relationship between Luther and his followers, providing powerful affective arguments to justify Luther's break with the Church and to induce others to do the same. Yet we have seen that this was not purely a propaganda creation, for there is evidence outside the propaganda itself that many people shared these perceptions. The propaganda both recorded such perceptions while it sought to arouse them in others.[50] In so doing, it attempted to touch many different levels of consciousness of the age. We shall investigate some of these levels more fully in later chapters.

3

ENEMIES OF THE GOSPEL

It is ironic that the most popular image of Luther during the early years of the Reformation should have been Luther as monk. From the beginning, monks were regarded as his chief opponents, and early propaganda for the evangelical movement was directed largely against the institution of monasticism. This is hardly surprising, for there was a long tradition of popular criticism of clerical laxity, and the humanists had already waged an energetic campaign against monasticism. It was only natural that the image of Luther as a man living a pious Christian life should have been juxtaposed to a picture of monastic vice.

Pre-Reformation criticism was blunt enough. An excellent example is a satirical depiction of monastic lack of sobriety, dating from the last quarter of the fifteenth century (ill. 26). An abbot reclining on a giant jawbone is pulled across the ice by nuns because he has become so swollen from drink that he cannot walk. Two others similarly laden break through the ice, and

26   *The Abbot on the Ice*, Albertina

the abbot advises caution lest he do the same.[1] Drunkenness and gluttony were held to be typical vices of monks, while the association of monks and nuns in such depictions alluded to sexual immorality. Sometimes monks and nuns were depicted taking part in a bacchic feast, or even engaging in love play.[2]

These ideas were taken up eagerly by the visual propaganda of the 1520s. A woodcut of 1523 by Leonhard Beck shows a monk purchasing a farmer's daughter to live with him as a concubine (ill. 27). Scrolls placed within the picture space provide a commentary from each of the characters, somewhat in the style of a modern comic strip. The monk holds the farmer's daughter firmly by the hand, and offers her father a coin from the pile before him:

> Father, I will hire your daughter
> And bring your affairs into order.

The daughter appears not unwilling to conclude the deal:

> Father, I know what's going on
> Else I'd not have let the monk come along.

The farmer angrily grasps the hilt of his sword, and growls:

> Monk, you have deceived me,
> And made my daughter leave me.

Behind him, the girl's mother weeps:

> Oh, what a shameful lot,
> For my child I'll plead to God.

27   Leonhard Beck, *The Monk and his Maid* (1523)

Behind the seated monk stands an older monk, perhaps his superior, who laments:

> This doesn't happen by my will,
> But I must watch and be still.

This work demonstrates the simplicity and directness of visual propaganda through its capacity to combine visual signs and primitive reading ability to tell a dramatic story. Its effectiveness is dependent on the skilful structural relationship between the various signs. The picture is constructed around the antithesis between two groups of characters. The two monks and the girl on the left are separated from the farmer and his wife on the right. They are, respectively, the offending and aggrieved parties. The table both links them into a larger group and separates them, for it partly impedes the angry farmer's threatening movement towards the monk.

The antithesis is reinforced by the socio-cultural code which identifies the characters. The farmer and his wife are clad in dress typical of the country-folk of the time, while the monks wear their readily recognisable habits. The daughter, in contrast to her mother's peasant dress, wears a more fashionable style, showing that she is no doubt a willing sinner. It is more the exploitation of their state of need by the proffered money and the outrage to the family sense of decency that causes offence. All this is made fully clear by the written text, which also adds the information that the monk has won the daughter by trickery.

The antipathy of the two groups is also established by a gestural code. The monk and the maid are seated; they have been drinking, perhaps in an inn. The peasant and his wife are standing, he in an aggressive, argumentative posture, the wife turning away in sorrow. The hand gestures are neatly balanced. The monk's left hand holds out the large coin, thus one of great value; the peasant's points in accusation and warning. The monk's right hand grasps firmly that of his prize, perhaps in parody of a wedding promise where right hands were joined; the peasant grasps the hilt of his sword, his only reply to this gesture of possession. The facial expressions complete the composition. The monk is calm, composed, sure of his victory; the peasant is angry, frustrated, willing to use force as his last resort. These are all visual codes which, when taken together, tell the story with sufficient clarity. The written texts add more information, making the visual signs wholly unambiguous. They confirm that the daughter is a willing party to the monk's lust, that the old peasant can do nothing, that the mother sorrows over her daughter's choice (although she does appear to smirk behind her handkerchief!), and that the monk has had his way through deceit. Important to their effect is that the texts are in rhymed couplets. They were easily read out to the non-literate and easily remembered.

Finally, one must be aware of the wider context in which this woodcut would have been read in 1523, for in that year it first became inescapably clear that a new wave of peasant unrest had broken. It was no less clear that it was directed largely against the privileges of the clergy. Our woodcut therefore invokes a broader social theme, linking clerical immorality to economic exploitation of a poor peasantry by an over-rich clergy, a favourite theme of printed propaganda. Nowhere can it have been more succinctly stated than in this single woodcut.

Further social criticism of monasticism is found in another woodcut by Beck from 1523, which condemns monastic life as parasitic (ill. 28). On the left, an old monk carries a nun on his back in a basket, perhaps intended to signify that she is his concubine. The monk carries a walking-stick and a wine sack as signs of an idle mendicant life. The nun attempts to spin yarn, but without success, for the ball of yarn falls onto the ground behind her, indicating lost effort. This is made clear by the inscription above her head: 'As one who would spin in a basket — much is lost and little won.'[3] On the right is seated an ass, successfully spinning on a wheel. It is clad in a fool's costume, indicating that even a fool and an ass can be more successful at useful work than the monk and the nun. The scroll again spells out the message: 'If I could not spin yarn thus, one would abuse me as an ass.'[4]

The construction is similar to Beck's other woodcut. The two sides are both contrasted and linked by the spinning-wheel. However, the binary struc-

28   Leonhard Beck, *The Monk and the Ass* (1523)

ture is used here to suggest equivalence rather than antipathy. This may also be suggested by the two flying birds on each side of the wheel. They seem to be ignoble birds, possibly ravens or crows, symbolising ill-fortune, dissension or uncleanliness,[5] signs difficult to relate to the overall message. The owl perched atop the wheel may symbolise ignorance, or may be intended in the sense once used by Hans Sachs, to represent the blind children of the world, who cannot see and stubbornly persist in their sins.[6] If this is the case, it links both sides of the picture. The mulish brutishness of folly is equated with monasticism, trapped by its uselessness and incapable of reform. More indirectly, the woodcut as a whole alludes to another social issue which the reader in 1523 would hardly have overlooked. This was the common grievance against the economic activity of nuns, whose spinning and weaving provided competition for town weavers, often the poorer element of urban society.[7]

Another broadsheet from the early 1520s proclaimed the same message by depicting the monk as spoon-seller (ill. 29). This presents monasticism as 'spoon-work', that is, as something trifling and useless.[8] This is an interesting case where the written text dominates the visual message, for it is only through the scrolls around the woodcut that we are able to unravel what it wishes to convey. The tone is set by the scroll in the top left-hand corner, which comments that it is a disgraceful state of affairs that the monks have become

29   *The Monk as Spoon-seller*, Dahlem

spoon-sellers. The scroll set sideways on the left-hand side continues the thought, apparently placing its words in the mouth of the monk seated in the centre of the scene. He laments that monasticism is worthless spoon-work; had he realised this he would not have entered the Order, but studied more to become a credit to God and the world. The small monk gathering up spoons from the ground has a similar lament in his scroll. He too thinks it is disgraceful; he must pick up all the spoons, but can sell none at all. He is everybody's footrag, perhaps a reference to his lowly position in the Order, indicated visually by his smaller size. He has decided, therefore, to put up his spoons, that is, to leave the Order.

The scroll in the centre top is another lament from the larger monk about the low general opinion of monasticism. His Order is so little regarded that even the old woman scolds him. The scroll in the bottom left-hand corner identifies her as a miller's wife (she wears a miller's sack and twenty-four keys), from one of the 'dishonourable' professions. She reproves the monk for his idle life, and threatens to 'pick off his lice' with her spoon. This adapts a common proverb, that one should delouse fools with a club, that is, that a fool's folly can only be beaten out of him.[9] Indeed, the old woman has set about this so vigorously that her spoon has broken with the impact.

A new thought is introduced into the schema by the scroll at the top left-hand corner, again spoken by the old woman. The monk should have stuck to his books, for the flies have almost eaten him. He should see to his pox or the flies will indeed turn him into a shadow. This reference to the pox invokes the sexual excess associated with monasticism, and calls attention to another overtone of the term 'spoon-work': striving for female favour. The sexual theme is echoed by another scroll given to the old woman, the one turned sideways on the right-hand side: 'What are you gawping at, look rather at the ape's arsehole.' The sexual connotations of this injunction are plain enough, but the ape showing his rear to the monk has been placed in the picture for another reason as well. His scroll reads: 'Do you know the old ape of Heidelberg?' This refers to a proverbial figure of an ape, which stood on the stone bridge in Heidelberg bearing the inscription: 'Why do you gawp at me, have you never seen an old ape? Look around Heidelberg and you will find many more!'[10] The folly of student or academic life is intended in the original, and the usage here applies it by analogy to monasticism. It also echoes Luther's condemnation of monasticism as an 'ape's game' and a 'fool's game'.[11]

The examples discussed so far have little in them that is explicitly evangelical. They represent a stream of social criticism and anticlericalism which welled up alongside the Lutheran movement. The Reformation certainly attacked monasticism, but so far we have seen it condemned as a social abuse, not as an affront to true belief. We enter a different dimension with a 1521 woodcut from Hans Sebald Behem (ill. 30). Three female figures, identified by Latin titles as Pride, Lust and Avarice, restrain a monk by means of a scarf around his neck. A ragged peasant, egged on by the figure of Poverty, has the monk by the forelock and attempts to force a book into his mouth. It is clear from the monk's hand gesture that he has refused to take hold of the book, and another book lying on the ground may also signify this refusal (although it may also be intended to indicate the monk's rule, which he has dropped in fear).[12]

The structure is similar to that in Beck's woodcuts. The action is divided between two groups, the Vices on the left, the peasant and Poverty on the right. The monk stands between both groups, uniting and dividing them. Indeed, the scene could be read as a contest between the Vices and the peasant, a tug-of-war between scarf and forelock. This is an unsatisfactory explanation, because the monk is not a passive object in between. The book-eating, which could be interpreted in two different ways, only partly clarifies the ambiguity. It could signify deserved punishment — a messenger who brought an unpleasant message was forced to eat it — but this does not quite fit the subject. It could also stand for energetic, forceful instruction, as in Ezekiel 3.1 or in Apocalypse 10.8. If the book is meant to be the Bible, this is the sense intended. The monk has been given a divine message, which, however unwilling, he must proclaim.[13]

There are also two possible interpretations of the woodcut as a whole. First, it could be read as an allegory of monastic life. The monk rejects the poverty which should characterise his way of life because he is held back by three vices all too common among monks. He must be forced to accept the Word of God, which he ought to proclaim as part of his profession.[14] This interpretation places less emphasis on the role of the peasant. A second

30   Hans Sebald Behem, *Allegory of Monasticism*

possible interpretation would emphasise the social criticism in the work. The ragged peasant, depicted in so much of the early pamphlet literature as the mainstay of the Reformation, is the major victim of monastic vice. Fittingly, he is the chastiser and admonisher of the monk, the layman reproves the religious, and he does so through the Word. This element is common to both interpretations, whether we emphasise the monk, as the central figure of the composition, or the peasant, as the approved party in the contest. The artist appeals to the same standard of judgment in both cases, the Word of God, signified by the book. It is the Word which the monk rejects, and which he must accept to overcome his vices.

There is no ambiguity in the next example, *Christ appears to the Monks* (ill. 31), which presents a clear-cut opposition of monks and Christ himself. Six monks, identified by an inscription above the four on the left as 'the servants of the high priest', guard Christ's tomb. The lid of the tomb, which might prevent Christ's resurrection, bears the caption 'the burdensome human doctrines, laws and prohibitions'. These are visualised in the fish on the top of the tomb, signifying fasting, and by the book held by the monk in the right foreground, signifying the rule of his Order. The monks' vices are indicated by

31   *Christ appears to the Monks*, GNM

the money sack held by the monk who falls backwards in the left foreground, and by the wine glass and flask on the top of the tomb.[15]

The monks shrink back in terror from the risen Christ, who has overcome all these obstacles and thrust back the stone. He stands before them as the Word of God risen in glory. On the right, a group labelled by an inscription on the gate-frame as the Christian host watch through the entrance to the graveyard. Two women at the front of this group carry vessels, alluding to the women who came to anoint Christ's body, only to find him risen. The depiction thus has a double message. Christ the Word has risen, and the monks are his enemies; though the monks will try to prevent it, the Word will soon be revealed to all true Christians.

It was not only monks who were singled out as enemies of the Gospel. A small woodcut by Hans Holbein the Younger shows how the norm of the Bible was used to condemn the entire Catholic hierarchy. The woodcut (ill. 32) depicts true and false forgiveness. On the right, the pope sits enthroned in a large hall, apparently the choir of a church. The coats of arms which decorate the choir-stalls, and the two banners above the pope's throne, contain the device of the Medici family, a cluster of six roundels, so that the pope is Leo X. Attended by a large retinue of cardinals and clerics, he grants a bull to a kneeling monk. In the right foreground of this half of the woodcut, two priests hear confession. One places his hand on the head of the penitent in a gesture of absolution, and indicates with his rod a money chest before the choir-stall. The penitent is expected to pay for his absolution. A stooping woman, possibly the previous penitent, is already placing her contribution in the chest. On the left side of the choir, monks are busy selling indulgences. A woman pays for her indulgence, a burgher waits his turn and a ragged beggar upon a crutch gestures towards a monk who is filling out indulgence forms. It is unclear whether he is merely asking for an indulgence, or pleading his inability to pay. The whole scene on this side depicts the forgiveness offered by the Catholic Church, forgiveness which must be purchased by cash.

On the left-hand side of the woodcut, one finds by contrast a depiction of true forgiveness. David and Manasses, Old Testament types of penitent sinner, beg forgiveness from God the Father. Behind them stands the simple figure of

32   Hans Holbein the Younger, *True and False Forgiveness*, BM

a 'public sinner', who bows his head in repentance.[16] Unlike the papal scene on the right, God's forgiveness is humbly asked for and freely given, especially to the simple sinner. As in other woodcuts, the binary structure suggests polar oppositions. The forgiveness of the papal Church is that of man, or at least of man intervening between the penitent and God. True forgiveness comes directly from God when man confronts him in penitence. The forgiveness of God is free, that of the papal Church must be bought. With the former, the poor man approaches God on his own, with the latter, he is forced into a cash transaction which he can ill afford. Holbein's work thus criticises papal exploitation of spiritual goods for financial gain. It also reflects Lutheran ideas on penance and forgiveness. Common to both themes is the use of a biblical norm. The forgiveness of the papal Church is compared to that of the Old Testament, and found wanting.[17]

In another woodcut, *Christ the Light of the World* (ill. 33), Holbein uses the same technique to show opposition between Christ and the papal Church. The risen Christ, with nimbus and the wounds of his crucifixion, points to a large candleholder from which the scene is lit. The base of the candlestand shows the symbols of the Evangelists − the lion, the eagle, the angel and the bull, the last obscured behind the stand. The stem bears figures of three New Testament writers, St Peter with the key, St Paul with the sword and St John with the scroll. The candle and stand are together a sign of the Word, embodied in the New Testament. It alludes to Matthew 4.15: men do not light a lamp and put it under a bushel, but on a stand where it gives light to all in the house. It is therefore a symbol of the Reformation rediscovery of the Word. Christ calls the attention of a crowd of peasants and burghers on the left to the light. On the right, a pope, a cardinal, a bishop, monks and a canon − the papal hierarchy − are led into a dark pit by two figures labelled Aristotle and Plato, wearing a Turkish and a scholar's cap respectively.

The central theme of darkness and light is suggested by Christ's claim to be the light of the world. In fleeing the light, the papal hierarchy flees from Christ. Darkness and light can also signify error and truth, signs used very effectively in the broadsheet *Luther leads the Faithful from Egyptian Darkness.*

33   Hans Holbein the Younger, *Christ the Light of the World*, BM

The pagan philosophers Plato and Aristotle here evoke the theme of error and truth, for they were deprived of the light of Christian truth, as will be those who follow their teaching. Finally, the woodcut presents a contrast between the laity who see the true light and the hierarchy who do not, between ordinary folk and great and powerful officers of the Church.[18]

Similar themes recur in the titlepage of a pamphlet by Haug Marschalck, *A Mirror for the Blind* (ill. 34), published in 1523. A blindfolded monk standing in a pulpit holds up a covered mirror to a bishop and a canon, both of whom also wear blindfolds. An inscription on the pulpit identifies the preacher as Scotus, so that he is teaching Scholastic doctrine, the futility of which is symbolised by the mirror he holds. It is covered so that the onlookers cannot see anything in it; in any case, they are blindfolded and the whole business is pointless. Behind them, identifiable by their dress, a peasant and a burgher have turned away from this hopeless situation. They reach up instead to the radiant figure of Christ as Lord of the world, seated in glory in the clouds. These last two woodcuts take us into the area of doctrine. The teaching of the papal Church is the belief of the pagan and the blind. Any attempt to follow it leads only to frustration and error. The true teaching is that of

34   Titlepage to H. Marschalck, *Ein Spiegel der Blinden* (1523?), BL

Christ, the Word. This opposition is also that between the hierarchy and the laity, between the great and the humble.[19]

The propaganda process we have observed so far involves the reader being led from one level of argument to another by a chain of association. A pre-Reformation tradition of anticlericalism and anti-monasticism is continued and strengthened by propaganda such as Beck's. The monk becomes a sign of unchristian life. The next step is to demonstrate that monks are not only unchristian, but that they are antichristian, enemies of Christ. The argument is then applied to all parts of the Church hierarchy, from the pope downwards. Important in the building up of these connotations is the use of biblical criteria. Monks are antichristian because they reject the Bible and the Word. In Behem's allegory of monasticism this is stated somewhat ambivalently, but in other works it is put bluntly: monks oppose the real, living Word of God, Christ himself. This imparts a theological depth to the propaganda, and raises the issues to eschatological significance. It is the risen Christ in glory whom the monks and the hierarchy oppose and reject. Finally, we must note the 'correction' or reshaping of biblical situations, parables or metaphors to convey the message. In *Christ appears to the Monks* the resurrection story is retold as a contemporary tale. The propaganda message is thus carried by a socio-cultural code most readily recognised by the people of that age: the whole range of biblical stories and metaphors.

We can see the uses to which biblical allusions could be put in a broadsheet entitled *Moses' Seat has become a School for Liars* (ill. 35). It is based on Matthew 23.2: 'The scribes and pharisees sit on Moses' seat, so practise and observe whatever they tell you, but not what they do, for they preach but do not practise.' The text to the left of the illustration gives the Gospel passage through which the picture is to be read, Matthew 23.4, 13–35, with some abbreviations. The text beneath the picture gives a glossary applying the verses to Catholic practice. The picture space itself is filled with separate scenes, each with its own caption naming, parallel to the written text, a pharisaical Roman practice. Half of the picture is filled with a papal throne. The pope places a bull of indulgence on the shoulders of a kneeling suppliant with the words, inscribed in the scroll above the throng: 'Receive this indulgence, and give us now our prescribed fee.' Beside the suppliant is a large sack of coin, the sum required for the fee. To the right and left of the pope sit other Churchmen, who lay different burdens on the shoulders of the laity. On the pope's immediate right, a bishop loads the heavy books of the law onto a kneeling layman, who is almost prone from the weight. 'Keep our laws', is the bishop's command. To his right, a canon places the heavy injunction, 'You must fast' on the back of a kneeling nobleman who holds a rosary.

To the left of the pope, a cardinal entreats: 'Go to church and sacrifice.' As a sign of this command, he places the model of a church on the shoulders of the man kneeling before him. Further left, a monk commands another lay-

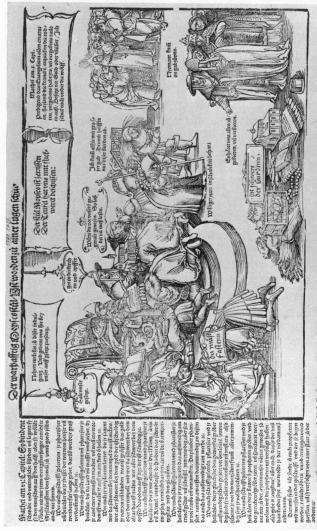

35 *Moses' Seat has become a School for Liars*, Berlin

man: 'If you will recover from our power, then have many masses read for you.' Further left, two figures walk away from the papal throne, bowed down under their burdens. One is a peasant loaded with his offerings, geese, doves, grain, doubtless representing the tithe. He pleads: 'I came here with large offerings; free me of this burden.' Beside him is a wandering friar, with cross and beads. Unlike the peasant, he is 'a willing fool hardened in knavery'. In the bottom right-hand corner of the woodcut stands a group of Catholic clergy, the pope, a cardinal, a bishop, a canon and a monk. Their caption states: 'Let no one come to us without an offering.' They point to a pile of objects to the left of the group with the words 'It is given unto us to allow or prohibit everything.' The objects in the pile are labelled by a caption 'the weight of burdens', containing a rosary, fish as a sign of fasting and abstinence, a bull of indulgence, the books of canon law, a church signifying, as it does elsewhere in this woodcut, the obligation to sacrifice, a mendicant's begging-box, and grain and fowl, items of the tithe. A sack of coin, the 'prescribed fee' mentioned by the enthroned pope, completes the pile.

This broadsheet has not forgotten to contrast such practices with the way of the Gospel. In the top right-hand corner the risen Christ prepares to send his disciples into this crowd of pharisees. The caption refers to Matthew 10: 'Preach the Gospel to all creatures, heal the sick, raise the dead; you received no pay, give no pay, take no gold or silver, I send you among wolves.' As propaganda, the work achieves a number of purposes simultaneously. It supplies a Gospel text, and interprets it both in words and pictures as it applies to the papal Church. Not content with this negative achievement, it further presents a positive norm, again based on a Gospel text. The reader therefore learns the Gospel, sees how it is contrary to papal practice and is shown the true practice of Christ, namely, the preaching of the Word.

The use of the Bible and biblical imagery is not at all surprising given the dominant role of the Bible in the culture of the age, and given that the Reformation was largely a biblical revival movement. We can see more clearly the particular contribution of propaganda to this movement if we examine the use made over a period of time of one special image, the good shepherd. The skilful articulation of this one sign provided the Reformation with a valuable weapon in its propaganda armoury. The image of the good shepherd has many elaborate layers of connotation, arising from its uses in the Old Testament, and from its New Testament use in John 10. It was an ideal image for a pastoral people such as the Hebrews, and could be applied with effect in a predominantly rural society such as sixteenth-century Germany.[20]

The parable of the good shepherd contains three basic images which could be adapted for propaganda purposes. First, there is the shepherd who lays down his life for his sheep, whereas the hireling flees at the moment of danger. Second, there is the sheepfold, in which the sheep may shelter and through whose door they may safely come and go. Beyond the sheepfold is danger, and he who does not enter the sheepfold by the proper way is a thief or robber. Third, there is the contrast between the sheep and the wolf, the member of the flock and he who preys upon it.

The first two images were used in three different broadsheets during the 1520s.[21] The first version, by Hans Brosamer (ill. 36), takes up the theme of the good shepherd and the hireling. In the left foreground, Christ and four apostles observe the good shepherd defending the flock, which is being attacked by wolves. The hireling flees (see John 10.12), here identified with the clergy through a priest's beret. On the right, the shepherd approaches a sheepfold, whose doorkeeper opens for him, while the thief attempts to enter through the roof. The flock follows the shepherd, but not a stranger. This depiction has a fairly low level of visual polemic, and the good shepherd image is used only to identify the hireling with the Catholic priest.

The second broadsheet appeared in 1524, with woodcut by Hans Sebald Behem and verses by Hans Sachs (ill. 37). The woodcut shows a sheepfold with Christ standing in the doorway, recalling John 10.9: 'I am the door; if anyone enters by me he will be saved, and will go in and out and find pasture.' A number of sheep already in the fold peer through the doorway or through a break in the wall. A number of the faithful approach Christ to seek entry: a peasant and a peasant woman, a scholar in his talar. Another figure, in a broad hat under the ladder, peering around the corner, resembles Charles V, perhaps intended to show his indecision about entering the right door with the faithful. Meanwhile a number of Catholic clergy, monks and a nun attempt to enter by scaling ladders onto the roof and breaking in from above. A mass-priest, holding a chalice, places his hand on one of the ladders to join them.[22] The reference is to John 10.1: 'He who does not enter the sheepfold by the door, but climbs in by another way, that man is a thief and a robber'; and to John 10.10: 'The thief comes only to steal, kill and destroy.' The angel at the

36   Hans Brosamer, *Christ and the Sheepfold*, Schlossmuseum Coburg

37   Hans Sebald Behem, *Christ and the Sheepfold*, Berlin

bottom left-hand side of the sheepfold tries to attract two women onto the right way by reading from a book, probably the Bible. The first woman carries signs of Catholic devotion, a rosary and a candle, so that it is adherents of the old belief whom the angel seeks to lead to Christ through the Word. Behind the first woman, a cleric stoops down, possibly in order to sneak past the angel and seize the lamb peering out through the hole in the wall.

The antipathy between the papal clergy and Christ is that between harmful belief and saving belief. This is the implication of the two verses John 10.1,10, and the contrast is spelled out by Hans Sachs' text, where passages are spoken by Christ, the angel and the 'godless band'. Christ's words develop the theme of the door and the sheepfold: Christ is the only way to salvation, through his taking man's sins upon himself and dying on the cross. The angel calls the godless band's attention to Christ's words. Why do they blindly reject the Word in favour of false human works and laws which only lead to damnation? The godless reply by attacking the 'new heretical teaching', which opposes good works and destroys divine worship, that has been established for four hundred years and followed by many folk.

It is thus only in Hans Sachs' text that the doctrinal opposition between the new belief and the old is brought out fully. In the visual text, the opposition is largely that between Christ and the papal clergy. But taken as a whole the broadsheet seeks to align the evangelical movement with the cause of Christ, and to identify this with opposition to good works. The vital links in the structure of the argument are the image of the sheepfold, the identification of Christ as the door and of the Catholic clergy as thieves and robbers.

The third version of the theme, by the Master MS, tries to convey the same message without any written text (ill. 38). The sheepfold is here shown as half barn, half church, making the analogy with the Church very obvious. The visual references to the text of John 10 are similar. Christ stands in the doorway, while the clergy attempt to break in from the roof. It is now more clearly the papal hierarchy which plays this role. The pope himself sits astride the church roof, giving his blessing to two figures climbing in through an upper window. Beneath them a cardinal and a bishop try to divert the attention of a group of believers who have come seeking the sheepfold, among whom is a peasant family. To the left of this group a pilgrim has gone astray, and he knocks on the wrong door, on the small door of the side barn, where customarily swine or cattle were kept.

To the left of the doorway a well-dressed man, perhaps a prince, discusses the question of good works with two saints, identified by their haloes. Good works are signified by the prince reaching into his wallet to give alms to the crippled beggar squatting before him. Immediately before the door, a kneeling man with a lamb beside him looks towards Christ, the sheep indicating that he is one of the faithful. The figure with Christ in the doorway indicates an article of evangelical belief. He is a layman, but holds a key, the symbol of the power to bind and loose, so alluding to the priesthood of all believers.

In the background left is depicted the theme of Christ the good shepherd, showing the flock following him alone.[23] In the background right we see the crucified Christ surrounded by the flock, an allusion to the good shepherd who lays down his life for his sheep. Behind this, the hireling flees as wolves ravage the flock. This visualises John 10.11–15 and stresses Christ's sacrificial death. If we compare this version with Behem's, it is much more effective visually in presenting both the antithesis of the old belief to Christ and certain doctrinal features of the new faith. We may well ask, however, which is more effective in introducing the reader to Reformation doctrines. The MS woodcut seems to presuppose some familiarity with Luther's teaching to read the visual signs. Behem's depiction does not attempt the same doctrinal complexity, but leaves this to Hans Sachs' text. Both are undeniably successful in establishing one sign, the denotation of the Catholic clergy as the thieves and robbers of the parable. The question of effective presentation of doctrine we shall return to in a later chapter.

The distinction between the good and the bad shepherd is taken up in another woodcut from an unknown Nuremberg master from sometime before 1530 (ill. 39). It depicts the pope and his 'temple servants', who exploit the flock for their own gain. The sheep are shorn by the three servants on the right, and slain and flayed by the servant in the foreground right. Meanwhile

38   Master MS, *Christ and the Sheepfold*, GNM

the princes of Germany do nothing and pretend not to notice by 'looking through their fingers', a proverbial expression for ignoring what is plainly obvious.[24] The written text, again from Hans Sachs, relates the scene to the long passage in Ezekiel 34, where the Lord complains of the shepherds of Israel who have been feeding themselves, but not their sheep. 'You eat the fat, you clothe yourselves with the wool, you slaughter the fatlings, but you do not feed the sheep' (Ezekiel 34.3). The text is placed in the mouth of the pope, who complains that he and his servants – cardinals, bishops, monks and priests – keep a good pasturage where they try to keep the sheep in the fold and away from strange pastures where they might be poisoned by the Gospel. If they remain with the pope they are placid and subservient, and can be milked, shorn, flayed and butchered. While the pope sits in glory, the worldly princes must be silent or suffer the ban. True, Luther has revealed papal practices and turned Germany away from the pope, and some princes and towns have taken these matters to heart. But these lost sheep will be sought out and driven with rods of iron back into the papal fold. Sachs ends with an admonition in his own voice to turn from lies to truth, from the pope to Christ and so to blessedness.

The third image which could be derived from the good shepherd story is that of the wolf who preys on the sheep. We have already seen this used in Luther illustrations, where the Catholic hierarchy was portrayed as ravening wolves menacing the flock of Christ. An anonymous woodcut from the 1520s copied this theme, while omitting the figure of Luther (ill. 40). It is unnecessary to describe the contents again, except to call attention to the two goats

39   *The Pope and his Temple Servants*

in the top right-hand corner, who stand for the damned who have been separated from the sheep. There is an eschatological tone in this reference which pervades the whole illustration. It is conveyed by the binary structure, by the darkness which clouds the right-hand side and the sunlight which floods the left-hand side. The trees on the left are in full bloom, those on the right stand desolate and barren. The sheep in their fold have ample pasture, while the ground on the darkened side is bare of foliage and strewn with rocks. The two wolves are placed in the centre of the depiction, trying to carry the sheep from the left to the right; indeed, we may well say: from the realm of the saved into that of the damned.

As in the earlier version which included Luther, this labelled the pope and his followers as spiritual wolves, so creating an image of great signifying power for visual propaganda. It was biting enough to stand alone, detached from the more elaborate frame of biblical reference, a self-sufficient sign which required no explanatory text. In the titlepage of a 1539 pamphlet, for example, it was enough to show a canon and a monk as wolves tearing at a sheep to evoke the wider connotations (ill. 41).[25] It was used with even greater effect in a trick-broadsheet in which a widow pleads with a monk for assistance (ill. 42). The top section of the sheet folds back to reveal first the monk as a wolf devouring a lamb, then to show the monk devouring the widow's house. The same sign is even used for an 'inverted world' depiction,

40   *The Spiritual Wolves*, Dahlem

to be discussed in a later chapter, showing the sheep turned into 'hounds' who hunt down the wolves – the pope, bishops and cardinals (see ill. 135).

It was a major task for the adherents of the early evangelical movement to identify their cause not just with Luther and the personal fate of one man. It had to be seen to involve matters of cosmic significance. Luther's enemies had to be seen as the enemies of the Gospel and so of Christ himself. They thus became the proponents of false religion, who might lead those who followed

41   Titlepage of U. Rhegius, *Wie man die falschen Propheten erkennen* (A. Goldbeck, Brunswick, 1539), UB Göttingen
42   *The Monk and Wolf as Devourers of the Widow's House*, UB Bern

them to damnation. This was essential if the movement was to avoid the stigma of false belief and heresy. By shifting onto its opponents the associations of wrong belief, it was able to occupy the positive ground of saving belief. On the other hand, its delineation of its own belief was often indirect and imprecise. In the examples we have seen so far it pointed to Christ, the Word and the Bible as leading to salvation. The Lutheran movement was right belief because it was associated with this. It achieved this purpose by drawing on a number of codes familiar to the time — anticlericalism, socio-economic grievance, biblical images, proverbs (in the case of *The Monk as Spoon-seller*), even what Victor Turner has called 'root paradigms', cultural stereotypes such as the opposition between darkness and light.[26] To gain a fuller appreciation of how such codes were used, we must now examine some of them more closely. In the next three chapters we shall deal first with a group of codes which may be loosely described as 'popular culture', then with another group which may be labelled 'popular belief'.

4

POPULAR CULTURE

'Popular culture' is an elusive concept, and in this period can be distinguished only arbitrarily from 'popular belief'.[1] It can mean common social custom, such as the practice of strangers sharing a common bed in inns.[2] It can be taken to be mass as opposed to elite culture, the village fair rather than the exclusive dances of the well-to-do.[3] Seen from another angle, it can be contrasted to 'official' culture, almost as a sub-culture outside socially controlled modes of behaviour.[4] This is the culture of wayfaring folk, journeymen, of the plebeian lower strata, as opposed to the regulated life of those organised in guilds or corporations. Another approach could define it as superstition, as a pattern of behaviour dependent on having access to and control over supernatural power.[5] The use of skin taken from a hanged man as a talisman against evil exemplifies this definition. Finally, it might be related to elemental aspects of material life, to basic biological rhythms such as reproduction, nourishment and the cycles of nature.[6] Shepherds' calendars and blood-letting tables illustrate this usage. The third and fourth of these definitions merge with 'popular belief', with attempts to contact or deal with the supernatural. Popular belief in this sense was often set apart from officially sanctioned belief, as unorthodoxy to which the Church either turned a blind eye, or which it sought to channel as far as possible away from heterodoxy. Popular devotion to the saints during the later middle ages was of this nature.[7]

In dealing with the uses made by propagandists of various signs from popular culture, we shall assume that popular culture relates largely to secular and temporal activities, and popular belief to sacred or religious activities. This represents only a convenient means of arranging the material, and the two will often overlap. However, it corresponds crudely to a distinction often drawn at the end of the middle ages, where the attractions of secular popular culture were seen to threaten good religion and Christian belief. This was exemplified by a growing suspicion of carnival festivities towards the end of the fifteenth century.[8]

Such suspicion of secular popular culture concentrated on play, an activity which Johann Huizinga saw as rooted in human culture, almost as an archetypal social institution.[9] Huizinga defines play as a voluntary and disinterested activity, set within a limited space and duration so that it is distinct from 'ordinary life'. It creates its own order and establishes its own rules, involving the temporary suspension of normal social life. At the same time, it is an intensely serious activity, involving an element of tension in which the players strive to decide an issue and so to end the play. It is in this sense agonistic, and often antithetical, involving two parties or teams, although the antithetical element need not always have an element of contest. It is also close to ritual and magic, for its element of seclusion, and so of secrecy and mystery, has the same effect of transporting the participants into 'another world' apart from the mundane. Here we may see one reason why the Church of the middle ages was often suspicious of play in popular culture – it challenged the Church's claim to control ritual, and so to provide exclusive access to the supernatural. More frequently, however, the Church accommodated itself to play, allowing it within a supervised and regulated framework.

The uses of play for a propagandist are numerous. As Erasmus discovered with the *Praise of Folly*, it was possible to make an intensely serious point under the guise of jest. Men were thus brought to see a point of view of which they might otherwise be unaware. There are risks in this procedure, for the propagandist must exploit the detachment of play, and divert it into 'deadly earnestness'. This may alienate the participant, who may see it as the act of a spoilsport. At its most skilful, propaganda must hover on the fringe between play and earnestness, and trust that the involvement demanded by the play draws the participant from one to the other.

A good example can be found in the titlepage to the pamphlet *The Lutheran Strebkatz* (ill. 43).[10] The Strebkatz was a popular game in which two opponents engaged in a tug-of-war by gripping between their teeth two rods, which were connected by cords. This contraption was itself called the *Strebkatz* and the players contended for its sole possession. In this version, the cords pass around the contestants' necks. The original form of the game is depicted in

Die Luterisch Strebkatz

43   Titlepage to *Die Luterisch Strebkatz* [P. Schöffer, Worms, 1524], BL

the titlepage of a 1522 pamphlet (ill. 44), where two monks contend for the prize, a wreath held by a watching damsel.[11] In the first instance, the contestants are Luther and the pope, who is helped by a crowd of supporters representing some of Luther's main opponents – Eck, Emser, Cochleus, Murner, Hochstraten, Lemp and Alfeld.[12] Although the contest seems unequal, Luther has dragged the pope to his knees so violently that his tiara has fallen off and his money purse has burst. Luther's victory is aided only by the crucified Christ, signified by the crucifix he holds aloft in the faces of his opponents.

This example shows how the transition from play to seriousness may be achieved without alienating the viewer. The action is transposed from the seclusion of play, not back to the mundane, but to a higher level of seriousness. The contest of the *Strebkatz* thus becomes a struggle between true religion and false. This is signified above all by reversal of the normal terms of contest. It would be expected that the pope and his helpers would easily overcome the lone figure of Luther, but Luther is aided by a stronger power, that of Christ, which gives victory in the struggle. Implicitly, then, the contest is not Luther versus the pope, but the pope versus Christ.

The scene at the top of illustration 44 uses a similar technique, based on another typical contest of the time, the tournament. Christ is shown jousting

44   Titlepage to *Verhor und Acta vor dem Byschoff von Meyssen* [J. Grunenberg, Wittenberg, 1522], BL

with the pope, who wears armour and is seated on a war-steed attended by a footsoldier—devil. Christ rides an ass, and is unarmed except for his cross, but the outcome again is the reverse of what we would expect, for it is the pope's lance which falls to the ground in defeat. The confrontation between Christ and the pope is now undisguised, but there is a further level of connotation in the contest. The pope carries in his left hand a letter hung with seals, signifying a papal bull, the weapon of the pope. It is from this hand that the lance has fallen, connoting that Christ is more powerful than papal condemnations.

The world of play was not always used by propaganda to elevate the mundane to high earnestness. As Mikhail Bakhtin has pointed out, another function of play was to reduce the high and the serious to the level of the comic and the mundane. This was a form of popular criticism of the mighty, robbing them of their aura of sanctity.[13] A good example is found in trick-depictions of a cardinal which could be inverted to show a fool (see ill. 134). The tournament, as a high cultural form, was also treated in this fashion. Normally the preserve of the social elite, the princes and the nobility, it was parodied at a popular level in mock tournaments, such as those found in the Nuremberg carnival.[14] In such forms as the contest between Carnival and Lent, immortalised in Pieter Brueghel's eponymous painting, it became almost an archetypal feature of popular culture, and was a common feature of the popular festive scene in Germany.[15]

The hunt was another form of high-society play which was both parodied by popular culture and assimilated into it. Mock hunts became an integral part of carnival festivities, in forms such as the hunting of old women or spinsters, or the hunt of the Wild Man.[16] These provided ready models for artists seeking forms to convey Reformation propaganda. Lucas Cranach prepared a sketch of women hunting clergy, which was probably intended for a propaganda broadsheet.[17] Earlier we mentioned another variant on the hunting theme, the Swiss broadsheet in which Moses, Peter, Paul and the Evangelists hunt down the clergy, using the flock of Christ as their 'hunting dogs' (see ill. 135).

One form of the princely hunt sometimes took place by hunting game into an enclosure, where it was picked off by the waiting hunters.[18] This form was parodied in a broadsheet showing monks, nuns and priests hunted by devils (ill. 45). They are being driven into an enclosure at the end of which stands a hell-mouth, where they are devoured. Some attempt to hide in the thicket but are hunted out, and a monk who has managed to climb the fence is hauled back. The pope is already seated in the jaws of hell, apparently unconcerned, giving his blessing to a devil kneeling before him. The hunted are in fact in league with the hunters, for the hounds used in the hunt are given the clerical attributes of berets and a monk's habit. Monks also run hand in hand with their concubines. Monasticism is shown to lead to hell, but it is the pope and the clergy who do some of the hellish work for the demons. This hunt scene was not the invention merely of the artist. In Zwickau in 1525, students staged a carnival hunt through the streets, with devils hunting monks in the same fashion.[19] There is no evidence that this event influenced the woodcut, but both clearly had the same source, forms of carnival play which suggested anticlerical polemic.

Another form of dignified ritual copied and parodied by popular culture was the 'triumph'. The triumphal entries of secular rulers into their towns were a familiar part of late-medieval pageantry. In popular and carnivalesque forms it appeared as the Triumphs of Venus or Folly.[20] The triumph was also a popular theme among humanists, who rejoiced in its classical associations. In celebration of Johann Reuchlin's expected victory over his opponents in the affair of the Jewish books, an illustration was produced depicting Reuchlin's Triumph.[21] It was in analogy to this theme, rather than to popular triumphs, that *The Triumph of Truth* was provided in support of the evangelical movement in 1520 (ill. 46).[22]

A triumphal procession enters a town to the joyous acclaim of the people. They have come out with palm branches, and lay their cloaks in the pro-

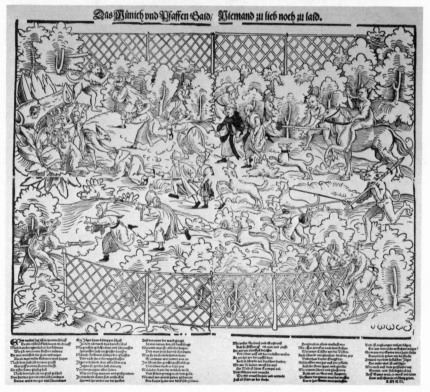

45   *Hunting the Clergy*, BM

46 *The Triumph of Truth*, GNM

cession's path, while trumpeters on the walls announce the entry. At the head of the procession is the Ark of Holy Scripture, carried by patriarchs and prophets, among whom can be recognised Moses by his horned headdress and David by his harp. Behind them march the apostles with their attributes, while Ulrich von Hutten, mounted and clad in armour, leads a group of prisoners bound by a chain. These include a pope, cardinal, bishop and several of Luther's opponents – Murner, Emser, Lemp, Faber, Wedel and Hochstraten.[23] At the end of the procession rides Christ as Saviour and Lord of the world on a cart drawn by the heraldic figures of the four Evangelists. Two attendants marching at the front of the cart are labelled as Luther and Karlstadt. A number of martyrs, bearing palms of thanksgiving, close the procession. Angels hover above Christ, holding a citation from John 14.6: 'I am the way, the truth and the light.'[24] An angel at the head of the cart bears a banner proclaiming the Lord of ages to whom all glory should be given, and identifying the group of prisoners around the pope as the sons of perdition.

The socio-cultural codes in this depiction are curiously hybrid. It draws in part on the solemn *joyeuse entrée* of a secular ruler, in part on the classical triumph of a victorious general, signified by Hutten with his chained prisoners. However, it also alludes to the Palm Sunday procession in commemoration of Christ's entry into Jerusalem. Indeed, the Christ figure seated on the cart resembles that used in such contemporary expressions of popular devotion.[25] This shows the difficulty of separating popular culture from popular belief, even where such an uncompromisingly humanist work as this is involved. Moreover, it shows that even classical and humanist models need not be remote from popular cultural forms, but that the one was often grafted onto the other.

Another combination of popular cultural elements with humanist and classical models can be seen in a parody attributed to Peter Fletner, directed against one of Luther's leading critics, John Eck. It was customary to have a triumphal arch erected to honour the person featured in a triumph. The most famous example is the triumphal arch planned by Dürer and other artists for Maximilian I. *The Triumphal Arch of John Eck* (ill. 47) was doubtless conceived as an analogy.[26] According to the accompanying text, Eck was said to have had such an arch erected for himself to celebrate his victory over Luther in the Leipzig Debate. It was allegedly set up in St Maurice's church in Ingolstadt. In the version depicted here on the left-hand side of the woodcut, it featured Eck's patron saints, John the Baptist, John the Evangelist and St John Chrysostom, famed for his oratory. The Latin inscription lauds Eck's academic titles and his famous victory over Luther. In the medallion above the arch, a cardinal's hat has been set above an empty shield, possibly in expectation of Eck being made a cardinal for his defence of the papacy in Leipzig.

Beside this alleged original is placed a satirical arch, which claims to be the real version. Eck's appropriation of the three Saints John insults them, for his patrons are really the bath, good wine and beautiful women. These appear in the arch as a bathhouse attendant, with a tub and bundle of leaves; as a fat Bacchus with a wine jug, decanter and a large loaf, who vomits from his excesses; and as Venus holding a fiery arrow, which Cupid tries to seize. The inscription above them now reads: 'In the cause of our faith, these are the patrons of Eck.' The inscription above this has been changed from 'The Triumphal Arch of Eck' to read 'Dedicated to Sardanapalus the Epicurean', a luxury-loving and effeminate king of Assyria. The medallion has been filled by a fool's cap in the shield, while above the cardinal's hat is a winged heap of excrement. This motif is repeated in a steaming heap of excrement placed on each of the top corners of the arch. The text celebrating Eck's achievements has also been parodied by additions or by substituting Latin puns for part of the text. The text is made to read:

John Eck, master of sacred $\frac{\text{theology}}{\text{sophistry,}}$ the $\frac{\text{doctor}}{\text{anguish}}$ of canon law, $\frac{\text{protonotary}}{\text{proto-fool}}$ of the $\frac{\text{apostolic}}{\text{apostate}}$ see ... not vicecancellarius but auto-nocellarius, suffragan of St Maurice, that is Wine-bishop ... returning home by goat from $\frac{\text{Saxony}}{\text{Leipzig}}$ after $\frac{\text{overcoming Luther}}{\text{being cut down to size,}}$ to the most

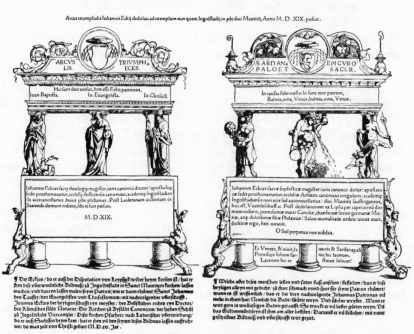

47   *The Triumphal Arch of John Eck*, Gotha Schlossmuseum

pious mother the sorceress, the sister of German folly and the most sweet sister of Philautiae, he took care to be set safely in the ranks of mortals, alive among the living, and so in folly.

The reference to 'Wine-bishop' is a pun on the German word for a suffragan bishop (*Weihbischof*). *Philautiae* is self-love, another form of folly. *Autonocellarius*, as a pun on *vicecancellarius*, seems to be a humanist neologism similar to other words created from *nocens*, 'harmful', during the fifteenth century. It is probably intended to mean 'self-abuser' (but without the sexual connotations of modern usage). 'Self-depraver' is perhaps an appropriate rendition. The reference to being cut down to size is to the pamphlet *Eccius dedolatus*, in which Eck has the evil cut out of him by being flayed alive. This links the satire to the theme of the *Narrenschneiden*, found in the Nuremberg carnival, and to the carnivalesque use of 'grotesque realism', which will be discussed in more detail below.[27]

The forms of play mentioned so far all have associations with carnival, the most popular form of play during the later middle ages.[28] Carnival is also synonymous with fools and foolery, especially in such well-known manifestations as the Nuremberg carnival, the *Schembartlauf.*[29] However, carnival was celebrated throughout Germany, from Basel and Regensberg in the south, down the Rhine into the Low Countries, and as far north and east as Danzig and Koenigsberg.[30]

Participation was not restricted to any single social group, although each class seems to have celebrated in its distinctive manner. The nobility, the urban patriciate and well-to-do artisans favoured the private feast and dance, although there is some evidence that this practice was sometimes followed among the lower orders. The broader levels of the populace in town and country took part in public celebrations, such as processions, the fetching of Shrovetide cakes or various forms of 'trick or treat' (*Heischung*). Another form which had both public and private character were various 'performances' such as carnival plays, sword dances, tournaments or customs such as the 'Butchers' Spring' in Munich. The tournaments could be eminently serious, in the case of the nobility, or mock tournaments, in the case of the lower urban classes and the peasantry.[31]

Like play, carnival involved suspension of the norms and rules of ordinary life, so that it became a form of release from mundane pressures. In this sense, it was akin to Church feasts, such as the Feast of Fools or the Feast of the Ass, in which monastic novices, for the rest of the year subject to a rigid discipline, could let off steam.[32] The agonistic feature of play is also present in carnival, most noticeably in the form of carnival versus its opponents, that is, those who refused to join in the festivities or criticised its excesses. This seems to underlie the custom of *Heischung*, where cakes or sweets were demanded under threat of having some prank played for refusal. The agonistic form also appears in various mock contests staged during the festivities.

Besides mock tournaments, and the harassment of unmarried girls and old women, there was the archetypal confrontation between Carnival and Lent. A German form is attested for 1505 in Zittau, where on Ash Wednesday two figures clad as Pickelherring and Hans Wurst wrestled until the former threw the latter into the town fountain, a sign of the victory of fast over feasting.[33]

Another carnival custom was the satirising of those in authority through parodies of official ceremonies, such as the election of a scholar–king in Nördlingen in 1511, or the holding of a carnival court in Pfreim in Bavaria in 1497. Elsewhere it took the form of a ritual of rebellion, with a mock storming of the town hall, and deposition of the government in favour of the rule of folly.[34] During the fifteenth century, parodies of the clergy were also frequent in carnival celebrations, especially through dressing up as monks and nuns in carnival processions. In Cologne in 1441 a mock reliquary was carried through the streets, accompanied by a carnival puppet with an asperger and banner, in mockery of a religious procession.[35] In Frankfurt in 1467 seventeen citizens were punished for parodying a religious procession. In Augsburg in 1503 several youths carried around a goat lying on a cushion bedecked with ribbons, which was baptised by a mock priest.[36] Such parodies were usually regarded with good humour by authority, although the more blatant cases of irreverence were punished. Towards the end of the fifteenth century, however, there was an increase in prohibitions of carnival mummers wearing monks' and nuns' costumes, of mockery of Church customs and of wearing masks during carnival.[37]

It was natural that supporters of the new evangelical faith should turn to these popular forms of mockery. They provided ready-made forms of irreverence towards a faith now held to be useless. Over twenty instances where carnival was used to attack the old belief can be traced in Germany during the first two decades of the Reformation.[38] The theme of carnival and its many variations was ideal for propaganda, and was taken up eagerly. The 1520 pamphlet *Eccius dedolatus*, describing how Eck had the evil cut out of him by being skinned alive, alluded to a carnival scene, the *Narrenschneiden*, in which a fool's folly is cut out of him. This had been used with great success by Thomas Murner in his *Exorcism of Fools*. Murner, a Franciscan from Strassburg, was the only able Catholic polemicist of the early years of the Reformation, and he used the theme again in his tract *On the Great Lutheran Fool* of 1522, where the folly of Luther's heresies is cut out of the Lutheran fool.[39]

The image of the fool was used frequently by Reformation propaganda, and we have already mentioned some examples: the cardinal–fool depiction, which was to become very popular as a motif for medals, or the equation of monasticism with folly in works like *The Monk as Spoon-seller* or Beck's *The Monk and the Ass*. The similarity of fool's cap and monastic cowl suggested the substitution of one for the other, creating a sign which recurs throughout evangelical propaganda (see ills. 71, 83, 166 for examples). Linked to the fool was the carnival puppet, and fools were often shown carrying fool puppets. A popular Nuremberg carnival float was a 'ship of fools', in which sat a large fool surrounded by several of these puppets.[40] The notion of folly combined with the mummery of the puppet was seized on eagerly by propagandists. Pious Christians, wrote Philadelphus Regius in a 1524 pamphlet, would not be fooled by false papal miracles 'like young children with carnival masks and straw dolls'. Luther has exposed the pope and 'torn from him his mummery mask, with which he has fooled and deceived the whole world'.[41] This even became a popular term of abuse for the Catholic clergy. In Ulm in 1524 a Catholic preacher who tried to open his sermon with an Ave Maria was abused by the angry congregation as a 'carnival puppet' (*Fastnachtsbutz*).[42]

The idea of the carnival puppet or mask as something to deceive only the young or the foolish was taken up in visual propaganda at an early stage. It was brilliantly used in the titlepage of a Swiss pamphlet of 1520, *Of the Old and New God, Belief and Doctrine* (ill. 48).[43] On the left-hand side, the pope is depicted as a carnival puppet held aloft in a procession by his supporters, some of whom are identified by name as Aristotle, Ambrosius Caterinas, Johann Faber, Eck and Sylvester Prierias: the last four were all opponents of Luther. The pope is crowned with his tiara by two devils, as are the cardinal and the canon to the left. The pope holds the key symbolising his office, and usurped symbols of Christ as judge, a bundle of swords and a rod. He represents the 'new belief', while the 'old belief' is depicted on the right. There we find the Trinity, represented by the Father, the dove and the risen Christ. A scroll links the Father to Christ, reading: 'This is my beloved son.' The upholders of this old, true belief are the four Evangelists, indicated by their symbolic figures, St Paul with the sword and book, and Moses and Aaron to the right and left of Christ respectively. In the bottom corner right stands Luther, holding a scroll which reads: 'One God and Father of all'.

Although crudely drawn, this illustration is very skilful in its layers of signification. The binary, antithetical construction immediately establishes the fundamental opposition between true belief and false. The new god is identified: the pope; for the old God any inscription is superfluous. The antithesis is established both horizontally and vertically in the graphic composition. On the right, everything flows down from the Father, through the Holy Spirit to the risen Christ, thence out through the figures of the New Testament to Luther on the fringe. On the left, the pope is propped up precariously from below by human strength, precariousness signified by the tilt of the stool on which he sits. The devils holding the papal tiara may also be contributing to the attempt to hold him aloft. The figures in the composition amplify these oppositions further. The human figures on the left signify human teaching; the non-human, the devils, signify the diabolical nature of the papacy. On the right, the divine figures and the assembly representing the

Old and New Testaments combine to associate Luther with right belief. But the most important connotation is imparted by the puppet. Whereas the belief of Luther is that in a true and living God, that of the 'new' papal belief is in something of straw and rags, well indicated by the raggedy, floppy legs of the papal doll. It is a diabolical belief, connoted by the doll's right leg, which has a webbed foot, a sign of the Devil. A sixteenth-century reader would above all have recalled the other important feature of the carnival puppet. At the end of the carnival it was burned and interred, a symbolic committal to hell, which was thus to be the fate of the 'new god'.[44]

Greater use was made of the carnival theme in a broadsheet which depicts

48   Titlepage to *Vom alten und nüen Gott* (1521), GNM

what was only implied in the last example, the papal journey to hell (ill. 49).[45] In the Nuremberg carnival tableaux were pulled through the streets in horse-drawn carriages. Here such a carriage is filled with Catholic clergy, pulled by horses with the pope as postillion. The tree in the centre of the carriage is a carnival tree, which was stripped of branches and left with only a tuft of greenery at the top. It is also reminiscent of a May branch, and could allude to the amorous activity of the clergy. It is here hung with three letters of indulgence, and below them is a larger letter with crossed papal keys indicating a papal bull. This recalls that each Nuremberg carnival was given a motif which recurred on the floats. The floats were often in the form of ships, and this carriage resembles a ship with its mast and 'sail'. The ship of fools was a popular theme for floats, and this carriage-load of clergy is perhaps another 'ship of fools'.[46]

The Nuremberg tableaux were accompanied by runners who played pranks on the crowd, pulled them along and beat them with tufted branches.[47] Here this role is carried out by devils, harassing monks beside the carriage. One devil carries a bishop in a basket on his back, and there is another similar figure in the left background. They recall a Nuremberg carnival figure, a devil carrying an old woman to hell in his basket.[48] The devil dragging a monk by his cowl in the foreground may refer to another carnival custom, the hunting of old women by devils.[49] The Nuremberg carnival ended with the tableaux entering a specially constructed set, the 'hell', which was demolished or destroyed by fire.[50] It is into exactly such a 'hell', constructed in grand classical style, that the pope leads his wagon. The 'hell' is overflowing with every kind of cleric, including popes, and is already being consumed by fire, laid by monks and devils, who stoke it with firewood. Despite the many unmistakable references to the Nuremberg carnival, there was no corresponding historical event, unlike the Zwickau 'parson hunt'. The Nuremberg government was too cautious about creating public disturbance or giving offence to Catholic authorities, such as the emperor, to allow such an explicit piece of propaganda. In 1522 it prohibited performance of a carnival play in which the pope appeared, and forbade the use of a 'hell' which might cause offence to the clergy. However, in the procession of 1523 one of the runners wore a costume made of bulls of indulgence. This was evidently considered allowable social comment, for there was a history of opposition to indulgences in Nuremberg since the fifteenth century, and there had been an indulgence parody in the carnival of 1516.[51]

More open attacks on the clergy or on religious belief were frowned upon. The Nuremberg Council inquired disapprovingly in 1525 into the satirical carrying of a crucifix during carnival, and carnival itself was prohibited entirely during the years 1525–38.[52] On its revival in 1539, it was immediately banned again by the Council. A satirical float was directed against the Lutheran preacher Andreas Osiander, a sober, puritanical man whom the

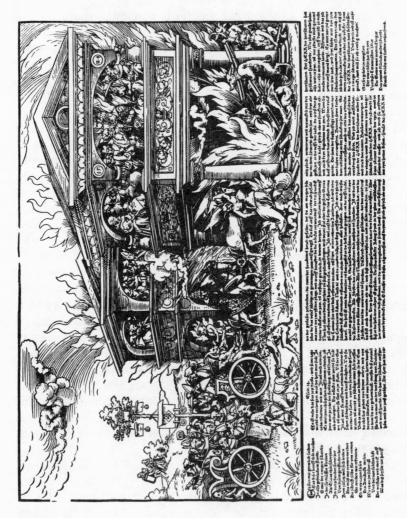

49   *The Papal Ride to Hell*

townsfolk clearly held responsible for restrictions on their festive life. In a 'hell' in the form of a ship of fools, Osiander was shown surrounded by fools and devils, holding a gaming board (ill. 50). He complained to the Council, which had the carnival organisers arrested and the carnival prohibited. In retaliation a crowd stormed Osiander's house, so driving home the message of the float that Osiander should go to hell with his strictures on popular games and sports.[53]

The incident reveals the wide gap between popular and official attitudes towards play and game that is important to an understanding of Reformation propaganda. Playful mockery of established institutions was allowed within certain limits. Once it stepped beyond the bounds of propriety, as defined by the authorities, the playing had to stop. This applied no less to propaganda which used popular forms, such as play and carnival, to make its points. It was prohibited when it became too biting. Nuremberg again provides useful examples. The Council kept a careful watch over the production of the printing press, and intervened against anything it considered offensive or indiscreet. In 1521 it prohibited the sale of Luther's portrait with the dove, in 1523 it forbade the sale of satirical songs, abusive literature and broadsheets featuring Luther and the pope. There were similar prohibitions for 1524, which were

50   *Hell from 1539 Schembart in Nuremberg*, GNM

also applied to visual propaganda — portraits of Luther, broadsheets, murals and even painted cloths. Up to 1555 such bans were repeated in eight different years, all directed against visual propaganda for the Reformation.[54] In one of the first towns to give allegiance to the evangelical movement, this sensitivity to strong attacks on the old belief is remarkable. It attests that broadsheet propaganda certainly was genuinely popular — in the sense that it met a continued demand in the face of official disapproval.

Carnival and carnivalesque occasions were to provide extensive material for Reformation visual propaganda, clearly because of their essentially visual nature. Besides the carnival procession and puppet, the carnival theme can be followed through several other signs which have less obvious links to carnival. The animal masks given to Luther's opponents, which were mentioned without further explanation in several woodcuts above, are similar to carnival puppets or masks.[55] We can examine them in detail through a broadsheet from the early 1520s, showing five figures arrayed before a colonnade, as if on a tribune (ill. 51). All are named by inscriptions at the top. The lion in the centre is Pope Leo X, the cat Thomas Murner, the goat Jerome Emser, the sow John Eck and the dog the Tübingen theologian Jacob Lemp.

The allusions in this woodcut are not just to carnival masks. Murner had taken on the form of the cat himself, as an onomatopoeic parody of his own name: Murner — miaow, a cat's cry. Emser's animal mask also comes from his name, which means goat, and Emser himself included a leaping goat on his

51   *Leo X, Murner, Emser, Eck and Lemp as Animals*, GNM

heraldic device. The associations of the others were not self-chosen, but applied to them by their Reformation opponents. Eck, shown holding an acorn, is a sow nuzzling in the dirt after his food, and living like a pig. Lemp, defeated in the Zurich disputation of 1523, is shown as a snapping cur, quarrelsomely wrangling over the bone he is holding.[56] These are natural polemical applications of animal characteristics to human beings, similar to the animal metaphors found in medieval literature. Such theriomorphism is close to personification of non-human and inanimate beings. Animal and human are amalgamated by attributing to personified animals the quality which the persons in question are thought to share with them.[57] A lion is synonymous with savagery, so to depict Leo X as a lion is to represent him as savage, an association made easier by his name. Similarly, the randiness of the goat was attributed to Emser, the text given to him making an ironic play on these connotations: 'Ah, virgin goat, you stink so bad of chastity in your long beard.'

Other representations of Luther's opponents as animals seem less inspired. In *The Lutheran Strebkatz* Johann Cochleus is shown with a snail perched on his head, but little use was made of the animal attributes of the snail, sloth or sexuality. Cochleus can mean either snail or spoon and, following this latter reading, Cochleus is also carrying a spoon over his shoulder in the *Strebkatz*. Hochstraten is attended by rats, in allusion to an arbitrary name given him as 'the rat king'. In *The Triumph of Truth* he even appears as a rat wearing a crown. Less enigmatic is the squirrel in *The Lutheran Strebkatz*. This is a theriomorphic depiction of Eucharius Henner, whose sermons were regarded with contempt, so that he could be dismissed, like the squirrel, as being of little significance.[58]

Animal representation could have many layers of connotation, including, as we shall see shortly, the demonic.[59] We can see some of these in a depiction of the pope as an ass attempting to play the bagpipe (see ill. 60). It draws on the brutishness and stupidity of the ass, which made it synonymous with folly, and the Reformation made good use of the term as a polemical catch-cry in abusive labels such as 'cloister-ass' or 'choir-ass' directed against monks.[60] It also recalls a popular proverb, 'the ass on the lyre', signifying the wasted effort of someone attempting a task for which they are not suited. The bagpipe may have been used here instead of the lyre as a sign of debauchery, in its role as a phallic symbol.[61] We are also reminded of the animal allegories in such highly popular works as Aesop's *Fables* and *Reinhard the Fox*. The characters of Reinhard the fox and Isengrim the wolf doubtless provided models for anticlerical satires showing a fox or wolf in clerical or monastic habit, preaching to geese or hens. It was a frequent motif in medieval church sculpture, and the fox preaching to the geese appeared on the Minster in Strassburg, and on churches in Braunschweig, Wismar, Lübeck and Ebstorf.[62] It was not surprising that the motif was taken over by the evangelical movement, as in the case of a priest in Annaberg in Saxony, who in 1524 found a drawing of a fox in priest's habit in his pulpit.[63]

A 1522 pamphlet, *The Wolf's Song*, shows how early the animal allegory was used for Reformation propaganda. The work instructs its readers on how to recognise spiritual wolves, and although the contents draw on the biblical parable discussed in chapter 2, the titlepage alludes to medieval animal allegory and the proverbs which grew out of it (ill. 52).[64] It shows the pope and cardinals catching geese, either through strings of beads, by means of a net or through music. It alludes to a proverb mentioned in a 1523 pamphlet by Heinrich von Kettenbach, where he says that priests 'preach as the wolf to the geese in the woods', that is, they seek to ensnare them by tricks and cunning.[65]

By the later part of the sixteenth century, these animal allegories were a stock part of the Protestant propaganda repertoire. A good example is a woodcut portraying Duke Christoph of Wurttemberg as a Christian prince, which gives a prayer invoking God's protection against the beasts which surround him (ill. 53). Six are depicted, each with the indicative sign of a different member of the Catholic hierarchy: a dragon is the pope, a lion a cardinal, a fox a bishop, a bear an abbot, a tiger a canon and a rabbit a chaplain. All are beasts of ferocity, except for the rabbit, which is a sign of laziness, for the written text speaks of the chaplain's willingness to sit in a benefice and enjoy its fruits without effort.

Das wolff gesang.

Ain ander hertz/ain ander klayd/Tragen falsche wölffin der haybd
Damit sy den gensen lupffen / Den pflum ab den kröpffen rupffen
Magstu hie bey garwol verston/ Wa du lisest die büechlein schon.

52   Titlepage to *Das Wolffgesang* [S. Grimm, Augsburg, 1522], BL

The fox, with its reputation for slyness, was probably used for propaganda more frequently than the wolf. But more interesting is the use made of a popular proverb about stroking a fox's brush as a synonym for flattery.[66] The titlepage of a 1524 pamphlet applied it to Erasmus, showing him stroking a fox-brush crowned with a triple tiara (ill. 54). This signifies his unwillingness to break with the papacy, and his desire rather to praise it in the hope of gain. The fox-brush was also a synonym for hypocrisy, and there are such over-tones in the attack on Erasmus. It is most clearly used to allude to hypocrisy in the titlepage of a 1538 pamphlet (ill. 55), the German translation of the report of the cardinals commissioned by Paul III in 1537 to study means of reforming the Church. It was printed in Wittenberg, with glosses from Luther attacking the inadequacy of the proposed reforms.[67] The illustration here shows three cardinals busily sweeping out a church with brooms made from fox-brushes, a sign of their purely hypocritical attempts at reform. A moral-ising broadsheet using the fox-brush as a sign of flattery and hypocrisy was printed in Augsburg during the 1530s, with a woodcut by Erhard Schoen, while a more elaborate polemical version in a Nuremberg broadsheet of 1545, *The Fox-brush Shop*, showed the attempts of the Catholic Church to win and hold its adherents by flattery and hypocrisy.[68]

Most of the examples examined so far have depended on the satirical adaptation of popular cultural forms, or were popular satires on high cultural forms. Such satire was an integral part of carnival and popular festivals,

53   *Duke Christoff of Wurttemberg and the Papal Beasts*, Dahlem
54   Titlepage to *Gesprech buchlein, von eynem Bawern, Belial Erasmo Roterodam* (1524)

which allowed a limited freedom for mockery and abuse within carefully controlled limits. There was usually an ambivalence about such festive occasions
which took much of the sting out of the mockery. But abuse could be used
not in this good-humoured way, but as a more serious form of insult, where
feeling ran high and tempers were short. A common form of serious insult
among the German nobility was the *Scheltbrief* or 'letter of insult', frequent
enough from the end of the fifteenth century for it to constitute an entire
genre. In an age when legal redress of grievance was difficult to obtain, such
letters provided an outlet for strong resentments and feelings of injustice.
They were usually accompanied by insulting depictions (*Schandbilder*) which
heaped abuse and libel on the enemy.[69]

A common form of insult in the age was association with hanging, particularly effective when directed against those with claims to social respect of pretensions to high power, for hanging was the mode of execution for the base
and low-born. In Italy a ritual hanging was used by many towns to insult their
enemies, and towns under attack would ceremoniously hang a depiction of
their attackers from the walls.[70] German *Scheltbriefe* often depicted those
they attacked suffering death by hanging, dismemberment or disembowel-
ment (ill. 56). In 1521 Aleander was depicted hanging upside down from the

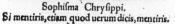

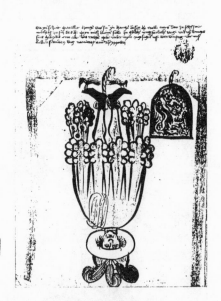

55   Titlepage to *Ratschlag . . . eins ausschus etlicher Cardinal*
(1538), GNM
56   *Scheltbrief* of Johann von Löwenstein to Landgrave Ludwig I
of Hesse, 2 November 1438, Stadtarchiv Frankfurt

gallows in this fashion.[71] Often it was sufficient just to allude to hanging to effect the insult. In February 1521 a depiction of Luther and Hutten as comrades in arms, doubtless one of those discussed in chapter 2, was nailed to the public gallows in Schlettstadt in Alsace, and the town had to apologise to Hutten for the affront.[72] Such forms of insult probably had the same force as burning in effigy, and may have been related to popular forms of image-magic.[73]

A direct adaptation of the *Schandbild* for Reformation polemic is found in a work issued by Luther himself in 1545, the *Depiction of the Papacy*.[74] This small work is a picture book, with nine illustrations and brief text; here we shall examine its fifth sheet (ill. 57), where the pope and three cardinals are being executed by hanging. Two cardinals have their hats dangling from their bodies, that of the third is tied to the gallows-beam on which he hangs. Devils carry off the souls of the expiring victims, while the executioner nails their tongues, which have been cut off, to the gallows as a sign of their criminal falsehoods. The Latin text at the top of the sheet announces that this is a fitting reward for the satanical pope and his cardinals.

The German text at the bottom proclaims, in imitation of a *Scheltbrief*: 'If the pope and cardinals were to be punished here on earth, their slanders would deserve what you see rightly depicted here.' The form 'as you see

57   *The Fit Reward for the Pope and his Cardinals* (1545), BL

depicted here' is a standard rendition of the *Schandbild*.[75] Moreover, the figures who have been so justly dispatched can be identified individually as Pope Paul III, Cardinal Albert of Brandenburg and Cardinal Otto Truchsess of Waldburg.[76] This too conforms to the style of the *Schandbild*, which not only names the crime for which those attacked deserve hanging, but which also identifies them by name and depicts them through their heraldic device. Coats of arms had a particular totem-like significance for men of the later middle ages, since they were regarded as a substitute for the person they signified. Indeed, they were even seen as a pictorial expression of the personality itself, something put to good polemical use in Eck's coat of arms.[77] The *Schandbilder* seized upon this feature and in some cases, as in illustration 56, hung the coat of arms alongside the person depicted as suffering death by hanging.

These features of the *Schandbild* are developed with some skill in a broadsheet showing the papal coat of arms, another work which originated from Luther (ill. 58). The arms have an heraldic shield with two crossed keys surmounted by a papal tiara. However, the keys have been shattered, a sign that the power of the pope has been broken. From the stock of one key hangs the

58   *Satire on the Papal Arms*

pope, from the other another famous victim of death by hanging, Judas.[78] The essential theme of the *Schandbild*, the deserved death by hanging, is thus established. The device within the coat of arms develops the theme. It shows a hand clutching money-bags, that is, 'Judas' purse', from which protrude bishops' mitres, in analogy to the thirty pieces of silver for which Judas betrayed Christ. Above the clutching hand is a cardinal's hat, and in the neck of the central bag are royal crowns. The verses accompanying the illustration are in dialogue form, and state that the pope has abused the power of the keys, the Church's power to bind and loose. Through annates and palliums, he has filled his purse with mitres and abbots' hats. He has even tried to purchase royal crowns, and wishes to make his cardinals everywhere supreme. He has, therefore, played the part of Judas, and so he is condemned to 'Judas' reward'. Henceforth, he shall bear Judas' purse in his arms.

Another variation of the *Schandbild* used a less refined form of insult. It showed the seal of the person under attack being pressed into a heap of excrement or into a sow's behind. The seal was a sign of personal commitment and good faith, like our present-day use of a signature. Such depictions thus expressed the injured party's conviction of the faithlessness of his opponent: his seal was worth no more than dung, fit only for an animal's behind.[79] The *Depiction of the Papacy* took up this feature in another of its pages to parody the papal arms (ill. 59). The crossed papal keys have been replaced by a pair of jemmies, which Germans called 'thieves' keys'.[80] The papal tiara which should be above the shield has been inverted, and a German mercenary soldier, a *Landsknecht*, defecates into it.[81] Two others adjust their dress after having done the same. The Latin title states satirically: 'The pope is adored as an earthly god.' The German inscription comments that the pope has treated the kingdom of Christ as the pope's crown is treated here. But do not despair, it continues, for God has promised comfort through his spirit. A reference to Apocalypse 18 shows what that comfort is to be: the proclamation that Babylon has been overthrown, that is, that the downfall of the papacy is at hand.

In this work the written text adds two varying messages to the visual message. The German text provides a quasi-doctrinal commentary; the Latin title, however, captures the woodcut's intention more closely: it is an ironic inversion, a reduction of the sublime to the mundane. This is what Mikhail Bakhtin has called the 'material bodily principle' in popular culture. The numerous references to basic human functions such as eating, defecation or intercourse have the effect, he argues, of reducing the elevated to the humble, of humiliating it so that it loses its ability to inspire awe.[82] Such 'grotesque realism', as Bakhtin calls it, is found throughout the pages of the *Depiction of the Papacy*. The seventh woodcut, which appeared as half of a double depiction with the ass on the bagpipe (ill. 60), used it to discredit papal plans for a General Council of the Church.

The pope rides on a sow, carrying a spiral of steaming excrement on his open palm. The Latin text at the top says that this is how the pope holds a council in Germany. The German text states that the sow must allow itself to be ridden and spurred from both sides. It wants a council, and in reply receives the excrement. There are two allusions here. Luther often spoke of Germany as the 'papal sow', to be force-fed with papal lies for the pope's sole gain. There was also a popular riddle in circulation, and which appeared in print in 1541: 'How do you ride a sow so that it does not bite? – Put dung on your hand, and when the sow smells it, it will chase it and not bite the rider.' The message, then, was that Germany may well seek a council from the pope, but all it could expect was lies and deceit.[83] This sheet uses Bakhtin's 'material bodily principle', but lacks the ironic inversions of the *Landsknecht* scene. It was used far more effectively in the third sheet of the series (ill. 61).

Two peasants bare their bottoms and fart at the pope, who is holding out a papal bull of condemnation, identified as such by the fire and brimstone it is emitting. The emission of the bull is thus answered by the emission of wind, a piece of grotesque realism worthy of Rabelais. The German text comments: 'No, pope, do not scare us with your ban, and be not such an angry man, or else we'll oppose you and show you a Belvedere.' 'Belvedere' here means to present a fair view, a satirical reference to showing the bottom to the pope.

59   *The Pope is Adored as an Earthly God* (1545), BL

This was itself a popular gesture signifying contempt.[84] The Latin text develops another thought suggested by the visual text: 'Here are lips fashioned for the feet of the pope.' This refers to the custom of kissing the pope's foot in reverence as a sign of subjection, and constitutes another inversion through use of grotesque realism. Lips here become the cheeks of the buttocks, so that the imparted meaning is that the pope's foot, far from being worthy to kiss, is fit only to fart upon, or even worse. A solemn custom has been reduced to the level of the crudely material, rendering it risible. Such attacks on papal customs could serve another purpose for Reformation propagandists, namely, to act as a profession of disbelief in its power and efficacy. To flaunt objects, persons and actions held to represent the divine order of things in such a manner could vividly demonstrate that they were without supernatural power.[85] The material bodily principle was thus used to desacralise the numinous and withdraw it from the realm of religious veneration. It found expression in polemical literature in injunctions to use indulgences for lavatory paper.[86]

We have evidence that such debasement of the opponents of the Reformation was applied literally. One pamphlet of 1528 told how Luther had been sent a copy of a work written by two Leipzig *Magister*, attacking in scurrilous terms his marriage to Katherina von Bora. This work was taken off

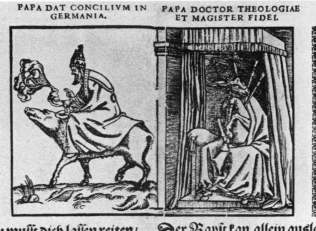

60   *The Pope rides the Sow; the Papal Ass on the Bagpipe*
(1545), BL

to the lavatory by various of Luther's supporters in Wittenberg, 'illustrated' there, and then returned to its authors.[87] There was, however, another dimension to this scatological humour than just an intention to demean and humiliate. In the popular mind it would also have served to link the pope and his followers with the demonic. In popular superstition the privy was the haunt of demons and evil spirits.[88] It is thus no surprise that the themes of defecation and the demonic should be linked in Reformation propaganda. Thomas Murner had tried to invoke the connection at the end of *On the Great Lutheran Fool*, where Luther is thrown down the privy, a popular ritual form of consigning him to hell (see ill. 190).

From the Lutheran side this was far exceeded in coarseness by an attack on one of Luther's most vehement opponents, Johann Cochleus (ill. 62). The theme is to show Cochleus as an instrument of the Devil, as the 'Devil's arsehole' as it is expressed in the text. The Devil, wearing glasses and with spoons in his ears, a play on Cochleus' name, defecates into Cochleus' open mouth, while a fool—devil holds aloft a mirror to enable him to adjust his aim. Cochleus is so full of devil's excrement, the written text tells us, that he is likely to burst, so that he in turn excretes this as his books against Luther. In the bottom left-hand corner, observers of the scene turn away in disgust. This is not just a reference to the excrement, but also to the unbearable

III.

61   *The Papal Belvedere* (1545), BL

stench associated with the Devil. Undeterred by this, a monk, a priest and a prince eagerly receive and devour Cochleus' works, while a circle of rejoicing demons dance around them. These have animal heads, in particular those of animals associated with the demonic — a dog, a swine and an ass. We have already seen such demons in the carnival parody of the pope's ride to hell (ill. 49). They add another dimension to the animal masks in which Luther's opponents are depicted in the illustrations discussed above (see ills. 43, 46 and 51) — these are linked to the demonic.

The associations of defecation and demons are used to greater effect in a broadsheet showing *The Origins of the Monks* (ill. 63). This also takes up the gallows theme, invoking the popular superstition about places of execution being also the haunt of evil spirits. Three devils perch on a gallows, one of whom is relieving himself by excreting a vast pile of monks onto the ground below.[89] The German verses expound this theme with a narrative. Once upon a time the Devil began to suffer severe abdominal pains 'as if he were preg-

62   *Satire on Johann Cochleus,* Dahlem

nant'. Climbing onto a gallows, he began to strain until he had relieved himself of the cause of his discomfort. Observing the result, he remarked that it was no wonder he had suffered so much. Such crafty and cunning knaves were worse than he and all his fellows. Should they all gather in his kingdom, he would be expelled himself. They should, therefore, not be allowed all to remain together. So saying, the Devil saw to it that the 'loose, tonsured monkish knaves' were scattered throughout the world. This provides an extra dimension lacking in the visual text, but there is another theme in the woodcut which the written text does not take up, namely, that the monks are also gallows-knaves, those born beneath the gallows who will end upon it. The broadsheet thus draws together three separate themes from popular culture: defecation, superstitions about the demonic and insults. It is thus simultaneously a *Schandbild* similar to those in *Scheltbriefe*, and a means of equating monks with evil spirits through popular superstition.

The theme of birth is also found in the *Depiction of the Papacy*, in its ninth sheet showing the birth of the pope (ill. 64). Here the link with defecation is weaker and a natural birth is intended. The woodcut shows a grinning and pregnant she-devil giving birth to the pope and a crowd of cardinals. This diabolical origin is further emphasised by showing the pope being

63   *The Origins of the Monks*, Berlin, BL
64   *The Origin of the Pope* (1545), BL

suckled, nursed and toddled by the three Furies. These are identified by the German text as Megaera, the Fury of hatred, Alecto, the Fury of matricide and patricide, and Tisiphone, the Fury of insanity and demonic possession.[90] The fox-brush of hypocrisy is also much in evidence, lying beside the cradle by the suckling pope, and being used by a Fury to keep the flies off as the pope is rocked in his cradle. The use of the classical Eumenides would seem to weaken the popular cultural appeal of this sheet. However, to the reader unfamiliar with the three names mentioned in the text, the three old hags would appear to be witches, so preserving the diabolical allusions, even if the subtleties of the association with the Furies were lost.

The notion of the diabolical origins of the papacy supplies the theme for another sheet, which was probably a companion piece to *The Origins of the Monks* (see ill. 63). This is called *The Origin of the Antichrist* (ill. 65) and shows two devils crushing up monks and priests in a huge tun, while two others flying through the air bring more to add to the number. In the background, two flying devils fetch another tun full of monks, who have been at least partly crushed, judging from the juice pouring from the tun. Beside the large tun, two devils breathe life into a fat, naked and bacchic pope. The scenes depicted are explained by the German text. The Devil has become incensed at Christ gathering about him a Church in which the Word of God is preached. Thus he has had a great host of monks, clergy and nuns gathered and crushed up. From these he makes an image into which he breathes life

65   *The Origin of the Antichrist*, Dahlem, BL

through black magic. This figure he calls the Antichrist, because he will always oppose preaching of the Word of God. This creature is made in the image of his creator, cruel and wild; and as soon as he is conscious of his strength, he decides himself to become prince of hell. Here then, concludes the text, is the Antichrist: he is nothing more than a monster formed out of monks and priests.

This sheet provides us with an excellent example of the complementary nature of written and visual text, much of the latter being only partly explicable without the former. The numerous elements on which it draws show clearly the blurring of the boundary between popular culture and popular belief. It relies on allusions to demonic creation, similar to the other examples we have just discussed, but adds the theme of black magic. It could be seen at one level as a magical parody of the communion, alluding to popular devotional representations of Christ in the winepress, which will be discussed in the next chapter. However, it is also full of allusions to carnival and carnivalesque satire. First there is the theme of the pope as a monster formed in a process akin to winemaking. The creation of the monster recalls the carnival puppet of illustration 48, the bacchic theme the excessive imbibing associated with carnival. The theme of crushing is a similar carnivalesque motif to the one of dismemberment that is found in medieval epics or in Rabelais.[91] The diabolical itself is also a carnival motif, most carnivalesque festivities featuring mummers clad in devil-costumes who were allowed to run loose in the streets, thus creating the atmosphere of unbridled freedom associated with carnival.[92] Seen in this light, the depiction has as much in common with popular festivities as it has with the more serious theme of the Antichrist.

Similar in its linking of carnivalesque and demonic motifs in anti-papal satire is a Low-German or Dutch watercolour dating possibly from the mid-sixteenth century (ill. 66). The devils are shown carrying-off to hell a wagon-load of souls, some of whom are monks. The souls, signified by their smaller size, are struggling to escape from a large tun, into which a devil is trying to cram them with the aid of a mallet. The other devil, with bird's beak and claws, rides as postillion astride a goat, a diabolical animal linked to witchcraft in popular superstition. The cart itself is formed by the body of the pope, his legs acting as the shafts in which the goat is yoked. The outstretched arms form the axles of the cart, while the wheels are locked into position by the papal keys held grasped in the papal fist. The spokes of the wheels are formed by members of the Catholic hierarchy, bishops, cardinals and monks, and a grease-pot for oiling the wheels hangs down from the pope's tiara at the rear. This bizarre cart recalls a carnival wagon, and the bird-beaked postillion resembles a popular form of carnival mask.[93] The devil crushing the souls into the tun is similar to the monk-crushing theme of the previous woodcut. As a single image, it imparts brilliantly the message that one will go to hell with the papacy, which is a vehicle of the Devil.

More elaborate in its use of these themes than any of the last few examples is a woodcut broadsheet showing the clergy feasting in the jaws of a grotesque she-devil (ill. 67). The demon is a giant figure, half bird, half beast, seated on a large letter with numerous affixed seals, signifying no doubt a papal bull. Its left leg is injured, for it supports itself with a crutch, and a sling and bandages are bound around the leg, which is resting in a bucket. The asperger in the bucket signifies that it is a vessel for holy water. In its outstretched hand it holds a collection box, and this and the remnants of a cowl draped over its head show that it is intended to represent a monk. The large-scale composition is thus a satire on indulgences and monks as their purveyors. These are revealed once again as diabolical.

The small-scale detail is more complex. In the gaping mouth of the demon a group of clergy are seated around a table – a monk, a friar, two nuns and a canon all preparing to eat. Lolling at their feet are two demons, while above them a number of demons on the head of the giant devil prepare food. The first course is already being handed down to a nun, who reaches up from inside the demon's ear. The other demons fly through the air, one propelled by breaking wind, bringing a canon and a pope to the feast. The pope carries his key of office, and a letter of indulgence or a papal bull. The cooking scene is elaborate. A large tree-branch, which seems to be growing from the neck of the giant devil, serves to suspend the food over the fire. There is a large pot,

66   *The Papal Cart*, GNM

67   *Devourers of the Dead in the Jaws of Hell*, Dahlem

and strung out alongside it what appear to be human limbs. On a branch to the right sausages have been left to smoke, while a demon on the left prepares more sausages and spitted carcasses for the fire. The latter seem suspiciously human in shape. At the very top of the branch are seated two devils who provide music for the feast with pipe and drums, while the entire feasting scene is illuminated by the rays from the fire.

This gruesome feast is especially difficult to interpret. The feasting and dismemberment themes are rabelaisian, and another version of the carnivalesque theme of crushing. This cooking-pot recalls the title of a pamphlet from around 1535, *A Fresh Compot from the Pope* (ill. 68), which speaks of the stew cooked up by the pope and his allies for German consumption. The illustration shows the pope stirring the pot with the aid of the emperor, two princes and a bishop. A cardinal behind the pope cooks up what appear to be cabbages in a pot in a fireplace, while a fool on the left-hand side places another cabbage in the large tun from a basket beside it. The devil uses a bellows to fan the flames of the cardinal's pot, while another flying devil blows with a bellows into the ear of the pope. The compot is thus the devil's stew.[94]

The cannibalism motif is suggestive of a similar monkish feast, in Pamphilus

68   Titlepage to *Ein frischer Combisst vom Papst*
[J. Cammerlander, Strassburg, 1535], BL

Gengenbach's play *Devourers of the Dead*, published in 1522, which has certain features of a carnival play.[95] Its argument is that the pope and the clergy, by their exploitation of indulgences, requiems and absolutions, 'feast on the dead', that is, exploit the dead for gain. The titlepage of this work (ill. 69) has a passing similarity with our woodcut, including the devil with the fiddle who provides music for the feast. In the text this devil comments:

> These are my chosen children
> On earth I have no better friends
> Thus I play on the fiddle
> So they can pass the time
> In dancing, piping or in song
> And spring with me to hell.

If any parallel between the two works is accepted as plausible, we can link the large-scale with the small-scale scene. Here once again we have a carnivalesque devouring of the dead, signifying the exploitation of indulgences, absolutions and papal remissions.

The feast of the devourers of the dead in the jaws of hell leads to a similar example from Luther's *Depiction of the Papacy* (ill. 70). This shows the pope enthroned in a giant hell-mouth, surrounded by demons. Some of these have heads recalling the animal masks given to Luther's opponents. There is one, half squirrel, half goat, another with a pig's head, a third is half goat and several others have goat's horns. One winged demon in the top left-hand

69   Titlepage to P. Gengenbach, *Die Todten fresser* (1522), BL

corner is clad as a monk with a prominent tonsure. The carnivalesque overtones are made more explicit by alluding to the figure of the fool. The devil
with the pig's head wears a fool's cap, while the pope has the ears of an ass.
Two demons hover above the pope and are about to crown him with a triple
tiara, which has a spiral of excrement for its tip. The ass's ears, of course,
refer to the depiction of the pope as an ass playing the bagpipes, the spiral of
excrement to the other depictions in the series based on this theme.

The main task of the demons in the depiction here is to prop up the papal
throne, which is breaking apart and collapsing into the jaws of hell. The
movement intended here is ambiguous, for it is not clear whether the pope
has just arisen from hell or is about to sink into it.[96] This is in many ways
inconsequential. What is signified above all is that the pope is suspended in
the hell-mouth about to be crowned, but at his moment of triumph his
throne collapses beneath him. It is this state of suspension to which the text
calls attention. The German text states: 'Here sits the pope in the name of all
devils; now it is plain that he is the true Antichrist who is foretold in the
Scripture.' The Latin title at the top gives the biblical proof by referring to
2 Thessalonians 2, and removes any doubt about the relevance of whether the
pope is arising or falling. What is depicted is the 'Kingdom of Satan and the

70   *The Pope Enthroned in the Jaws of Hell* (1545), BL

Pope'. This points forward to our next chapter, where the role of popular belief in propaganda will be discussed. It is worth noting here, however, that the naming of the pope as Antichrist is not suggested or confirmed by the visual text. The visual signs are rather those of popular culture, evoking carnival, the grotesque and the demonic.

What is the importance for Reformation propaganda of these elements that we designated as derived from popular culture? We have propaganda drawing on several popular cultural codes: play and game, carnival, popular festival forms, insults, theriomorphism, grotesque realism and the demonic. These were all systems of signs readily recognisable to the common folk of the time. The creators of the propaganda worked largely by taking these familiar signs and reassembling them as 'images in syntagma' which could then be read by the unlettered as easily as we recognise the visual allusions of television commercials today.[97] However new the message they were presenting, the codes were age-old and customary. If Reformation popular propaganda was highly successful, it was because it relied so heavily on what was taken for granted in popular culture.

What of the content of the message? In the context of popular culture it possessed no great theological profundity. It merely amplified the traditional message of popular festivals. Those in positions of authority who laid claim to respect, reverence and awe because of the dignity of their person or office could be reduced, by popular satire or parody, to the level of the meanest or humblest objects − puppets, carnival fools, dung. To the extent that this 'material bodily principle' reflects forms of popular resistance to the ruling elites of society, the Reformation tried to present itself in the form of a popular movement. To the extent that popular festivals provided a 'safety valve', a form of expression allowed by authority to neutralise popular passions, it represented a channelling of any broader discontent the Reformation might have aroused.[98] Reformation propaganda directed itself against the papal Church and its officers, not against authority, rule or social elites. Above all, it was the papacy which was to be deprived of its ability to inspire awe or demand reverence. In this sense, the propaganda sought to achieve the opposite to that of building up charisma around the figure of Luther that we have seen above. It sought to destroy the charisma of the papacy and the Catholic hierarchy, whether charisma of office or charisma of persons. In counterpoint to the development of Luther's image, his opponents and those of the evangelical movement were provided with an anti-charismatic image.

This process occurred, in the examples we have seen in this chapter, not by arousing religious emotions, but by invoking the secular beliefs and activities of the people. In this age, however, it is always difficult to separate the religious from the secular, and there is a danger of distortion by drawing this boundary too rigidly. To fill out our picture we must now examine popular belief and the use made of it by propagandists.

5

POPULAR BELIEF

Popular belief may, in general, be regarded as the belief held by the mass of the people, by contrast to that held by the religious elite who make up the clerical hierarchy of the Church, the 'professional men of religion'. But this distinction should not be too rigidly drawn. The rural parson or the wandering friar, for example, may well have shared the belief of the masses, or at least have adopted some of their attitudes, rather than those officially approved by the Church. This concept of popular belief is expressed clearly enough in the medieval saint and miracle cults. Such a definition, however, tells us only where popular belief is to be found, but little about its nature. One of the most persistent dilemmas in the study of religion is whether to approach it as a set of held beliefs or as a set of practices. The dilemma is the more acute in the case of popular belief, where the ideas behind religious practices are rarely formulated clearly and concisely in any formal conceptual structure. Often they appear only through the practices, yet they also give meaning to them. The two must be studied as inextricably linked.[1]

A useful means of doing so is to look at popular devotion and the images through which it was expressed. It was less formalised than ecclesiastical ritual, and certainly less regulated. It was the point at which the individual believer invoked and paid homage to the sacred. It embodied in practical form the way in which the individual conceived of the more elaborate and systematised structure of belief to which he or she gave allegiance. Nothing exemplifies this point better than the late-medieval statues of the Virgin, which opened up to reveal the Trinity inside. They attempted to visualise for the ordinary believer the doctrine of the incarnation. In so doing, they crossed the line of Christian orthodoxy (Mary was the mother of Christ, not of the Trinity), but it is doubtful whether the pious believer would have been too concerned about this.[2]

Because it is less structured and more fluid, popular devotion is a kind of liminal area where beliefs are volatile and susceptible to new suggestions and influences.[3] It also involves individual and collective expressions of faith at the same time, best exemplified in the pilgrimage. This made it an ideal ground for propaganda that sought to influence opinion and behaviour. This chapter will examine how popular belief and its codes were drawn upon to disseminate the Reformation message, and especially how popular devotional imagery was reshaped to this end.

One of the most common forms of communal devotion was the religious procession, which occurred with such regularity throughout the year that it was almost a defining characteristic of the sixteenth-century small community. Besides the processions on major feasts, such as Corpus Christi or Whitsun, there were those of the church fairs held even in small villages. At times of exceptional distress — war, plague or famine — the community held a religious procession to beseech the intervention of God to alleviate their suffering. Such occasions were an expression of communal solidarity, and a manifestation of social and spiritual relations within the community.[4] For evangelical belief, these events epitomised Catholicism in its most superstitious form, the notion that God's intervention was at the disposal of man's behest. It was the more offensive because processions involved the display of the Sacrament, the chanting of litanies invoking the saints and display of the Church hierarchy.

It is hardly surprising that the religious procession should have featured in evangelical propaganda. It was essentially Catholic and preeminently visual: an irresistible theme for the propaganda broadsheet. The best example is a satirical church fair procession by Peter Fletner (ill. 71). A procession of monks, nuns and priests passes across an open space between two churches, a reminder that religious processions usually wound their way from church to church, making a halt for prayer at each in turn. This procession seems to have little of religion in it: it is bacchic and carnivalesque. It is led by a swine and a very fat priest swinging an incense burner. Behind him a curate sprinkles holy water from a kettle held by a woman in secular clothes, doubtless a priest's concubine. Here any resemblance to a religious procession ceases. Next in the parade come two friars, vomiting copiously and behind them two canons drinking from huge beer steins, thus indicating the cause of discomfort of the two ahead.

71   Peter Fletner, *Satirical Procession* (1535?)

The central place in the procession is taken up by a very fat abbot being borne on a litter. He is preceded by two child monks, bearing candleholders in which the flame is represented by spirals of excrement. The abbot is carried by two fools, the foremost of whom has a profusely running nose. Behind the litter, a nun carries a spit packed with sausages, behind her are two nuns with hay-forks, from which hang cod-pieces in parody of the banners carried in religious processions and making a jibe at clerical sexual licence.[5] Two other nuns sing from a gaming-board instead of from a hymn book, and yet another holds aloft a large roast goose. The procession is closed by two nuns, one holding a wine decanter and glass, the other a swaddled baby, a nun's illegitimate child.

This procession is a brilliant carnivalesque parody of the immoral excesses of the clergy. The abbot is so stuffed with goose and wine, the printed text tells us, that he could scarcely be carried by two horses, much less by the straining fools. He seems to be a similar figure to the abbot on the ice, discussed in chapter 3 (see ill. 26). The work thus embodies the anticlericalism through which evangelical propaganda sought to discredit the opponents of the Gospel. To this end it uses themes drawn from popular culture: excessive eating and drinking, folly, grotesque realism and carnival parody. As with earlier examples of carnival themes, we can find historical parallels to such works of propaganda. In Naumburg a comic procession of monks, nuns and the clerical hierarchy was held through the streets during carnival in 1525. A similar satire on a religious procession was held in Münster in carnival 1532, while another occurred in a small village outside in 1534. An elaborate series of carnival satires on Catholic belief was held in Hildesheim in 1543, including a mock procession in which figures dressed as monks sang a mock Kyrie from gaming-boards.[6]

Exemplum wir geben / auerst taceatis:
Perinde als wir leben / also faciatis.
Lus mundi sein wir noch / alles improbitatis:
Nazarei sein wir doch / auerst ne credatis
Omnia sein vns vicij / durch Bullen cuulgatis
Jdcirco dragen wir / heilichbom sanctitatis . 3.

Auff wir doch schon in Teuten singen /
Das vns der Nloten tzum hals aussspringen:
Kommen wir das gar weder abslaen /
Mit heilich Wasser / vnd ander dingen:
Die wir mit Ablase dar vnder mingen /
Das wir dem Aben / reine Schweinen slaen . 4.

So far the example highlights the influence of popular culture, and the church fair was certainly as much an occasion for communal feasting and festivity as it was a religious event. However, several features direct our attention to elements of popular belief in this pair of woodcuts. First, there is the parody of the religious objects themselves, by which hymn books, candle-holders, banners and possibly the relics often carried in processions have been replaced by objects of gluttony. There is also the retention of the incense and holy water at the beginning of the procession, thus associating these items with the irreligious. Second, there is an association of folly with vice, a familiar theme of popular moralists of the later middle ages, such as Brant and Geiler von Kaisersberg. Folly here is no longer laughable stupidity or mere brutishness: it is sinful excess. Later, we shall see how this is developed into association with the diabolical.

If we turn from the visual to the written text, we find that the religious theme is more fully stressed. Come to the church fair, the first verse entreats, where indulgences are earned by monastic life. One can be 'holily impure', but if one honours the abbot one's sins can be swept away. This refers to one of the great religious attractions of church fairs, the indulgences attached to the performance of the religious activities which took place there. The second verse alludes to the excessive bulk of the abbot, but the third returns to the theme of Catholic belief. Written as a parody of a litany, it invokes the clergy as those who give an example of religious life. They are the light of the world, the Nazarenes, true followers of Christ. The 'light of the world' reference alludes to the spirals of excrement in the candleholders, echoing a quip made by Luther in 1524, that the pope sits in Christ's place in the church and 'illuminates as dung in a lantern'.[7] Thanks to papal bulls, the verse concludes, all things are free to the clergy, and they carry around holiness. The fourth verse also refers to the visual text. The monks sing so that 'the notes rise up in

72   Peter Fletner, *The New Passion of Christ* (1535?)

our throats', exemplified no doubt by the two vomiting monks, but this can be relieved with holy water and other things mixed with indulgences.

Perhaps the most important feature of this procession is what is omitted, for it includes only clergy. The only lay figure is the concubine holding the holy-water kettle. The religious procession is thus identified with both vice and with the clergy. The layman can stand outside it as an uninvolved critic. Religious practice can be condemned without embarrassment to the lay reader, who is encouraged to transfer his antipathy to the clergy onto the religious forms associated with them. Such satirical depictions of public religious practice encouraged the layman to distance himself from it.

The use of private religious devotion for polemical ends was a more sensitive matter, for it had to avoid including the reader in its condemnations. A second pair of woodcuts by Fletner, *The New Passion of Christ*, attempted this by drawing on popular devotion to the stations of the cross intended as a pious aid to meditation on the suffering of Christ (ill 72). Reading from left to right, Christ is brought before the high priest, who is depicted as a bishop through his mitre. This was common enough in late-medieval depictions of the high priest in the stations or the Passion, and probably has no polemical intent. Christ's captors, however, are monks, and in successive scenes across the two woodcuts he is scourged, crowned with thorns and then crucified by the monks as the pope in each case looks on. In the crowning with thorns, Christ is mocked by a canon, who with outstretched arms offers him a beer mug. In the last scene, Christ rises in glory from his tomb, despite the guard of monks placed there to prevent it. This is clearly copied from the woodcut *Christ appears to the Monks* discussed above (see ill. 31). By contrast with the satirical church fair, this work uses a form of devotion to make its point without calling the devotional practice itself into question. Indeed, as we shall see later, the crucifixion was one motif taken over by Protestant devotional

iconography and reshaped to suit its own emphases. Stress on the suffering of Christ was an element common to Catholic and evangelical belief. To depict monks and the pope as the tormentors of Christ thus invoked popular religious emotions to condemn the clergy and the Church hierarchy.

A similar use of private devotion is found in a depiction showing the pope as the bad thief crucified beside Christ (ill. 73). This draws on late-medieval interest in the good and bad thieves, the companions of Christ's suffering, often taken as types of repentance and stubborn unrepentance.[8] Depicting the pope as the bad thief thus stresses his refusal to recognise Christ as true God even in the throes of death. So much may be read from the visual text, but the printed text provides a more elaborate exposition. The good thief, it tells us, is the evangelical movement, for it preaches Christ crucified and recognises him as head and Lord. By this means each man can recognise the true Church, which is not that of the Jews, the Turks or the Papists, but only of 'those whom one now calls the new Christians, the Lutherans'. These alone preach the Gospel, penance and forgiveness of sins in the name of Christ. The bad thief is he who recognises not Christ, but the high priest of the Jews for his head. The bad thief stands for those who persecute the Gospel and reject Christ with stubborn and unrepentant hearts. Their Church is that of the Antichrist and the Devil. This written text concludes with a version of the popular song *O poor Judas*, driving home the theme of rejection of Christ.[9]

Several features of the depiction are explained by the written text. The soul of the good thief will join Christ in paradise, illustrated by the angel receiving a small child from the mouth of the expiring good thief. The bad thief's soul will be torn from his mouth by the Devil, also depicted in the woodcut.[10] Using another biblical simile, the text identifies the papal Church with the barren figtree, which will be cut down and cast into eternal fire. This is represented visually by merging this motif with the cross on which the pope is hanging. A demon is cutting it down, while flames lick around its foot, in anticipation of its fate.

Another devotional image which enjoyed great popularity immediately before the Reformation was the image of the instruments of Christ's Passion. This is a recurrent theme in pious meditation, depicted in small pictures which served as aids to private devotion.[11] Devotion to the instruments of the Passion became itself a means of gaining remission of punishment for sin through indulgences. One such depiction from the fifteenth century (ill. 74) promises a massive amount of indulgences to be gained by honouring the picture with a Pater Noster: fourteen dozen years, plus six years granted by each of forty-three popes, and forty days granted by each of forty bishops. Another familiar form in which these 'arms of Christ' were depicted was the mass of St Gregory, commemorating his vision while celebrating mass of the suffering Christ.[12]

A work known as *The Seven-headed Papal Beast* is based on such depic-

73 *The Pope as Bad Thief*, GNM

tions (ill. 75). It appeared both as a single broadsheet about the size of a small folio and as a book illustration, as well as being published with a text from Hans Sachs in 1543.[13] It shows the arms of Christ: the instruments of the Passion, the cross, the nails, the scourges and the crown of thorns grouped at the head of the cross, and the spear and sponge on a staff placed on the crossbeam. In parody of the inscription INRI commonly found on the crucifix, an indulgence letter has been attached to the cross, with the motto: 'For cash a sack of indulgences'. The altar usually found in the devotional pictures has been replaced by a cash chest, the repository of proceeds from the sale of indulgences. It was thus an altar of mammon, and upon it, in the place usually taken by Christ, is seated a seven-headed monster, flanked by flags bearing the papal arms, crossed keys and a papal tiara. The arms of Christ are thus mocked by the arms of the pope. The seven heads of the monster are those of a pope, two cardinals, two bishops and two monks. From beneath the cash chest appears a demon, and to underline the message, the artist has placed the title *Regnum diaboli*, the kingdom of the Devil, at the sides of the chest.

The printed text equates the monster with the beast of the Apocalypse, although the description does not quite match the illustration. Just like the papal beast, the apocalyptic beast has seven unequal heads. All are crowned, signifying the tonsures of the clergy; it has ten horns, signifying spiritual power; it bears a blasphemous name, which the text interprets as the seductive

74   *Indulgence Broadsheet*, early fifteenth century

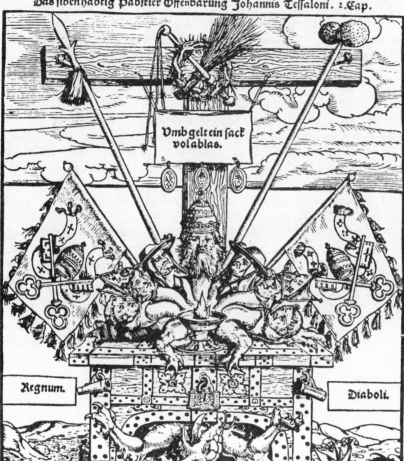

Das sibenhabtig Pabstier Offenbarung Johannis Tessaloni. 2.Cap.

Vmb gelt ein sack
vol ablas.

Regnum.

Diaboli.

Schawet an das siben hewbtig tier   Bedeüt jr verfürische zung   Den doch gar nie erfüllen thetten
Gang eben der gstalt vnd manier   Das thier was aim pardel gleich   Zples/pallium noch annatten
Wie Johannes gesehen hat   Bedeüt des Bapst mordische reich   Rann/opfer/peicht/stifft zů Gotsdiensi
Ein tier an des meres gestat   Das auch hinricht durch tiranney   L'and vnd leüt Rünigreich rent vn zinst
Das hat siben vngeleicher haubt   Alles was im ent gegen sey   Das es alles hat in sich verschlunden
Eben wie diß pabstier gelaubt   Auch so hat das thier peren füß   Das thier entpfieng ain tödlich wunden
Die waren all gekrönt bedewt   Deüt das das Euangeli süß   Deüt das Doctor Martin hat gschriben
Die blatten der gaistlichen lewt   Ist von dem bastum vndertretten   Das bapstum tödlich wund gebieben
Das thier das het auch zehen horen   Verschart/verdecket vn zerknetten   Mit dem otem des Herren mund
Deüt der gastlig gwalt vn cumoren   Das thier het auch ains löwen mund   Gott geb das es gar ger zů grund
Das thier trüg Gottes lesterung   Bedeüt deß bapstum weiten schlund   Amen.

75   *The Seven-headed Papal Beast*

tongue of the papacy. The beast is like a leopard, that is, the tyranny of papal rule. It has feet like a bear's, to tread the Gospel underfoot. It has a lion's mouth, which signifies the papal gullet never full with all that its great maw swallows – indulgences, palliums, annates, offerings, foundations, the proceeds of the ban. The beast bears on one of its heads a mortal wound, which signifies the deadly harm done to the papacy by Luther and his writings.

The written text thus applies the description of the beast of the Apocalypse to the papacy, although the visual text makes the same point more succinctly. By reworking the theme of the arms of Christ, it shows the papal beast usurping the place of Christ in the popular devotional image. This message is spelt out by the reference to 2 Thessalonians 2.4 in the woodcut's caption, which speaks of the son of perdition who takes over the rightful seat of God in God's own temple. Through this alone, woodcut and caption, the papacy is identified as the Antichrist. The popular devotional image has not been attacked, but a perversion of it has been used to show the papacy as a perversion of Christianity.[14]

This reworking of familiar devotional imagery became a frequent device in Protestant propaganda, capable of indefinite extension. Two examples illustrate this practice: the mill and the ship images. A common means of representing graphically the doctrine of transubstantiation was *The Host Mill*. This showed Christ placed in the hopper of a grain mill and communion wafers emerging from the tray. Together with an associated depiction, *Christ in the Winepress*, it served to visualise an extremely abstract doctrine.[15] It was in direct imitation of this image that the illustration *The Divine Mill* was used as the titlepage of a Swiss pamphlet of 1520 (ill. 76). It was one of the earliest

76   *The Divine Mill*, titlepage to *Dyss hand zwen schwytzer puren gemacht* (M. Ramminger, Augsburg, 1521), BL

visual expressions of the role of the Bible in the revival of evangelical belief, and appeared in six editions.[16] Christ shakes the grain of the Word into the hopper of the mill. The grain is St Paul with the sword, and the symbols of the four Evangelists, all signifying the New Testament. Production of the flour is supervised by Erasmus, a reference to his 1516 edition of the New Testament, which was decisive in the revival of biblical theology. The flour emerges as Faith, Hope, Charity and the Church, indicated by small scrolls which Erasmus is ladling into his sack. The flour sack itself, over which hovers the protective dove of the Holy Spirit, bears a symbol which is probably a millwheel surmounted by a cross. Just as a miller is identified by the sign on his sacks, so one can recognise the produce of the divine mill as that made from the grain of divine wisdom.

Behind Erasmus is Luther, who has baked the flour into the bread of the Bible and is shown trying to distribute it to the Catholic clergy, helped by a peasant. The pope, a cardinal, a bishop and a monk reject it in horror, while a diabolical bird–dragon above them screeches 'Ban! ban!', in allusion to papal condemnation of Luther. Behind Luther is Karsthans, the figure of the 'evangelical peasant', wearing a sword and wielding a flail in defence of the Gospel. From the heavens, Christ as Lord of the world, identified by his cruciform halo, looks down, adding a note of eschatological urgency to the confrontation occurring below. A Catholic devotional image, simplifying and popularising a central doctrine, has here become a means of expressing an evangelical message.

The mill as an image of refining or rejuvenating was also a secular image, often used satirically.[17] Iconographically, it was close to the fountain of youth, in which old men or women are turned out young, and closer still to the oven in which fools are newly baked. They are all images of transform- ation.[18] In a sheet from Hieronymus Resch, dating from the 1550s, the satirical possibilities of the mill image are merged with the devotional image of the divine mill (ill. 77). Entitled *The Spiritual Mill of Fools*, it develops the notion that folly is close to sin, vice and the diabolical. It depicts a large and spacious mill, at which arrive a stream of carriers bringing sacks of spiritual fools, the Catholic clergy. These are shaken into the hopper and emerge into the trough, 'refined' into their better form, as demons. The dross from the process is shaken out in the milling, falling onto the floor before the vat. These are the signs of Catholic authority: mitres, crooks, cardinals' hats, a triple tiara. Some of the corn unfit for grinding is carried in a bucket by a figure on the right-hand side, and is fed to pigs, shown guzzling in a bucket in the bottom right-hand corner. This poorer grain is comprised of monks and bishops. The grain sacks and the mill-hands carry the symbol of the mill- wheel, similar to that in *The Divine Mill*, although the cross is lacking. This symbol links the two works sufficiently to suggest the influence of one on the other. That the mill is here intended to signify the divine Word is shown by the figure of the miller, standing on the right-hand side, clad in the robes of a prince and pointing in an open book. It is the process of the Word which reveals the true nature of the papacy and of Catholic belief. This reading of the visual text is reinforced by the title on the sheet, from Proverbs 27.22: 'Crush a fool in a mortar . . . yet his folly will not depart from him.'

The divine mill theme was reworked further in a 1577 broadsheet by Tobias Stimmer, with text from Johann Fischart, *The Weird and Grotesque Mill* (ill. 78).[19] The caption supplies the central idea: as the corn is, so is the flour. The diabolical nature of the Catholic clergy is again revealed by the refining process of the mill. Here death delivers the sacks on a bony, emaciated steed, recalling the images of death in the devotional *memento mori* genre. Three demon-like monsters act as mill-hands, pouring the sacks of clergy into the hopper, whence they emerge as monsters and demons. Here, however, we have an inversion of the original devotional theme of the divine mill. We are now in the diabolical mill, Satan's mill, to which the clergy are delivered by death. The work is thus a *memento mori* for the Catholic clergy, and a revelation for the incautious believer. Milled into their true nature, the Catholic clergy are exposed as demons.

Another motif frequently used in popular devotion was the image of the ship. This was no doubt based on Luke 5.3, in which Christ teaches from a boat, works the miracle of the prodigious shoal of fish and promises the

77   H. Resch, *The Spiritual Mill of Fools*, BM

78　T. Stimmer, *The Weird and Grotesque Mill* (1577), Dahlem

apostles that they will be fishers of men. The ark of Noah, as a prefiguration of the Church, would also have contributed to the connotations of this image, and by the late fifteenth century it was a standard topos for the Church. It became more explicitly so with the development of the ship of St Ursula into a representation of the papal Church, seen in the illustration provided by Peter Fletner for the *Hungarian Chronicle* (ill. 79).[20] The perils of sea travel in that age added another connotation, the precarious and dangerous nature of ship voyages, which could be adapted for devotional exhortation. A wood-cut from around 1512, *The Ship of Salvation* (ill. 80), gives an elaborate exposition of the motif, explained in great detail by the text on the dorsal side of the sheet.[21] The ship sails over the sea of life to the places of salvation, such as Jerusalem. This suggests a further influence on this metaphor, the perilous sea voyages undertaken by those on pilgrimage to the Holy Land. The first ship of life was made by God, but the first sailors, Adam and Eve, ran it onto the rock of disobedience. Baptism provided a second ship, but this is all too easily breached and sinks through sin. Penance is the third ship, which each man can make for himself with the aid of Christ the carpenter. This ship sails the sea of the world, in which lurk the numerous monsters of vice. These often overturn or swamp the ship, but the sailor can bail out the water with confession. Faith, with the infallible needle of belief, is the compass; the rudder is God's commands and precepts; the mast is Christ's cross; the sails are laid on with free will, but not in every wind, only in the fair wind of piety. There is the anchor of hope, and the ship's hands are the holy angels who take good care for the barque.

These two images, the ship of the Church and the ship of the individual believer, are joined by the third common ship image of the early sixteenth

79   P. Fletner, *The Ship of St Ursula* (1515), Dahlem

century, the ship of fools. In his brilliant image of an overloaded ship en-
trusted to the folly of its becapped crew, Sebastian Brant has skilfully combined both of these images. In chapter 103 of *The Ship of Fools* he contrasts
St Peter's barque with the ship of the Antichrist. The latter is frail and easily
wrecked, endangering those foolish enough to board it. This is depicted
vividly in the illustration to the chapter (ill. 81), showing the Antichrist
seated upon the wrecked vessel, while the fools who capsized in it seek to
escape drowning. Such is the folly of mankind that another ship of fools try
to attach themselves to the sinking vessel, lured perhaps by the sack of gold
held by the Antichrist in his right hand. This depiction from the 1498 edition
of Brant's work was striking enough for it to be copied in another sheet by
Erhard Schoen, and shows a visual contrast between the frailty of the ship of
Antichrist and the solidity of St Peter's barque. The latter brings its comple-
ment safely to land, the former places them in mortal danger. However,
Brant's pessimism led him to express in his written text the fear that even St
Peter's ship might founder: 'St Peter's ship is swaying madly. It may be
wrecked or damaged badly.' This doom-laden sense of impending disaster was
expressed through another ship image used as an illustration to a popular
prophecy published in 1508.[22] It shows the ship of the Church going under in
a storm; the pope and the clergy throw up their hands in terror, while a king
and a canon attempt to trim the wind-filled sails, which bear the image of the
crucified Christ.

80   *The Ship of Salvation* (1512), GNM

The ship image was firmly established as a popular devotional sign by the eve of the Reformation, and it is not surprising that it should have been adapted for evangelical propaganda. The 1508 illustration reappeared as a titlepage in 1522, making a more polemical point than its earlier use (ill. 82).[23] The sensitive spot touched by this particular image is attested to by the fact that it was used again as an illustration for a work published in Leipzig in 1523. Here, however, the papal tiara was cut away, plainly to avoid giving offence to the Catholic ruler of Leipzig, Duke George of Saxony.[24] This further attests to the importance of visual signs in the period, for the content of the pamphlet itself, a mock prognostic by the physician Johannes Copp, was strongly evangelical.

An undated broadsheet, probably from the early Reformation period, attempts clumsily to blend the ship and the fishers images (ill. 83). It shows four ships full of Catholic clergy, one of them bearing the papal arms, engaged in catching laymen. These ships are so heavily laden with all kinds of clergy, especially monks and friars, that they are about to sink under the weight. Those laymen who attempt to board these ships of the Church are beaten back. They are intended, rather, to be caught up in the trawling net operated

Spiegel der naturlichen himlischen
vnd prophetischen sehungen aller trubsalen/angst/ vn not/die vber alle stende/geschlechte/ vnd gemayn den t er Cristenheyt / sunderbar so dem Krebsen vn Scorpion auß naturlich seinfluß des himels vnderworffen sein/ vn in dem sibenden Clima od circkel begriffenn/ in kurtzen tagen geen werdenn/ Durch den wirdigen hern Joseph Grünpeck zu Nurmberg beschriben.

81   Illustration to *Doctor Brants Narrenschiff* (1499), BL IA 37957, fol. s iii.
82   Titlepage to J. Grunpeck, *Spiegel der naturlichen himlischen und prophetischen sehungen* (W. Stockel, Leipzig, 1522), BL

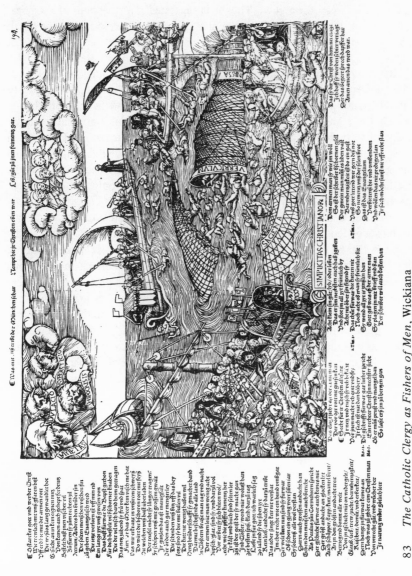

83   *The Catholic Clergy as Fishers of Men, Wickiana*

by the two boats on the right, and trapped by the giant lobster net between them. Certainly, individual laymen may be taken on board, as indicated in the bottom right-hand corner, by acquiring the monastic cowl in exchange for a sack of coin. This cowl closely resembles a fool's cap, and the monk in the prow of this boat, who is pulling on the trawling net, seems to have been given a fool's cap for a cowl. Thus it is suggested that the ships of the papal Church are ships of fools. They are also the ships of exploitation, by which the laity are caught for sale. They are propelled by vice, indicated by the figures of the four winds in the top left-hand corner, representing impiety, flattery, hypocrisy and superstition. What enables this prodigious draught of fish, however, is explained by the Latin caption bottom centre, the simplicity of Christians. From the heavens, a group of saints clad in monastic habits watch the scene with anguish. They clearly represent the original monastic ideal of Christian simplicity, now perverted by their successors. The written text of the broadsheet fails signally to make full use of this range of visual images. It touches, however, a central point made by the depiction, that the Catholic Church is for the clergy, while the laity exist only to be exploited by them.

The ship of the Church was used more simply and effectively in the 1540s in two woodcuts by Mathias Gerung. One shows the shipwreck of the papal Church (ill. 84). A ship bearing the pope, a cardinal, a bishop and a monk, with two cardinals holding papal bulls standing on a bridge in the prow, breaks in two. The other half contains the emperor and princes. In the background, a sea monster swims towards the ship, or perhaps has caused it to sink, while another ship of the Catholic clergy goes down in the background. It expressed the simple message that the papal Church is doomed, and may be taken as a companion piece to the second illustration, the ship of Christ (ill. 85). This shows the ship of the Catholic clergy and that of the Turks foundering in the foreground, a double message about the fate of false belief. The centre of the depiction is occupied by the ship of Christ, which sails on invincibly. Manned by the apostles, its main cabin is a church, from which two angels repel attacks on it. These come from demons on the prows of two ships of Catholic clergy in the background, which attempt to impede the course of Christ's ship.

The ship of the papal Church was used with brilliant inventiveness in an engraving from the latter half of the sixteenth century (ill. 86). Here we see a papal ship setting sail from land, the body of the ship formed by a grasshopper-like creature lying on its back. Six of its legs support a church, whose steeple forms the mast for the sail. The comb and spike on the creature's forehead provide a rudder with which the pope steers his barque, which is rowed by seven sets of clergy. The rowlocks for these clerical oarsmen are supplied by rows of teeth along the side of this 'boat', and give it the appearance of the jaws of some great monster. It thus has iconographical links to depictions of the pope enthroned in the jaws of hell which we discussed in the previous chapter. Clearly the papal ship is a diabolical craft, confirmed by the winged demons who assist its passage by pulling it forward and driving it through the water by means of a fan, a pair of bellows and a trumpet.

This ship is not, however, just a ship of papal clergy. It is as much the ship of Catholic practice. The church, supported by the legs of the monster, has three idols and the papal arms above its entrance. A pilgrimage church is perhaps intended, for votives can be seen through the windows on the side. In the prow of the ship there is a procession, with the host exposed in a monstrance. On the shore behind the departing ship stands a nun holding a cloth stuffed full of the items of Catholic belief. She also carries under her arm a swaddled child, the result of illicit sexual activity. Finally, two owls perch on the sail of the ship, birds of ill-omen, doubtless signifying the fate of the Catholic Church.

In contrast to this polemical use of the ship image, we can also find the later Reformation adopting it again as a pious image. *The Ship of the Apostles* by Matthias Zundt from 1570 provides an example (ill. 87). Here we have a ship of the Church or ship of faith, not dissimilar to the version of 1512. On the prow are the four Evangelists, on the stern the other apostles. Peter and Paul are the steersmen, John the Baptist the lookout in the prow. On a raised deck is Christ with the cross, beside him the Protestant sacraments – baptism,

84   M. Gerung, *Shipwreck of the Papal Church* (1545), BM
85   M. Gerung, *The Ship of Christ* (1548), BM

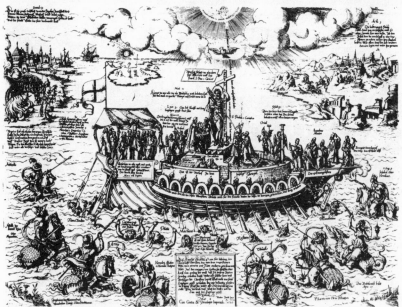

86   *The Ship of the Papal Church*, Munich, Staatl. Graph. Samml.
87   M. Zundt, *The Apostles' Ship* (1570), Dahlem

the Lord's Supper, confession and absolution. Four archangels bear the instruments of the Passion, recalling Christ's salvific death. The ship is rowed forward by the Christian emperors since Constantine, an appropriate theme for the age of the territorial Protestant Church. In the sea encircling the ship, swimming or riding on sea-horses, are the hostile and heretical powers: Nero, Caiphas, Pilate, Sergius, Nestorius, Pelagius, Arius and Mahomet (all swimming), Antiochus, Attila, Genserich, Herod, the Turk, the Tartar, Jezebel and the whore of Babylon (all on horses). These are all persecutors or opponents of the Church, a theme continued by two scenes on land. On the left, the three children in the fiery furnace, saved from persecution by the intervention of the Lord; on the right, St Paul another persecutor of the Church, struck down on the road to Damascus. Thus the Protestant Church is depicted as the true Church, whose enemies will not prevail against it.

The role of the visual image in popular devotion was to call the mind of the pious believer to spiritual truths, and to concentrate his attention on them. The examples of evangelical propaganda we have discussed above all depend on this principle. Often working through satire or parody, they nonetheless serve to call attention to the truth about the old and new belief, and to concentrate the reader's attention on it. The process involved is one in which familiar images are set in new surroundings or given new connotations. The viewer is thus led from the familiar to the unfamiliar and is asked to ponder the implications of this revelation. Its content is that the Catholic clergy and the papacy are sinful and vicious, opposed to Christ and inimical to salvation. This is a pious message, but it depends heavily on anticlerical feeling, which makes the reader the more susceptible to its argument. Yet one may question whether such a process of itself would be capable of arousing any deep and passionate religious feeling which might dispose the reader to shun Catholicism and embrace the new belief. How far did Reformation propaganda seek to touch stronger religious emotions, the impulses which led men of that age to turn to popular devotion of whatever kind?

One of the major preoccupations of the Christian believer of that time was the salvation of his soul and the time when this was adjudged. For this reason, eschatology was a dominant theme of sixteenth-century religion, the reminder of the last things of life and the last days. This took two forms, the general judgment of all men at the end of the world, and the judgment of the individual soul. Eschatology is a persistent motif in evangelical propaganda. We have seen the general judgment alluded to in several works discussed above. There is the motif of the sheep and goats in illustrations 20 and 40. The appearance of Christ as Lord, and so as the judge of the world, is suggested in other woodcuts: *The Complaint of the Godless, The Divine Mill, Two Kinds of Preaching* and Behem's *The Fall of the Papacy* (see above, ills. 22 and 76, and below 132 and 166). We can see an example of the use of the individual judgment in a titlepage from a pamphlet of 1525 (ill. 88).

The judgment of the individual soul was often represented by a weighing in a pair of scales. The saved soul is weighed against personified evil in the other tray — either the Devil, wicked souls or personified sins or vices. Until the sixteenth century this weighing up of souls was a component part of depictions of the Last Judgment.[25] Our titlepage shows a pair of scales suspended from the heavens, held by the invisible hand of God. On one tray sits Christ, so much outweighing the combined bulk of a pope and cardinal in the other tray that they are flung high into the air. The pope clutches a bull of indulgence, affixed with the papal seal, but this is of no weight compared to the true remission of sin provided by Christ, shown handing such a remission to three simple laymen. Christ's letter of indulgence is sealed with a true token of forgiveness, the image of the Saviour. Beneath the pope, two devils examine the indulgences presented to them by a naked soul, one of whom makes a gesture of rejection — papal forgiveness will not save one from hell, for the second devil places a possessive arm around the suppliant figure. On a near-by tree two animals, perhaps a cat and a squirrel, thus possibly signifying Murner and Henner, leap up to catch bulls dropped by the pope in his involuntary flight. This woodcut cleverly combines the notion of the Last Judgment, through the weighing up of papal and Christian belief, with the idea of personal judgment, through the plight of the single soul. For the believer concerned about salvation, its message was direct and simple.

The emotive force of such eschatological references for a sixteenth-century

88   Titlepage to *Ein schöns tractetlein von dem Götlichen und römischen Ablas* [J. Schmidt, Speyer, 1525]

reader can be understood only by examining the greater sense of immediacy about the last days which prevailed at the beginning of the sixteenth century. Wilhelm Peuckert has pointed out that the Reformation occurred in an apocalyptic age, an age which expected a great change in the world.[26] This may have been understood as the end of the world or as the coming of a new epoch of the world's existence. In either case, the imminence of this great change was proclaimed continually by prophetic works found in rich abundance during the two generations before the emergence of an evangelical movement. This generated an apocalyptic fervour whose significance has been largely unexplored. A number of different elements went into the making of this apocalyptic fervour, each reinforcing the others in their cumulative effects. Taken together, they form the most characteristic elements of popular belief during the age of the Reformation. First, there was a strong sense of pessimism and fatalism; second, there was the powerful influence of astrology; third, there was a deep-rooted belief in signs and omens; fourth, there was a tradition of mystical prophecy which offered a cogent spiritual interpretation of these events; finally, there was a broad stream of one particular kind of prophecy, Joachimism, which enabled men to locate this great change historically and to link it to hopes for spiritual and secular improvement. In the context of our present discussion, such elements can best be understood through their iconographical representation.

Fatalism was embodied in the wheel of fortune, a motif of classical origins which the middle ages struggled to reconcile with the Christian idea of providence. One feature of the wheel of fortune was its warning against pride and haughtiness on the part of the mighty. The wheel of fate turns inevitably, and brings down those who believe themselves invincible. Thus most fifteenth-century depictions of the wheel of fortune show a king riding high on the wheel while another topples from the pride of place, and a third rises on the turning wheel, soon to take his position of honour for a time. This concept of fate was essentially non-Christian, but was reconciled in the iconography with Christian belief by showing a rein or scarf attached to the wheel handle or to the figure of Fortune who turned it. This rein was held by the hand of God, so that ultimately it was he who set the wheel in motion, and his providence which decided men's fortunes.[27]

Thus a woodcut from the 1530s by Georg Pencz combines the theme of the fatalism of the wheel with that of hope for the underdog (ill. 89). A king and two princes sit atop the wheel, the prince on the left clutching two wine glasses to signify luxurious living. Two artisans clamber on the wheel, while a noble on the right has reached a point where he must fall from it. The wheel is turned by the blindfolded figure of Fortune, guided by a rein around her neck, held by the hand of God in the clouds. Two ragged figures, representing the poor, respectively pray for and greet the turn of the wheel. To the left, a crowd of well-dressed burghers and clergy are engaged in discussion, in apparent ignorance of the scene being acted out behind them. One figure alone, bearded and holding a stick, perhaps a peasant, draws the reader's attention to the scene with a hand gesture. It is a warning to the complacent and well-to-do of the way in which fate would sooner or later turn against them.

Sebastian Brant also made use of the theme in chapter 37 of *The Ship of Fools*, reminding those fools who climb too high that a turn of the wheel will soon tumble them to earth. The illustration to this chapter (ill. 90) shows three asses with fools' caps, one climbing the wheel, a second atop the wheel, triumphantly holding aloft a crown, a third being pitched headlong as the wheel comes down. The figure of Fortune or Fate has been dispensed with here, and the hand of God alone turns the wheel by means of a rope attached to the handle. The artist uses theriomorphism skilfully to depict the cycle of fortune. The fool riding up on the wheel is changed into an ass above the waist; at the top, he has become completely an ass; as he falls, he is still an ass below the waist; by implication, he is completely a man again as he falls to the ground, into the open grave awaiting him below.

The wheel of fortune could be linked to pessimism in two ways, by showing the wheel as the ages of man, depicting his inevitable decay and the unavoidability of death. Thus, in one version of the theme, death in the form of a mockingly laughing corpse turns the wheel. In another it is linked to the idea that death comes to all men by an accompanying depiction of a corpse in a grave.[28] If it was pessimistic, this motif was also intended to provide con-

89   G. Pencz, *The Wheel of Fortune*, UB Erlangen-Nürnberg

solation: death is the great equaliser, reducing all men to the same level. However, the motif was also capable of bitter social comment, shown by a woodcut from around 1480 (ill. 91). At the top of the wheel sits Reinecke Fuchs,
crowned with a triple tiara to signify the pope. On each side of him is a monk,
a Franciscan on his right in the form of a bear, signifying Begging and Greed;
on his left, a Dominican in the form of a wolf, representing Avarice. On each
side of these are two mounted figures, on the left Pride, on the right Hatred.
Seated on the horizontal spokes of the wheel are a man with a sickle representing Falsehood and a priest with a host and chalice representing Self-
conceit. At the bottom of the wheel lies Constancy, broken by the fall and
naked but for a loin-cloth. Behind the wheel is the giant figure of Patience,
who will turn it in due course, aided by the figures seated bottom left and
right, a Samaritan monk representing Love and a beguine representing
Humility.[29]

This sheet is remarkable for several features. It adapts the animal allegories
of *Reinecke Fuchs*, Isengrim the wolf, Braun the bear, and the wily fox
Reinecke himself to attack the financial and political pretensions of the
papacy and the monastic Orders. The nobility and the priesthood are also
targets of attack, while the author is clearly sympathetic to the sufferings of
the common man, crushed at the bottom of the wheel. It is anticlerical and
anti-papal, and indeed the written text castigates the pope's pretensions to

90   Illustration to *Doctor Brants Narrenschyff* (1499),
BL IA 37957, fol. f6v

91   *The Wheel of Fortune and Reinecke Fuchs*, Albertina

rule all lands, an anticipation of the more virulent Reformation attack on the papacy. For the common man it is consolatory: if he is patient, the wheel will turn and his time on top will come.

A direct descendant of this work can be found in the titlepage of an anonymous pamphlet published in early May 1525, during the height of the Peasant War (ill. 92). The centrepiece of the depiction is a wheel of fortune, on which the pope, clad in armour, rides up on the right-hand side. Behind him are his supporters, armed cardinals, bishops and knights. These are identified by the inscription above them as Romanists and Sophists, stock Lutheran epithets for papalists and Scholastic theologians. The wheel is turned by the figure of Dame Fortune. On the other side stand men armed with pikes and spears, onto whose upraised points the turn of the wheel will deposit the pope. Clad as *Landsknechte*, these are identified by the caption above as 'Peasants and good Christians'. The caption under this scene reads: 'Who increases the Swiss? The greed of the lords.' This refers to the Swiss as the symbol of those who threw off overweening authority, and rejected the yoke of feudal lords for a republican federation of yeoman farmers and independent towns. The Swiss were invoked in prophetic literature of the late-fifteenth century, the astrologer Johann Lichtenberger using much the same words to prophesy the spread of Swiss republicanism, because rulers

92   Titlepage to *An die versamlung gemeyner Bawerschafft* (1525), Nat. Lib. Edinburgh

would not moderate their behaviour. The pamphlet itself follows this line, supplying biblical justification for peasant resistance, using ideas close to those of Zwingli. The titlepage, however, preserves the uncertainty associated with the wheel of fortune, in that it was never sure where the wheel would come to rest: 'Here is the hour and time of the wheel of fortune. God knows who will remain supreme.'[30]

This mixture of fatalism, social criticism and evangelical inspiration can be seen in another woodcut, *The Poor Common Ass* by Peter Fletner (ill. 93). The poor ass, signifying the common people, is ridden by Tyranny, Avarice and Hypocrisy. The last, in the form of a monk clutching a money-bag, has been thrown off the lands ignominiously on the ground. However, Avarice in the form of a Jew is still seated astride the ass, flaying it alive, while Tyranny is also firmly seated in the saddle. In the centre stands the figure of Reason, holding a cloth before the eyes of the ass. Behind her, Justice is locked in the stocks, her scales hanging uselessly on a nail, while her right hand, in which she holds the sword of justice, is pinioned to the block by a handcuff. To her left stands another figure clutching a sword and a book, the Word of God.

As we have seen in a similar allegory by Behem (see ill. 30), the interpretation is not unambiguous. The common folk have thrown off the rider Hypocrisy, that is, they have rebelled against monasticism. But they are still subject to Tyranny and Greed. Justice is unable to assist, but the Word of God may intervene with the sword of the Bible. The role played by Reason is ambiguous. Is she removing the blindfold from the ass, thus enabling him to see the state of affairs: that Justice is bound and one has only the Word of God on which to rely? Or is she obscuring his vision, even about to tie the blindfold on? The latter would accord with a Lutheran, Augustinian reading of the visual text, the former with a humanist reading. The structure of the scene gives little clue here. If it is taken as an antithesis between the three riders and the three figures, Reason would seem to be unbinding the eyes.

93   Peter Fletner, *The Poor Common Ass* (1525), Dahlem

However, Reason stands in the centre of the composition, and thus may serve to separate the two groups and so to impede vision. It is this ambiguity which gives the work its fatalistic tone. The Word provides hope of release, but it is no unconditional hope, but a hope tinged with warning of a struggle to come which may be won or lost by the common folk seeking their liberation.[31]

Fatalism may well have been one result of the widespread interest in astrology which dominated the age. This involved the belief that man's fate was influenced by the heavenly bodies and consequently that future events could be read from their movement.[32] Two kinds of heavenly event were of particular interest. The first was the regular and predictable course of the planets, the second the extraordinary occurrence, such as a comet or meteorite. Among the regular movements of the planets, eclipses and conjunctions attracted most attention. Eclipses, however, provided only a minor theme in astrological literature, although there was some revival of interest in them during the 1520s. Thus an astrological work published by the Erfurt physician Johann Copp in 1523 warned of eclipses in that year which would lead to disturbances of the common man against the clergy and to a rebellion of the peasants against their lords.[33]

Popularisation of Arabic astrological tracts in western Europe at the end of the fifteenth century stimulated the overwhelming interest in conjunctions. From around 1470 these formed the subject-matter of the small printed works, *Praktiken* or prognostics, which foretold events for the coming year or years, based on the anticipated movements of the planets and their conjunctions. From the beginning of the sixteenth century, this belief was concentrated on the year 1524, when no less than twenty planetary conjunctions were expected, sixteen of them in the sign of the fish. The first prediction concerning these conjunctions dated from 1499, by the Tübingen astronomer Johann Stoeffler. He called attention both to the large number of conjunctions and to the momentous effects these would have on world affairs.[34]

By 1517 oral tradition had embroidered this prediction, directing attention to the influence of the sign of the fish to foretell a great deluge caused by the conjunctions. This in itself occasioned a flood of literature about the conjunctions, in total some fifty-six authors taking up the discussion in 133 works in six languages. The high point was reached, naturally enough, in 1523–4 with fifty-one works published in 1523 and sixteen up to February 1524. German interest was strongly aroused in 1521, when the first work in German was published. The conjunctions were much discussed at the Reichstag of Worms, where large illustrated broadsheets were put on sale. In fact the peak of interest was reached in Germany, where the effects of the conjunction were linked both to social unrest and to the emergence of the evangelical movement. In foretelling imminent disaster for the clergy, and in particular for the papal hierarchy, prognostics dealing with this conjunction provided propaganda for the new religious movement. Vivid titlepages and illustrations made these points visually.[35]

One of the most expressive was used for a 1523 prognostic by Leonhart Reynmann, taking as its central theme the great flood predicted for February 1524 (ill. 94). It shows the conjunction of several planets in the sign of the fish, producing a deluge which sweeps away a town and its inhabitants. The planets are identified by their astrological symbols as Saturn, Jupiter, Mars, Venus, Mercury, the Sun and the Moon. The figures grouped to the left and right of the flood represent Saturn and Jupiter as the major opposing forces. The astrologers regarded these as the two 'superior planets', which because of their slower orbits came only rarely into conjunction, indeed in the same sign only once in every 960 years. This was regarded as a 'great conjunction', producing particularly radical effects. Saturn was said to bring great misfortune for the State, and for the Church as well when in conjunction with Jupiter, which was held to rule over religion. The conjunction of February 1524 was to be such a 'great conjunction', bringing disease and death, the significance perhaps of the corpse inside the fish. In this illustration, however, the flood is subordinated to the prediction of a crisis threatening Church and State, linked to the danger of a peasant rebellion.

Saturn was said to rule over lowly professions and occupations, such as

94   Titlepage to L. Reynmann, *Practica* (H. Höltzel, Nuremberg, 1523), BL

rural workers; over criminals, the diseased and the crippled. Saturn himself is frequently depicted as an aged cripple with a sickle or scythe; clearly he is intended to be represented by the figure holding the scythe and banner at the head of a band of peasant followers. The emperor, pope, cardinal and bishops opposing them stand for the children of Jupiter. The astrological significance of other planets in the conjunction emphasises the threat of war and disorder implicit in the aggressive stance of the followers of Saturn. The Moon represents changeability and restlessness, and is an unfavourable influence when in the sign of the fish. The Sun may stand for contentiousness, while Mars, the constant companion of Saturn, is the planet of war, standing for murder, violence, arson and theft. Venus is the counterforce to Mars, and represents morals, manners and fair behaviour, which is threatened by war. These astrological allusions to the chaos resulting from the 'great conjunction' are reinforced by the presence of the two figures with pipe and drum in the background. These refer possibly to the folk belief that the sound of pipe and drum presage the imminence of war. This is confirmed by the comet, shaped like a star but given a comet's tail by rounded cross-strokes, to the left of these figures. According to Reynmann, the advent of a comet in that year would bring a peasant rebellion with it. Saturn's banner and the band of armed peasants at his back confirm and complete all these allusions.[36]

Comets or meteors, as extraordinary events in the heavens, were held to presage some momentous occasion, even to exercise some influence causing it. Thus the fall of a giant meteorite at Ensisheim in Alsace in 1492 was taken to prefigure great changes in the politics of the Holy Roman Empire, ranging from the death of the Emperor Frederick III to the inauguration of a new golden age. Sebastian Brant, in particular, took it as a sign that the time was propitious for Maximilian of Austria to act boldly against his foes: fate now favoured him, and he should seize the spokes of the wheel of fortune and arrest its course to his own advantage.[37] Heavenly lights seen in Vienna for five days during the first week of January 1520 prompted Pamphilus Gengenbach, an able evangelical polemicist, to issue a broadsheet interpreting their significance. Gengenbach called attention to the fact that similar lights seen in 1514 were followed by several disasters – epidemic, floods and a great battle in Milan. The Vienna lights were a warning to Charles V that the Church was in danger; but Luther was on the right path, and one should follow him gladly. Gengenbach especially pointed out the dangers expected for 1524, and warned the monastic Orders to prepare for reformation. There was a danger of a new Hussite movement.[38]

Comets were also interpreted in the same prophetic manner. In general they were held to foreshadow disturbance and war, dearth and plague, floods, storms and earthquakes.[39] A comet of 1523 appearing in the signs of Capricorn and Sagittarius was taken as predicting a rising of the lower orders against the clergy and nobility. An illustration to this work interprets this in an anti-papal sense (ill. 95). In the top right-hand corner the comet is flanked by the goat and the archer. In the top left-hand corner a peasant attacks a knight with a flail. In the foreground a burgher or a scholar beats a monk, while a *Landsknecht* prepares to strike down the pope with a sword. A second *Landsknecht* points to the heavens, as though justifying these acts of rebellion by divine command.[40]

Belief in comets as signs of momentous events to occur in the near future was but one aspect of a wider belief in omens and portents which was shared even by Protestants during the sixteenth century. These ranged from signs in the heavens, such as strange lights, curious cloud formations and rains of blood or crosses, to misbirths, monsters and deformations of nature. A virtual encyclopedia of such phenomena was put together in 1557 by Conrad Lycosthenes.[41] In a preface to the German edition of this work, the Lutheran publicist Johann Herold attempted to define the spectrum of such 'wonder works'. Herold lists signs, miracles, visions, prophecies, dreams, oracles, predictions, prodigies, divinations, omens, wonders, portents, presages, presentiments, monsters, impressions, marvels, spells, charms and incantations.[42] Herold's desire for comprehensiveness clearly led him to stray beyond the bounds of mere omens, especially in the last three categories, where he slips into talking about magic. He was sceptical about many of these signs, some of which he saw as pure superstition, others as the work of the Devil to lead astray the incautious believer. Surprising, however, is the amount of credence he was willing to give to the majority of such signs and wonders. 'Wonder signs' were 'the true witnesses and certain confirmation of the Word of God, which must also flow from cold belief. So we find that these are produced by God himself and by his creatures.'[43] Even here he took care to warn against

95   Erhard Schoen, *Illustration for a Prognostic*

diabolical trickery, and advised testing such signs by their consonance with Scripture. The conviction that they were some kind of divine warning seems to have been not incompatible with evangelical belief. Luther held this view, even if he carefully avoided applying them to any specific event.[44] Omens and portents could thus be understood as a call for men to repent and undertake moral improvement.

Monsters and misbirths were accorded special significance in the canon of signs and omens. They were usually taken to signify misfortune, although they could also be regarded as political allegories. Sebastian Brant in 1496 published two broadsheets dealing with misbirths, one on Siamese twins born near Worms, the other on the birth of a sow at Landser in the Sundgau with two bodies, but one head. Brant interpreted both events as political omens.[45] On the other hand, a much-publicised misbirth to a nun in Florence in 1512 was interpreted as a divine punishment for her denial of her pregnancy.[46] A broadsheet by Lorenz Fries on a misbirth near Rome in 1513 cast the net more widely, seeing it as signifying God's wrath, expressed in plague, disunity of Christians, advances of the Turk and loss of money from the land. But God also looked on man with pity, and had given them a pious, wise and learned pope, who would turn all to good. The 1513 misbirth thus becomes a sign of hope, associated with the accession of Leo X in March that year.[47]

Skilled publicists such as Brant and Fries knew how to make the most of misbirths, and it is not surprising that Reformation propaganda should have seized eagerly such opportunities. Two monsters, one a real misbirth, the other half legendary, provided ammunition for evangelical propaganda in 1523, a year when popular opinion was especially susceptible to ominous portents. The first was a calf born near Freiberg in Saxony on 8 December 1522, the second a fabulous monster allegedly found in the Tiber near Rome in 1496. The calf misbirth had a large bald patch on the head, with two horny knobs on it. It was covered with blotches or bald patches on its body, and had a long lolling tongue and only one eye. A large flap of skin on its back resembled a cowl, and from this and the bald patch on the head resembling a tonsure it was known as the Monk Calf.[48] It was first interpreted by someone around the court of Margrave George of Brandenburg as applying to Luther, although the sign was seen as directed against the Catholic clergy.[49] One pamphlet treated it as a misbirth which might symbolise the clergy, but did not mention Luther. Rather it was a warning to the Catholic clergy about their greed and high living. The author admonished them to live according to evangelical principles. This is not exceptional for treatment of a misbirth, and in its moral point is not too dissimilar from the sheet on the Florence misbirth of 1512.[50]

A second work was a broadsheet published before September 1523, which applied the calf to Luther (ill. 96). This depicts the monster being shown to the pope by a number of clerics, although the explanation is contained wholly within the printed rhymed text.[51] Two interpretations are offered, one by the clergy, the other by the pope's fool. First, the clergy interpret the omen. The calf is identified as Luther. The two warts on its head are the two swords of the papacy, which Luther would have taken away from the pope. That the beast cannot see signifies that Luther has blinded the whole world with his teaching, the long tongue the great trouble brought to the papacy by his slanders. The 'cowl' can be nothing other than what was foretold long ago by Reinhard, that a monk would bring a great heresy. The monster is thus linked to the popular prophetic literature of the fifteenth century. Indeed, the text continues, this prophecy is attested by the beast and by Luther. The pope should beware lest his great power be lost, for such births also marked the coming of Mahomet, who robbed Christendom of two empires and twenty-four kingdoms.

The fool then steps forward to contradict this interpretation. He reminds them that great disturbance has arisen from the monastic Orders, indeed that all evil flows from them. The beast is indeed a figure of Luther, but must be seen in a different light. The two warts signify the pride and avarice character-istic of the monks, against which Luther has written continuously. The beast has but one eye, signifying the sole evangelical doctrine which Luther teaches. The long tongue signifies how far his godly teaching has spread throughout Christendom. The cowl indicates the monks and nuns, whose abuses he casti-

96   *The Monk Calf before Pope Adrian* (1523), Wickiana

gates. That the beast resembles an ox is a sign of Luther's robustness, for he charges forth like a bull. The fool concludes his interpretation by bidding Pope Adrian to do the Christian thing and to release all monks from their Orders, so that a reform may be possible. The fool's interpretation, although favourable to the new religious movement, is far from Lutheran. Like the pamphlet mentioned above, it sees the calf as a warning to the Catholic clergy, and uses it to express anti-monastic feeling. However, it stands closer to a reforming Catholicism, reflecting the optimism for internal reform aroused by the accession of Adrian VI in 1522. Although it is sympathetic to the aims of the Lutheran movement, it shows no sign of the latter's implacable hostility towards the papacy as a whole.

The Monk Calf was also taken up by Luther and Melanchthon in a pamphlet of 1523. Melanchthon had first published an interpretation of the 1496 monster, the so-called Papal Ass, and then at Luther's instigation it was re-published alongside Luther's interpretation of the Monk Calf.[52] This pamphlet depicts first the Papal Ass (ill. 98), then the Monk Calf (ill. 97), followed by the two interpretations. Luther's explanation stressed the multiplicity of signs

Das Münchkalb zu Freyberg   **Der Bapstesel zu Rom**

97   *The Monk Calf*, in P. Melanchthon, *Deuttung der czwo grewlichen Figuren* (J. Rhau, Wittenberg, 1523), fol. Aii, BL
98   *The Papal Ass*, in P. Melanchthon, *Deuttung der czwo grewlichen Figuren*, fol. Ai, BL

to be found at that time.[53] Although he explicitly avoided a prophetic explanation, he was convinced that such signs foreshadowed some great change in the affairs of the world. He mentions specifically a similar misbirth at Landsberg, which he dubbed the Parson Calf because of its resemblance to a priest. This was a sign appropriate to the priestly estate, he argued, which he would not attempt to explain; he would be content, rather, to stick to that appertaining to his own, the monastic estate. As he saw it, the misbirth revealed what kind of folk the monks were, and he proceeded to give a detailed allegorical interpretation, taking each feature of the misbirth in turn.

First, the monster was no joke, but revealed the false appearance of spiritual and godly life found in monkery. The Monk Calf is 'the false idol in their deceitful hearts'. The calf is depicted in anthropomorphic fashion, standing on its hind legs, one front leg hanging at its side, the other stretched out like a hand. This feature Luther interprets as the gestures of a preacher, with his head thrown back, his tongue out and his hand gesturing. The Monk Calf thus depicted what kind of preacher the world had hitherto had to hear, the apostle and pupil of the pope. Is it not fitting that the ass-headed pope should have a calf-headed apostle? The calf is also blind, recalling the warning of Matthew 23.16: 'Woe to you blind guides.' The ear-like shapes of the 'cowl' signify the tyranny of confession, the tongue that monkish teaching is nothing more than idle, useless gossip.

The two knobs on the head are a sign that the monks have only the appearance of the Gospel: horns signify the Gospel and its preaching, but the calf has only the merest hint of them. That the knobs are on the 'tonsure' shows that the Gospel must conform to the tonsure, that is, to the will of the monks. That the cowl is wound so tightly around the neck signifies stubborn, stiff-necked monkery; that it is closed behind but open at the front shows that monks are only spiritual for the world, which stands behind them. The lower jaw is like that of a human being, the upper that of a calf's snout. This shows the nature of their preaching of divine law, for the two lips should signify the two kinds of preaching, the lower the divine law, the upper the Gospel. But instead of God's Word they preach the calf's snout, that is, their own good. The calf is smooth all over, signifying their hypocrisy. Finally, that it has now come forth from the cow means that they are revealed to the whole world, and can no longer hide themselves.

Taken by itself, Luther's interpretation of the Monk Calf could be seen as the application of spiritual allegory to a natural phenomenon, and so as a careful avoidance of appeals to popular superstition. However, it was published alongside Melanchthon's interpretation of the Papal Ass, a creature more lurid both in its appearance and in the interpretations which could be extracted from it. This curious monster was composed of an ass's head, a female torso with one human hand and the other an animal limb. One leg ended in a hoof, the other in a claw. It was covered in scales, with a dragon-like tail. This fantastic assembly of animal and human parts seems to have been invented in Italy at the end of the fifteenth century as part of a campaign to exploit signs and omens for political polemic. In particular, the original depiction of the monster seems to have been directed against Alexander VI. The building flying the papal flag in the background is the Castel Santangelo, built as a fortification by Alexander VI. The square tower on the right has been identified as the Tor di nona, a tower across the Tiber used by Alexander VI as a papal prison. Both were taken over unchanged in sixteenth-century copies of an Italian original. There was also a series of omens or portents throughout most of the years of Alexander's reign which were interpreted in connection with his rule. The alleged discovery of the monster in the Tiber after a flood in 1496 seems also to have been intended as an omen directed at him. The monster was used to attack papal power, and may have been part of a pasquillade mocking Rome's pretensions as 'head of the world' at a time when the papacy had suffered defeat by invading French forces.[54]

The depiction of the monster probably came to Germany via an engraving by the Bohemian artist Wenzel von Olmutz, made before the end of the century. It was doubtless used as propaganda for the Bohemian Brethren's opposition to the papacy. In any case, it seems to have come to the attention of Luther and Melanchthon from Bohemia, and Luther mentioned it late in 1522, perhaps also coining the name Papal Ass. Luther certainly had a hand in reshaping Melanchthon's first published attempt at an interpretation in order to make it accessible to as wide a public as possible. It attests both Luther and Melanchthon's firm belief in such signs and omens as not just allegories, but genuine foreshadowings of future events. In his second Advent sermon of 1521, Luther stated that such a mass of signs as then appeared would bring about things that reason could not imagine. In 1525, he wrote of a new monster that it filled him with dread.[55] Melanchthon began his exposition of the Papal Ass with a reminder that God always revealed his favour or disfavour in signs. In evidence, he pointed to Daniel 8.3 with its description of the beast of the Antichrist, and to Matthew 24, with its rich description of the signs of the last days. The Papal Ass was just that kind of sign, depicting and exemplifying papal rule.[56]

Melanchthon interpreted the Papal Ass along lines similar to those used by Luther for the Monk Calf. The whole stood for the papacy, the ass head for the pope. The Church should have no bodily head, and the ass head on the human torso was as fitting as the pope as head of the Church. The right hand is an elephant's foot, signifying the spiritual power of the pope, with which he treads all consciences underfoot, for the right hand usually signifies the inward, the soul and the conscience, which should be ruled by the gentle rule of Christ, not that of the ass head. The human left hand signifies the secular power of the pope, something acquired only by human means. The right foot is an ox foot, signifying the servants of the spiritual power who oppress the soul. These are the papal teachers, preachers, parsons, confessors and especially Scholastic theologians. The left foot resembles a griffin's claw, signifying the servants of the secular power of the pope, the canonists who repress the whole world. The female belly and breasts signify the papal body, cardinals, bishops, priests, monks and like whorish folk who lead unashamed lives, just as the Papal Ass shows its naked female belly.

The scales on the arms, legs and neck signify the secular princes. These cling to each other, and although they do not dare to protect open lusts and desires, signified by the parts they do not cover, they nonetheless tolerate them, and hang the more firmly on the arms, legs and neck of the monster, the papacy. Moreover they protect it, both as spiritual and secular power. The old man's head on the rear of the beast signifies the decline and end of the papacy, that it will grow old and pass away. The dragon spewing out fire behind it is nothing other than the poisonous bulls and abusive books of the papacy. Finally, that the beast was found dead in the Tiber indicates that the papacy's end has come, that it was found in Rome is confirmation of all the foregoing interpretation. Throughout his explanation Melanchthon also relates the beast to descriptions of the Antichrist in Daniel 8, the beast which Daniel saw in a vision, and to Job 41, the vision of Behemoth and Leviathan. The Papal Ass, Melanchthon argues, confirms and extends identification of the papacy with the antichristian beasts described there.

The Monk Calf and the Papal Ass both show the importance of visual signs in Reformation propaganda. Both descriptions depend for their exposition on the printed word, but this is unthinkable without the visual representation of the two figures. They provide an excellent example of the way in which a visual text could be expounded orally for a non-literate reader by the use of the printed text. However, they could also be detached from dependence on the printed word as self-sufficient visual signs. This was done most noticeably in Luther's *Depiction of the Papacy* of 1545, where the entire series of nine illustrations was opened with the Papal Ass (ill. 99). The Latin caption mentions that the monster was found dead in the Tiber at Rome in 1496; the German text contains the brief but essential message: 'What God himself holds of the papacy is shown by this terrible picture. Everyone should therefore shudder as he takes it to heart.' The iconic power of the image is adequately captured in this short verse, its rhymed form easily committed to memory. The propaganda value of the two works can be seen in the number of editions published. There were nine editions of both works together, five of the Papal Ass on its own, and two of the Monk Calf alone. There were also translations in French and English of both works, a Dutch translation and a seventeenth-century German edition of the Papal Ass.[57] Both monsters also passed into collections, such as Lycosthenes *Wunderwerck* of 1557.[58]

Such widespread interest in this kind of propaganda was probably a result as much of the appearance of the monsters themselves as of the allegorical interpretation attached to them. However, this interest was not just idle curiosity or thirst for sensation. It came, rather, from the conviction that nature reflected the rule of God. Monsters were an infringement of nature and so a perversion of God's creation. God permitted them as signs of disorder, although their essence was contrary to him. In this sense, there was a close relationship between monsters and sin. Sin was a disfigurement of God's image in man which transformed him into a monster. The monster thus stood close to the very origin of sin, the Devil, and the monster could itself become a visible expression of evil.[59] The monster motif could then be used to associate the papacy and its supporters with the Devil. This process can be seen in the animal masks given to Luther's opponents, discussed in an earlier chapter.[60] The mask fulfilled the function of transforming men temporarily into monsters, but they could also turn into real monsters, something for which there was biblical authority in Daniel 4.33.[61] Thus Lycosthenes cites a pre-Reformation legend, according to which Pope Benedict IX was turned on his death-bed into a bear with an ass's tail, because during his life he had lived like a wild beast.[62] The same notion was involved in the creation of the theriomorphic shapes of Luther's opponents in the *Lutheran Strebkatz*. Murner, Eck, Lemp and the rest are changed into beasts by the Devil's power.[63] In evangelical propaganda the role of the Devil in the creation of such monsters is an integral part of its polemical appeal.

We can see this concept expressed in the depiction known as *The Devil's*

99   *The Papal Ass*, in M. Luther, *Abbildung des papstums* (1545), fol. I, BL

Bagpipe (ill. 100). This shows a devil playing his tune through the ears and nose of a monk, identified by his broad tonsure. But the basis of this illustration is not a devil perched on a monk's shoulders. It is the monk as two-headed monster, for the devil has grown into one creature with the monk whom he uses as his instrument. The identity of the Devil with the monk as monster became a commonplace of Reformation propaganda. It could be indicated as simply as in the titlepage of a work by Pamphilus Gengenbach from 1522, showing a monk with large claws beneath his monastic habit (ill. 101).[64] This kind of depiction itself probably went back to a popular pre-Reformation proverb linking monks with the Devil. 'Misfortune has broad feet, said the peasant, as he saw the monk coming.'[65] The representation of monks as the Devil in disguise leads us to another feature of monsters in propaganda. The notion of a mask could be turned around, and the humanity of the opponent regarded as a mask hiding a monster underneath. This is the thought involved in a famous broadsheet depicting Alexander VI (ill. 102), which had a flap that could be lifted up to reveal who the pope really was (ill. 103).[66]

A more complex variant of the monster theme is found in an engraving by Melchior Lorch from 1545, showing the pope as a monster (ill. 104). Here the figure depicted is a two-headed demon. One is a human head with ass's ears, the other an animal head, possibly that of a dog. It wields an uprooted tree-

100   *The Devil's Bagpipe*, BM
101   Titlepage to P. Gengenbach, *Wie der Hailig Vatter Bapst
Adrianus ein geritten ist* (M. Ramminger, Augsburg, 1522), BL

stump as a club, which has three cross branches signifying the papal cross. In its left hand it holds a papal key, which is shattered at the end, and is crowned with a papal tiara whose peak ends in a spiral of excrement. The papal signs are completed by the slippers on its feet, bearing an embroidered cross. The creature has a long demonic tail and bat-like wings, and from its mouth flows a stream of flame, bearing reptiles, toads, lizards and snakes. This appears to be a reference to the figures in Apocalypse 16.13, where the beast, the dragon and the false prophet release three foul spirits like frogs. The beast stands astride a carpet of flames in which writhe suffering souls, and this diabolical identification is rounded off by a demon wearing a cardinal's hat, seated on a papal bull, bottom right, on which it is defecating. The bull bears the words 'Keep clear, God and man, I and the Devil are the lords.'[67]

This engraving draws on several traditions. The figure of the Wild Man, found in popular superstition and in popular art and literature, is clearly alluded to by the club and the matted, tufted hair which covers the monster. The Wild Man had strong links to the demonic, so it was fitting to represent the pope as both Wild Man and as demon.[68] The ears recall the Papal Ass, but

102   *Broadsheet on Pope Alexander VI*, Munich Staatsbibliothek
103   *Alexander VI Revealed as Devil*, Munich Staatsbibliothek

the two heads also allude to the monster as the embodiment of satanic evil, seen in *The Devil's Bagpipe*. Finally, the figure is linked to the beast of the Apocalypse, and so to the Antichrist. The written text, from the hand of Luther, labels the pope as Wild Man, and contains a prayer that God will aid man in the distress caused by papal condemnations.

The monster was an ambivalent figure, for it was both a sign and a direct revelation.[69] As a sign it could connote a range of implied meanings, which could only be unravelled by an allegorical interpretation, similar to allegorical exposition of Scripture. However, it could also denote, revealing its true nature without further exposition, similar to the 'literal' interpretation of Scripture. Thus the Papal Ass and the Monk Calf revealed the papacy and monkery as monstrous, without further recourse to the complex allegorical readings of Luther and Melanchthon. Nonetheless, evangelical propaganda exploited both features of the monster. It was more cautious about a third feature, the prophetic purpose of monsters.[70] We have already seen the prophetic emphasis in heavenly signs and omens, in conjunctions and comets. Evangelical propaganda was no less cautious about the prophetic nature of these phenomena, perhaps because it smacked too much of superstition. Two other forms of prophecy were less cautiously treated, for both were more

104   M. Lorch, *The Pope as Wild Man* (1545), Dahlem

intrinsic to the Christian tradition than the other signs. These were mystical visions and mystical prophecy.

There was an exceptional interest in mystical visions during the years just before the Reformation. The visions of St Bridget of Sweden exercised a strong influence on art, especially painting, while visionaries such as St Hildegard of Bingen were part of the stock repertoire of popular prophecy in the later fifteenth century.[71] These found a ready market in popularised printed form during the early decades of the sixteenth century.[72] Visions also played an important part in occurrences such as the movement of the Drummer of Niklashausen, where Hans Boheim claimed to have had a vision of the Virgin, or in the notorious Jetzer fraud in Berne, where a Franciscan claimed to have had a vision of Christ, in which he received the stigmata.[73] A vision which attracted attention in Reformation circles, and which was adapted for propaganda purposes, was that of the fifteenth-century Swiss hermit Nikolaus von der Flühe, or Brother Claus. A small booklet about Brother Claus published shortly after his death in 1488 contained an enigmatic diagram of his reputed vision.[74]

It consisted of two concentric circles joined by six spear-shaped spokes, like spokes of a wheel joining the outer rim to the hub. The tips of the spokes pointed alternately towards and away from the inner circle or hub. Later in the same work, in an attempt to interpret this device allegorically, a bearded face wearing a crown was placed inside the inner circle (ill. 105). The spears

105   Illustration to *Bruder Claus* [P. Wagner, Nuremberg, 1490], BL IA 8022, fol. A5v

were now arranged so that three points emanated from the eyes and mouth of the face, the three blunt ends, however, merely from the edge of the inner circle, one rising through the crown. Each spear led to a roundel illustration intended to provide a pious explanation of the vision, which was taken to symbolise the works of corporal mercy.[75]

In 1503 a Parisian professor of theology, Charles Bouvelles, visited the hermit's cell, and described the vision in a letter published in 1511, with a woodcut illustration. Although clearly modelled on the earlier depiction, it introduced small significant changes. The inner circle disappeared, leaving only the face in a large circle. The simple crown became a triple tiara and the beard was forked in three. The spears emanated from the eyes and mouth as before, but the three blunt ends now emerged from the two nostrils and the forehead, and resembled rays of light, made plausible by what seemed to be rays emanating from the pupils of the eyes. Bouvelles had sought an interpretation of this vision from an acquaintance, Nikolaus Horius, Bishop-elect of Rheims, who interpreted the face to signify a cruel ruler, perhaps a pope. The sword emanating from the forehead stuck into the cross, and so showed his opposition to Christ. The points sticking into the eyes signified that he was blinded by greed and unchastity, the blunt ends in his nostrils his indifference to heavenly things, which he could not smell. The point entering his lips indicated his unwillingness to proclaim the Word of God. That the swords had no handles signified that his vices could not be removed without injuring him, and so arousing his anger. The three-forked beard Horius interpreted to mean that this figure was the cause of evil which would befoul all people.[76] Horius' interpretation was given in 1508, and seems to have contributed to forming the conviction in Bouvelles' mind that the messianic age was imminent. In 1509 he wrote to Cardinal Ximinez of Spain, proclaiming the coming of a great reforming pope, and he attempted to inspire his Spanish friends with his prophetic excitement.[77]

This vision was taken up by Luther in 1528, after a friend had brought Bouvelles' work to his attention. Luther published a small pamphlet, with an illustration of the vision, the various letters from Bouvelles and Horius, the letter from his friend Speratus which called his attention to it, and his own interpretation.[78] In Luther's version (ill. 106), the illustration has undergone a further change. The outer circle has become two circles close together, the rays are now unmistakably sword points, and two of them now emanate from the corners, not the pupils of the eyes. For Luther, the vision now represents not a pope, but the papacy. The angry features signify the tyrannical, murderous and bloody rule of the papacy, which rules both body and soul with force. The sword from the top of the head signifies human teaching, invented by the human brain, which is against Christ's teaching and strikes at the Word of the cross. The sword from the right nostril is spiritual power, that from the left secular law; both are angry laws, for the nose signifies anger. The other three swords have no beginnings, and signify the spirit and the Gospel, which strike the papacy in the face. That coming into his mouth from below is the Word of God, which punishes his lying human teaching and opposes his hypocrisy. The point in his right eye is the Word striking at the papacy's spiritual power, that in the left at the secular power. That the figure has no body signifies that Christ and his Church do not adhere to the papacy, nor recognise it for its head, although it must suffer under him. The three-forked beard signifies the three groups which do adhere to the papacy: the hypocrites, such as the monks, nuns and priests; the scholars, such as the jurists and theologians; and the powerful, such as the princes. But they only hang there and do not touch neck or body, a sign that they do not belong to him, but to the Church. That the swords are without handles signifies that the pope depends on sayings taken from Scripture, possibly an allusion to the Word being like a sword; but they are broken, just as the pope breaks and mutilates Scripture.[79]

This work made far less impact as evangelical propaganda than the Papal Ass. It saw only two editions in 1528, and when two broadsheets on the vision of Brother Claus were produced, they preferred to adopt the interpret-

106   Titlepage to *Ein gesichte Bruder Clausen ynn Schweytz* (N. Schirlentz, Wittenberg, 1528), BL

ation given by Horius rather than that of Luther.[80] This tells us something of importance about visual propaganda. Interpretation of the vision required pictorial representation, but Luther's was far too allegorical. It could not be married to an equally effective literal interpretation which could stand beside the longer and more elaborate literary exposition. The Horius' version simply related the vision to 'some high spiritual prince' – in the broadsheet, to '*the* high spiritual prince'. This seems to refer to the pseudo-pope who was one of the manifestations of the Antichrist. This was more direct and accessible to the unlettered viewer than Luther's intricate allegory. In the last resort, however, it was probably less successful as an image because it was less of a curiosity, and far less sensational than the fantastic monster.

The vision of Brother Claus shows how persistent belief in popular and mystical prophecies was during the first half of the sixteenth century. In dealing with the vision, Luther believed that he was explaining a genuinely prophetic work. Far from seeing it as incompatible with his desire to restore true religion and remove superstition, he saw it as confirmation of the rightness of the evangelical movement. A similarly 'genuine' prophecy is seen in the work by Albrecht Dürer known as *The Michelfeld Tapestry* (ill. 107). This is in the form of a *Bilderbogen*, in three scenes set on six blocks, intended to be joined together into a long frieze.[81] In a text about the central panel, Dürer claimed to have seen the scenes depicted in a tapestry discovered in 1524 in a castle on the Rhine. It had been produced, he argued, a hundred years before, and revealed what the ancients had foreseen about Dürer's time. Although no Castle Michelfeld can be traced, Dürer does seem to have worked from an original tapestry. It was nowhere near one hundred years old, but may have dated from the end of the fifteenth century. This does not reduce the prophetic force it was regarded as possessing for interpretation of the events of the early sixteenth century. The willingness to accept the reality of such prophecies combined with the 'discovery' of such works as the tapestry or the vision of Brother Claus to create firm conviction in their genuineness. The Brother Claus vision, of course, still had to be interpreted. The Michelfeld Tapestry, on the other hand, was self-evident in its meaning.

The series of scenes is opened at the left by the wheel of fortune. Three ignoble birds are on top, the jay, the pheasant and the crow, which wears a crown in honour of its supreme position at the very peak of the wheel's course. At the bottom are the noble birds, the eagle, the falcon and the peacock. Time turns the wheel, but this is resisted by the figure of the fox to the left. Besides the connotation of cunning usually attached to the fox, this creature is given overtones of sexual licence through its erect male member. Thus, the ignoble not only rule, but fleshly vice seeks to stay the course of time to maintain that rule.

The next scene represents the estates – the knight and the noble, and seen between these two, the burgher, with the round high hat, the artisan, repre-

107   A. Dürer, *The Michelfeld Tapestry*, BM

sented by a smith with his hammer and tongs and the peasant with the flail. They regard the central scene where Justice, Truth and Reason sit locked in the stocks. Justice has her hands bound to a rod, thus preventing her using her scales and sword. Truth has her lips sealed with a padlock, while Reason has her hands pinioned to the stocks. To their left sits the figure of Deceit, enthroned and ruling with a rod the three virtues imprisoned in the stocks and the infant figure of Piety swaddled in a cradle at his feet. He holds one end of a banderole, which attributes to him the words written above the virtues: 'With my agility I have subjected Justice, Reason and Truth.' The representatives of the estates protest about this state of affairs: 'Deceit, burden us not so. Piety has slumbered too long. Awake her, or it will go hard for you.' The estates thus call for the revival of piety and warn Deceit of his fate once it has been awakened. In expectation, Truth and Reason have their eyes turned toward the cradle.

To the right of Deceit are two figures representing secular and spiritual law, the first an advocate with his high cap, the second a canon holding his breviary. These speak the words, addressed to Deceit: 'Lord, we hear your words willingly. We desire to learn in your school.' The law is thus the willing pupil of deception. These two have their backs turned on the final figure of the series, who is identified as Divine Providence. This figure stands with folded arms, rays darting from his eyes in a shape similar to a nimbus. The inscription embodies the neo-platonic idea that all creation is an emanation of the eternal light of the divine. The figure is divine justice, which both secular and spiritual law ignore in favour of deceit. Taken as a whole, the depiction expresses the sense of grievance against injustice dominant in the 1520s, and the hope placed in a revival of piety to redress this. Cunning and vice have brought the ignoble to dominance, but hope reposes in slumbering piety, which time will bring to maturity as the wheel turns again. It could thus be read as a prophecy of hope, that the reign of deceit will come to an end. The striking figure of divine justice signifies that the time is at hand, adding an eschatological note to the whole composition.

Dürer's propaganda for the new ideas was less polemical than many of our examples. He was content to evoke a mood — in this case, the mood of prophetic expectation attached to revival of piety. Other works were more polemical in tone, although they too bore the stamp of the apocalyptic outlook of the time. One of the most interesting can be seen in the small booklet published in 1527 by the Nuremberg pastor Andreas Osiander, the *Wondrous Prophecy of the Papacy*.[82] This was based on a pseudo-Joachimist work, the *Vaticinia de summis pontificibus*, two copies of which Osiander discovered in Nuremberg libraries. The work consists of two sets of illustrated prophecies. Each set contains fifteen pictures, each picture representing a pope, accompanied by a key phrase and an enigmatic description. These prophecies mentioned holy and unholy popes, and referred also to future popes, intended

to represent the Antichrist. The sequence of popes is arranged roughly chrono-
logically, with the antichristian popes at the end of the second set. Somehow
both sets were merged into one collection, but with the later set first, so that
the antichristian popes to come were placed in the middle of the collection.
The entire series was then interpreted merely to prophesy a series of angelic
popes.[83]

Osiander seems to have paid little heed to the commentary in the edition
he discovered. He interpreted it according to Lutheran views, reshaping the
prophecy completely to fit the needs of evangelical propaganda. As the basis
of his edition he retained only the thirty pictures, added a new, brief commentary for each, with an accompanying verse by Hans Sachs. This raises the
question of how seriously Osiander took the prophetic nature of the original.
His preface to his 1527 edition certainly sounds a sceptical note. Christians
should be adequately informed from holy Scripture of things that are to
come, but in the strange times in which they now live men look more to
human words and prophecies than to those of God. This is proved by the
great interest aroused by the prophecy of Johann Lichtenberger (who had
foretold, on the basis of a conjunction of 1484, the coming of a monk who
would cause a revolution in the Church – Luther's birth date was 1483!).
Osiander therefore publishes this prophecy so that, even if men ignore God's
own prophecy, they may turn away from human prophecies.[84] This work
will help them to do so. The preface thus remains ambiguous about whether
the work is to be regarded as 'human prophecy' or as something more reliable; however, Osiander continues as if it were clearly the latter.[85]

Osiander explicitly envisages the work as a pictorial prophecy, one
expressed 'not in words, but in pictures alone'. He has dispensed with the
written text because the pictures are older than it and, as has often been the
case, the prophecy has thereby been misunderstood. To aid the simple, an
interpretation has been supplied, but all people of reason will see plainly what
it means without any exposition. In sum, it shows the progress of the papacy
from the time it became a tyranny until the end of the world. It thus
becomes a pictorial history of the papacy with a prophetic gloss. Although its
impact is best understood through reproduction of the whole series, space
dictates that only a selection can be illustrated here. The argument of those
omitted we can refer to in summary. Pictures 1–3 argue that the pope has
turned away from the Holy Spirit and placed his trust in warriors. He becomes
a secular prince with his own power, and represses the emperor with the aid
of France. His courtiers hold him back from following God's Law.

In picture 4 (ill. 108) the pope has the emperor by the neck, and holds the
other princes down with his triple sceptre, that is, his power to bind and loose.
The monk behind him signifies that he seeks to uphold this power with
Scripture. In picture 5, Satan speaks to the pope from a bush, as God did to
Moses. The pope has rejected God's Law, but finds that he cannot rule with-

out law, so he receives new laws from the hand of Satan. The pope then abandons piety and justice for a sinful life and, moved by Satan, upholds injustice in return for rich gifts. Meanwhile, the secular powers are content to look on and merely to defend themselves, rather than to punish the pope as is fitting (pictures 6–8). The pope uses the keys of the law according to the Devil's instructions, forcing the Holy Spirit to flee, while the sword of false doctrine issuing from the pope's mouth wounds the lamb of Christ, the Word and eternal truth (picture 9, ill. 109).

The pope now sets his own power above that of the emperor but, not content with this, he also invokes spiritual Law. He thus represses the imperial crown, persecutes the Gospel and uses his keys to gain riches. His worldly sword he entrusts to ravening wolves, who wield it as the flaying knife of deceit (pictures 10–12). The pope is now as self-satisfied as the peacock, but God condemns him secretly, so that his word no longer binds before God. He is deposed and the world may attack him – but only with spiritual weapons (pictures 13–14). When attacked with the sword of the spirit, the Word, it is clear that the pope is the beast of Apocalypse 12 and 16. It has a fair countenance in front, but is cunning behind – but its jaws are bloodied from biting the sharp edge of the Word (picture 15, ill. 110). Knowing that he can

Der Bapst der sebt den Keyser fein.
Mit eydes pflicht der krönung sein.
Macht ybn auch matt durch seinen Ban.
Als er viel Keysern hat gethan.

Der Bapst hat mit dem Sathan gmeyn
Regirt durch das eynsprechen seyn.
Vnd wer seyn lere widder redt
Der wird von ybm veriagt/getödt.

108   Illustration in *Eyn wunderliche Weyssagung von dem Bapstum* (H. Guldenmundt, Nuremberg, 1527), BL 3906.bb.40, fol. Bi r
109   *Eyn wunderliche Weyssagung*, fol. Biii r

defend himself with Scripture no longer, the pope surrounds himself with
warriors. The Word disputes with the Devil while the pope looks on anxiously
(pictures 16–17).

Osiander's exposition now moves from allegorical to historical interpretation. The pope, hearing confession, is attacked by that most placid of
beasts, the unicorn, which knocks off his tiara, a challenge to confession and
indulgences (picture 18, ill. 111). The next picture (ill. 112) depicts the
opposition to the pope, based on three strong pillars. The horn is the Word in
God's hand, the monk is he who preaches the Word, the king is secular authority which takes the Word to heart and protects the monk. These references
to Luther are made explicit in the next picture (ill. 113), which identifies the
monk. The rose is Luther's heraldic emblem, the sickle signifies that he cuts
down the fleshly, shown by the severed leg. But he will ignite the love of
Christ again, using the branding-iron.

The next five pictures (21–25) are related even more closely to historical
events. The patient folk, signified by an ox, have long borne the burden of
papal financial exactions without complaint. Now they learn from God's
Word that this is unjust, and refuse to bear it any longer. When the pope
refuses to hear them, they are changed from the patient ox into the angry
bear, with all the ugly impatience of the common folk. To appease this
impatience, a Reichstag was called at Worms, but human not divine law ruled
there, under the influence of troops. But the mandate from Worms was with-

Wen man den
bapst mit dem
fewrigē schwe
rd des geystes(
das ist mit got
tes wort/das d
heilge geist dur
ch die fewrigē
zungen geschie
ckt vnnd reden
hat lassen)also
angreifft / So
wyrd es offens
bar/das sein re
giment die Be
stia odder das
thier ist/dz mit
seinem schwätz
den dürren teil
der stein zeucht
vnd ynn die ver
dammis gehet/
Apocalipsi. xiii
vnnd.xvij.hat
forn eyn erber
angesicht / aber hinden mit dem schwantz heymlich/tückisch/
vnd mit listen beyst es yn das schwerd des wortts/das yhm das
maul blut/vnd kan yhm doch nichts abrechen.

Das geschicht so yhn Gott greyffet an
Mit seynem wort für yederman
Denn wird entdeckt seyn abentewr
Das er eyn grewl ist vngehewr.

Wie mus es dē
zugehen ? das
der Bapst vns
tergehe ? Sihe
da/er sitzet/ hö
ret beycht/ vnd
absoluirt/ das
ist/er teylet Ab
las vnd vegeb
ung der sunde
vmb gelt aus/
wie seine gewō
heit ist / Wo er
selbs nicht hyn
kömpt/ schickt
er seine Boten/ vn
left sie solche
war feyl tragē
Vber diser wot
das ist/eben vß
er dem Ablas /
greiffe yhn das
aller freydigste
thier/das Eyn
horn an / mitt
grossem ernst ;
was aber das Einhorn bedeut /leret dich seyn der xciij. psalm/
Den liese mit vleys/ wirstu dester bas verstehen/ was hernach
folget.

Als nu kam die versehen zeyt
Schickt Gott auff yhn/seyn wort gemeit
Ob dem Ablas der kampff anfieng
Für aller welt ynn offnem ring.

C ij

110   *Eyn wunderliche Weyssagung*, fol. Cii r
111   *Eyn wunderliche Weyssagung*, fol. Ciii v

out force, for God's Word was stronger. Two further Reichstags were held at Nuremberg, where God's Word prevailed, as can be seen in the Recesses from these meetings. In these affairs, the papal side was led by the pope's courtiers, the foxes — Eck, Emser, Alfeld, Faber, Cochleus, etc., but so unskilfully that even more about papal rule was revealed to all.

The last five pictures now move to future events, arguing that the prophecy so far has been fulfilled by historical fact. It secures, therefore, credence for its further predictions. The pope will be robbed of all his power, and sit so naked and alone that even the poor peasant will mock him. He must finally confess that he is not a lord, but only a servant of the flock, and must give up his crown to his sheep. God will set other folk in the apostolic office, but the crown will then signify all the virtues of the Spirit. When this is done, the servants of the Word would be honoured by the world once more, and a Christian rule set up which would last until Christ came. Then all the servants of the Word would return their power to Christ, who would have all power on earth and in heaven.

Osiander's pamphlet is thus a remarkable attempt to shape the pseudo-Joachimist original into a prophecy of the evangelical movement, in the process providing it with prophetic legitimation. This legitimation is twofold: the old prophecy is fulfilled to date in the appearance of Luther and subsequent events of the 1520s, and the evangelical movement is a promise of the apocalyptic fulness of all things, leading to the last age before the coming of Christ.

Der handel wi der den Bapſt ſtehet auff drey ſtarcken ſeulen damit er vnter ſtützt vñ erhalten wird . Die erſte iſt/ Gotes wort/ynn Gotes hand/durch ein horn bedeut Die annder iſt ein Münch/der es frölich vnnd vnuerzagt predigt.Alſo ſpricht Jeſaias am lviij . Schrey/ erhöhe deyne ſtimme wie ein horn/etce . Die dritte ſewl iſt weltliche öberekeit/die es höret vnd zu hertzen nympt/den Münch ſchützt/odder yhm ia nicht weret etc.

Damit man ay ber ſehe/ wer d Münch ſey/ ſo ſtehet er da ynn ſeiner kleidung vnd hat ſein zei chen/ die Roſen ynn der handt/ ich meyn ia es ſey der Luther. Die weyl aber Jeſaias ſpricht am . xl . Alles fleyſch iſt wie gras Stehet er da mit einer ſi cheln/ vñ ſchnei dets ab / nicht gras / ſondern fleiſch/ vnd al les was fleiſch lich iſt/ Deñ da widder predigt er/vnd weil es ausgereutet iſt wird er mit de fewer/ eyſen/das fewer der Chriſtlichen liebe/ das erloſchen iſt/ widder auff ſchlagen vnd anzünden.

Das Görlich wort was kreffrig ſtarck
Vnd decket auff das Babſtumb arck
Mit gunſt etlicher Stedt vnd Fürſten
Die auch nach Gottes wort was dürſten .

Das thet der heldt Martinus Luther
Der macht das Euangeli lauter
All menſchen leer er gantz abhawt
Vnd ſelig ſpricht/der Gott vertrawt.

112   *Eyn wunderliche Weyssagung*, fol. C4 r
113   *Eyn wunderliche Weyssagung*, fol. C4 v

To achieve this result Osiander had to reinterpret the original, but he also had to reshape some of the pictures to suit his exposition. The most noticeable case is picture 20 (see ill. 113). Compared to the original Italian edition which Osiander used, the branding iron has been substituted for a large letter B (ill. 114), while the monk has been given the habit appropriate to Luther's Order. Similarly, the previous illustration in the series has been altered, by placing the horn in the hand on top of the third column, instead of what appears to be a blade in the original. The horn has then been placed in the ear of the monk, something not at all indicated in the Italian edition, and the monk has been given a cowl similar to that of Luther's Order.[86]

The *Wondrous Prophecy* shares the characteristics of other works of propaganda seeking to invoke the apocalyptic mood of the time. Whether dealing with comets, conjunctions, omens, monsters, visions or prophecies they were ambiguous about the amount of credence to be given to such phenomena. Reformation aversion to superstition led to attempts at spiritual interpretation, but these depended enough on literal belief in such signs for the matter to remain ambivalent. Thus, evangelical propaganda did not break with pre-Reformation apocalyptic feeling, but rather exploited it. In terms of the religious emotions it aroused, the propaganda confirmed and extended these elements of popular belief. This is proved convincingly by two themes which are of sufficient importance to deserve separate treatment in the next chapter: the Antichrist and the world turned upside-down.

114   Illustration to *Joachimi abbatis Vaticinia* (Bologna, 1515), BL 3836.b.37, fol. Dii r

6

ANTICHRIST AND THE WORLD
TURNED UPSIDE-DOWN

The Antichrist is one of the most fascinating figures of late-medieval popular thought, and illustrates the very broad penumbra between official faith and doctrine and popular belief. In essence, the Antichrist was a diabolical answer to the incarnation, for he was the antithesis of Christ, his personal history a black parody of the Saviour's.[1] He is born in Babylon from the tribe of Dan, the son of a whore and the Devil. Like Christ, he spends his youth away from the place of his birth, and is brought up by witches and magicians who initiate him into the black arts. At the age of thirty he goes to Jerusalem and is circumcised. He proclaims Jesus to be a fraud and himself to be the true messiah, convincing the Jews of this claim by promising to revive the Mosaic Law. He rebuilds the destroyed temple in three days, sets up his throne there and proclaims himself as God. Through miracles, bribes and force, he quickly gains a huge following, but his rule lasts only three and a half years. During this time he is not unopposed. God sends two prophets, Enoch and Elias, to preach against him, but he slays them. In parody of Christ, he stages a fake death and resurrection, but in trying to ape Christ's ascension from Mount Olivet, he meets his end. He is overcome and slain by the archangel Michael, and thrust down into hell.[2]

The origins of this legend are found in the obscure history of early Christianity, but its biblical foundations were strong enough for it to seem plausible to the Christian middle ages. It drew so skilfully on the classic apocalyptic texts — the Book of Daniel, 2 Thessalonians and the Apocalypse — that theologians of the calibre of Aquinas and Bonaventure felt obliged to sort out the acceptable from the unacceptable parts of the story. For example, they rejected the belief that the Antichrist was born of a virgin as an un-fitting parallel to Christ. They were also in some doubt about his miracles. If they were not fake miracles, they were worked by the power of the Devil. Given the seriousness with which such prominent theologians took the Anti-christ, we need not be surprised that he looms so large in popular belief. Belief in the Antichrist reached such a pitch that it could even be spoken of as an article of faith.[3]

Interest in the legend was certainly stimulated by any kind of eschato-logical feeling, for the Antichrist was intimately linked to the last days. His appearance is a sign that the last days are at hand, his defeat indicates that the end of the world is nigh. The identification of the Antichrist and his exact relation to the last days, however, remained extremely vague, despite the precision with which his biography was set out. First, it was unclear whether he was to be regarded as a single person or as a collectivity. Second, the appearance of the Antichrist could signify either that the world would end with his defeat, or that this defeat would inaugurate the millennium before the end of the world. These ambiguities helped to keep the legend fresh in the minds of medieval Christians, for it was always possible to show its relevance to the time at hand.[4]

By the end of the fifteenth century, he was as common a figure in popular religious thought as the Devil. He appeared in at least three fifteenth-century religious dramas, and even in a carnival play, an indication that he was familiar enough to invite jest. He forms the subject of several editions of the block-book, the forerunner of the popular picture book, where his history was linked to the fifteen signs of the last days. He is mentioned in numerous popular prophecies at the beginning of the sixteenth century, features in works by popular writers such as Brant and Geiler von Kaisersberg, and turns up on the very eve of the Reformation in Pamphilus Gengenbach's rhymed prophetic work of 1517, *The Nollhart*. A Latin summary of his life appeared in nine printed editions between 1473 and 1505.[5]

The Antichrist was just as popular with the broad stream of heterodox and oppositional Christianity dating from the Franciscan Spirituals and Joachimite-influenced movements of dissent. In this tradition, he is mentioned in the *Onus Ecclesiae*, a semi-prophetic, Joachimist work critical of the state of the Church, written around 1519 and first published in 1524. The Hussites also gave the Antichrist a prominent place in their thought. He was discovered among the Catholic clergy and in individual popes. They did not go so far as to identify the Antichrist with the papacy, but they did conceive of a diabolical antithesis to the mystical body of Christ, the *corpus mysticum Antichristi*. If Hussite writers did not agree whether the Antichrist was an individual or an aggregate personality, a person or a mystical tendency, they did agree that the Antichrist was thriving under the papacy.[6]

The figure is found in the evangelical movement from its earliest days. He provided the basis of the most successful work of visual propaganda produced by the Reformation, Lucas Cranach's *Passional Christi und Antichristi*. As one of Luther's closest friends, the Saxon court painter was close to the central ideas of the Reformation from its inception. In May 1521 he created the small illustrated pamphlet composed of twenty-six woodcuts, each with a brief commentary written by Philipp Melanchthon. Much of the inspiration for the work can be found in Luther's manifestos of 1520, but the central theme of the booklet was extremely simple. A *Passional* was a small picture book depicting scenes from the life of Christ or the saints for pious meditation by the unlearned. Cranach adapted this idea to juxtapose the life of Christ with that of the Antichrist, the pope. In thirteen contrasting pairs of woodcuts the reader could see for himself the difference between the two. The first in each pair depicts a scene from the life of Christ, amplified by a written text, usually a passage from Scripture. The second presents a similar scene from the life of the pope, amplified by passages from papal decretals and explanatory comments by Melanchthon.[7] This work was of such significance for the major themes of evangelical visual propaganda that it is worth extensive analysis.

The first pair of woodcuts depicts Christ fleeing the Jews' attempt to make him their king, while the pope is shown defending his claims to secular rule with cannon and sword (ills. 115—16). This claim, Melanchthon tells us, is upheld by the spurious Donation of Constantine, the document on which papal secular power was based. It had been exposed as a forgery by the Italian humanist Lorenzo Valla, and the exposure popularised in Germany in 1520 by Ulrich von Hutten. Valla's work had some influence in confirming Luther's belief that the pope and the papacy were the Antichrist, and frequent reference is made to the forgery throughout Melanchthon's commentary.[8] The ironic contrast in the first pair of woodcuts is developed further in the second. Christ is crowned with thorns, while the pope is crowned with the triple tiara, the sign of his secular power, said to be inherited from Constantine. Extend-

115   Illustration in *Passional Christi und Antichristi*
(Johann Grunenberg, Wittenberg, 1521), BL C53.c.6, fol. Ai v
116   *Passional Christi und Antichristi*, fol. Aii r

ing the contrast again, the antithesis between Christian humility and worldly pride forms the basis of the third set. Christ washes the feet of his disciples, while the pope presents his foot for princes and kings to kiss.[9]

The message of the fourth set is less visual. It states, largely through the printed text, that Christ commanded in Matthew 15 paying the authorities their dues, a command echoed in Romans 13. The pope, however, claims exemption for all his followers. Worse, he orders the interdict on those who follow Christ's command by levying tax on clerical persons or their property.[10] The fifth antithesis depicts Christ among the poor and lame, emphasising the humility of Christ in taking the form of a servant. The pope is shown presiding in princely state over a tournament. The commentary gives a nationalist twist to the contrast. The pope considers it beneath his dignity to humble himself, believing that the humble man brings contempt upon his government. Such an argument is fit only for fools, Melanchthon comments, but the pope must think Germans to be fools, to try to rule them as he does.[11]

In the sixth set, Jesus tells his disciples that whoever wishes to follow him must take up his cross and do so. So Christ and his followers go their way on foot, but the pope carries his cross in quite a different fashion, being borne aloft in princely state (ills. 117–18). Melanchthon's ironic comment is that

Christus.

Als Jhesus ist an weyten wege gangen / ist er müd worden. Johan. 4. Der mir wil nach volgen / der nem seyn Creutz uff sich und volge mir. Mathei 16.

Er hatte ym seyn Creutze selbst getragen und ist zu der stell die Caluarie gnant wurde / gangen. 19.

Antichristus.

Das capitel Si quis suadente und dergleychen zeyge genug an wie gerne der Bapst das creutz der wyder wertigkeyt duldet / so er alle die thoren / die hand an die pfaffen an legt vormaladeyet und dem teuffel gibt. Und also ouch tregt der Bapst das creutz das ynnen getaufft Christen uff ynen achselen tragen müssen.

117   *Passional Christi und Antichristi*, fol. Bii v
118   *Passional Christi und Antichristi*, fol. Biii r

this shows how willingly the pope suffers the cross of adversity.[12] The next pair contrasts starkly Christ preaching the kingdom of God, while the pope, who has forgotten this duty, feasts in a royal manner (ills. 119–20). The humble origins of Christ are recalled in the eighth set, showing a nativity. The pope is shown, however, armed and ready to wage war against a town. Such are the lengths to which the pope will go, the commentary informs us, to ensure clerical possession of property – he is willing to spill Christian blood, and even to overturn civil authority. Authorities who imprison clergy will find that the pope releases their subjects from their oaths of obedience, and he will allow the defence of clerical goods with the secular as well as the spiritual sword.[13]

The ninth set provided a contrast which became a stock antithesis between Christ and the pope (ills. 121–2). Christ's peaceful entry into Jerusalem on the ass is opposed to the pope riding in state on a steed, claiming that he had this right from the emperor, and that it placed him above the emperor. The two soldiers accompanying him indicate the military measures he is willing to take to uphold the right, although the demons in the top right-hand corner suggest that this is also a papal ride to hell, similar to that in illustration 49.[14] The tenth pair contrasts Christ's injunction to his disciples that they should

Paſſional Chꝛiſti vnd

Chꝛiſtus.
Jch muß ouch andern ſtetten pꝛedigen das reych gotts dan ich von des wegen geſandt byn vñ hab gepꝛedigt yn den Synago-gen durch Gallileam Luce 4·

Antichꝛiſti.

Antichꝛiſtus.
Es geſchiecht offt das die Biſchoff mit vidæl hendeln Sclabē ſeyn vnnd von wegen Jrer ʃ hedern / auch zum geytten komen ſies nit/das dan nit ſeyn ſoll mogen des pꝛedigens nit gewarte Sonderlich wan yꝛe Biſthumß groß ſeint dan mogen ſie ande-re wol ſich Beſtelle die do pꝛedigēe. Jnter cetera de offi · oꝛdina. Das ſeynd die Biſchoff die yꝛes oꝛdelichen ampts vergeſſen/ſint woꝛdē aniali̇a vētꝭ. 3. vñ ſpꝛechē/Fōmet vñ laßt vns ſchlēmē v·ꝛd tꝛmmer vnd alßo fur vnd fur gut leßen haben. Eſai. 56·

119   *Passional Christi und Antichristi*, fol. Biii v
120   *Passional Christi und Antichristi*, fol. B4 r

go poor into the world with the papal command that no bishop should preside over any but a great town, and that he should be given sufficient provision, worthy title and great honour.

The eleventh pair turns to the question of external religious observance. It depicts the scene in which the pharisees murmured against Christ's disciples for eating with unclean hands. Christ reminded them that the kingdom of God was not in externals, but within us. In keeping the laws of men, such as papal disciplinary laws, one may transgress the laws of God. The pope is shown seated on his throne, issuing commands about such externals. The commentary asserts that papal law is wholly concerned with externals – the ordering of clothes, tonsures, feast days, consecrations, benefices, monkish sects and priests. Yet the clergy call themselves and the property Christ's Church, and regard themselves as the elect of God, just as if the laity were not in the Church.[15] The twelfth set provides another vivid pictorial contrast (ills. 123–4). Christ drove the money-changers from the temple, the commentary tells us, but the pope has come to take their place. One sees the pope presiding over the sale of indulgences in a church. The identification as Antichrist is underlined in the commentary with direct biblical evidence: the Antichrist sits in God's temple, displaying himself as God. As Daniel foretold, he alters

paſſional Chꝛiſti vnd

Antichꝛiſti.

Chꝛiſtus.
Sich an /dein konigk kompt dir demütigk vff einem jungē eſel Mathei 2c. Alſo iſt Chꝛiſtus kommen reyttende vffinn frāmbs den eſell arm vnd ſanfftmütigk vñ reydt nicht zu regiren ſonder vns allen zu eynen ſeligen todte Johannis 12.

Antichꝛiſti.
Die geyſtlichen ſeint alle konnige vnnd das bezeygt die platten vffun kopffe. dno 12 q .1.
Der Bapſt magk gleych wie der keyſſer reytten vñ der keyſſer iſt ſeyn trabant vff das biſchoffliche wirde gehalt nicht ganus bert werde c. conſtantinus 10 . c . 6 . diſ.
Der Bapſt iſt allen volckern vnd reychen voꝛgeſatzt er vann ſich goттes Johannis 22.   C ij

121 *Passional Christi und Antichristi,* fol. Ci v
122 *Passional Christi und Antichristi,* fol. Cii r

all divine ordinances, suppresses holy Scripture, and sells dispensations, indulgences, palliums and bishoprics. He dissolves marriages, makes laws and then breaks them in return for suitable payment; he raises up saints, burdens consciences, blesses and damns to the fourth generation, and demands that his voice be heard just as that of God.[16]

This quasi-scriptural summary of the Antichrist's activities provides a context for the final pair of woodcuts, the fate of Christ and Antichrist (ills. 125–6). While Christ ascends to the Father in heaven, the Antichrist is dispatched to hell. The last picture in the work is that most clearly influenced by iconographical representation of the legend, where his attempt to imitate Christ's ascension is defeated in mid-flight, and the Antichrist is thrust down into hell. We can see what appears to be almost a direct model for Cranach's depiction in an illustration from Schedel's *World Chronicle* of 1493 (ill. 127).[17] On the left the Antichrist is preaching, inspired by the Devil; on the right, Enoch and Elias preach against him. In the centre is Mount Olivet, from which he attempted his ascension to heaven, and above it is depicted his fall. Cranach has taken over only the fall for the second half of his antithesis, and suggested the attempted ascension by showing Christ's ascension as the

123   *Passional Christi und Antichristi*, fol. C4 v
124   *Passional Christi und Antichristi*, fol. Di r

other half. The new element in the schema is the identification of the falling Antichrist as the pope.

This little book is an extremely complex work, which presents the reader leafing through its pages with themes on several levels. At its simplest, it is a *Passional*; indeed, it can be seen as an illustrated morality play, its scenes not unlike those which would have been familiar to the common man from the religious drama of the day.[18] The Christian virtues of humility, simplicity and unworldliness are opposed by the vices of pride, pomp and desire for possession. So much could have been read adequately from the visual text alone. At a second level, visual and printed text present a religious message, the difference between true Christianity and false. The religion of Christ is contrasted to that of human laws and externals. The testimony of the Word of God in Scripture is opposed to that of the pope in canon law and to the mendacious Donation of Constantine. A third theme found in both visual and printed text is the highly emotive issue of anticlericalism. Throughout the work, this most potent cause of social discontent is singled out for criticism — the privileged position of the clergy, upheld by papal law, backed by the sanction of the ban, the interdict and even war.

125   *Passional Christi und Antichristi*, fol. Di v
126   *Passional Christi und Antichristi*, fol. Dii r

A fourth theme had an even stronger emotional appeal than social anti-clericalism, the depiction of papal pretensions to empire, to political supremacy and to over-riding secular power. The papal claim to be the direct heir of the Roman emperors could not fail to arouse those who felt so strongly about Roman exploitation of Germany and the German Church. German political mythology had long taught the direct descent of the Holy Roman Empire of the German Nation from Charlemagne, from the Roman Empire, sometimes, indeed, from Adam himself.[19] Cranach's work drove home the antipathy between this tradition and the claims of the papacy, and set it in a broader religious context of the struggle between true and false belief. A fifth theme is almost subliminal. Throughout the work there is a running attack on warfare as unfitting to the Christian, echoing the vibrant propaganda against war of Erasmus of Rotterdam. In print and in picture, the pope is continually associated with war or warlike things. War is thus the instrument of the Antichrist, and it is shameful for Christians to resort to its use.

The final theme is the identification of the Antichrist. This is achieved in two ways. The reader is presented with cumulative evidence of how the life

127   Illustration in H. Schedel, *Buch der Chroniken*
(A. Koberger, Nuremberg, 1493), BL IC 7458, fol. cclix v

of the pope is contrary to that of Christ. This essentially visual contrast is then driven home by the commentary which shows how such behaviour is antichristian. The last pair of illustrations provide the conclusive proof, showing the pope visually as the Antichrist. All these themes, existing side by side in the work, making their point simultaneously at different levels, explain why it was such an effective piece of propaganda. It advances separate but interlinked criticisms of the papacy, introduces them through strong and simple contrasts, and does not attempt to raise any complex issues of theology. The pope is identified as Antichrist largely by the antithesis of his life to that of Christ. A more simple form of communication could scarcely be imagined within the scope of twenty-six woodcuts with a minimum of text.

The impact of the work can be seen in the large number of editions it quickly ran through, no less than one Latin and ten German editions within a few years. However, it can be seen more remarkably in the extensive influence it was to have on later works of visual propaganda. It established, with the visual contrast between Christ and the pope, an iconographical tradition which extended into the seventeenth century.[20] This formed the basis of numerous works of visual propaganda examined throughout this book (see ills. 33, 35, 38, 44, 72, 73 and 88). One of the most interesting in its adaptation of Cranach's basic antithesis is the depiction of Christ on the ass facing the pope on horseback (ill. 128). We have already seen an early version in the titlepage of a 1522 pamphlet showing Christ jousting with the pope (see ill. 44). However, the version here takes up the motif more or less as Cranach presented it in the *Passional*. Christ, clad in a simple garment, rides barefoot on an ass which is followed by its foal. The pope is clad in a splendid cloak and mounted on an elaborately decorated steed. The triple tiara is matched by Christ's crown of thorns and halo. Christ is barefoot, the pope wears slippers.

The depiction also draws on other signs from popular culture and popular belief. Each figure is given his coat of arms in the top corners of the woodcut. The pope has the crossed keys and tiara with the Medici roundels. Christ has the instruments of the Passion, the *arma Christi*. In the shield, which has the shape of a heart and perhaps recalls devotion to the Sacred Heart, are the cross and the scourges. The shield is surmounted by the crown of thorns, another reminder of the devotion to the Sacred Heart, which was often depicted crowned with thorns.[21] The counterpart to the crossed keys of the papal arms is provided by the spear and sponge. The written text summarises these contrasts as the comparison of lord and servant. It also recalls other contrasts from the *Passional*: the kissing of the pope's foot and the washing of the disciples' feet, the scorn heaped on Christ and the honour demanded by the pope, the poverty of Christ and the wealth and power of the pope and, finally, a doctrinal contrast, the freely given grace of Christ with the indulgences which must be purchased from the pope. This very effective depiction was copied for a broadsheet of the first half of the seventeenth century.[22]

Another depiction of the Antichrist which had its origin in the *Passional* is the figure of the warrior-pope. It is suggested in the 1522 image of the jousting pope, if not by the pope's dress, at least by the demon with a pike who attends him (see ill. 44). Portrayal of the pope clad in armour was doubtless suggested by Julius II, whose warlike reign provoked Erasmus to bitter comment about the incongruity of a warrior-pope. Not surprisingly, the figure was revived during the reign of Julius III (1550–5), at a time when German Protestantism faced military challenges from Catholicism. A broadsheet from this period portraying Julius II as a warrior links him both to the Devil and to the Antichrist (ill. 129).[23] Diabolical overtones are supplied by demonic faces on the breastplate, elbow- and knee-guards. Connections with the Antichrist are supplied by the written text. This informs the reader that the illustration was occasioned by Julius issuing a silver coin with his likeness and with the inscription 'The nation and kingdom that will not serve me shall perish' (Isaiah 60.12). One must fear that he will fall upon Germany with legions of Turks, and destroy it with fire and sword. The commentary thus echoes Cranach's view of the warlike nature of the papacy, that it will turn to

128   *Christ on an Ass Confronts Pope on Mule*, Dahlem

war to uphold its claims to power. There is an implicit reference to the Christ—Antichrist antithesis in the closing comment that it is better to die a thousand times than to turn from Christ to the Antichrist, for God alone is king of kings and lord of lords.

Another broadsheet from this period is more clearly influenced by the *Passional*, with a comparison between Christ and Belial (ill. 130).[24] On the left we see the warrior-pope trampling underfoot the crucified Christ, the papal sword raised aloft as in the previous example, about to deliver a mortal blow. The scenes behind the pope show how the image is to be interpreted: evangelical believers are martyred for their faith, one at the stake, another by beheading, a third by being scourged. Separating the left- and right-hand sections of the antithesis is the Trinity, God the Father through the Holy Spirit blessing Christ, who is baptised by John the Baptist. This is the promise of Christ's victory, which is fulfilled on the right-hand side, where Christ has risen in triumph. He stands above the tomb, under which is a skull and a serpent, representing death and the Devil. In the foreground, then, it is the risen Christ who has overcome the pope, who now lies trampled underfoot. He has been overcome by the cross of Christ's suffering, which the Saviour

129 *Julius III as Demonic Warrior*, Berlin

holds in his left hand, and by the Word, signified by the book held aloft in his right. Moreover, the pope has been exposed as the Devil, for in his fall his tiara has been lost, revealing the horns underneath. As in illustration 129, the elbow- and knee-guards have traces of diabolical visages which indicate these links. The visual structure adds emphasis to this, for just as the foreground and background scenes are linked on the left-hand side, so they are linked on the right. The pope represents death and the Devil, conquered by the risen Christ. To this skilful visual message, little is added by the printed text.

Although both warrior-pope broadsheets were suggested by the reign of Julius III, the notion of the warrior-pope was not linked just to that name.

130   *Comparison of Christ and Belial*, Berlin

The figure also turns up in a woodcut by Matthias Gerung from the mid-1540s, where the pope, clad as a *Landsknecht*, pursues the poor, and it was used in the titlepage of a 1546 pamphlet (ill. 131).[25] This places the warrior-pope in the context of the Apocalypse, astride the seven-headed beast, accompanied by the whore of Babylon. The scene is more appropriate to a depiction of the whore, which is thus equated with the papacy. Both are here adored by secular rulers and by a monk and nun representing the clergy. However, the scene is reminiscent of the nationalist themes of Cranach's *Passional*, for the pope carries the imperial symbols, the orb and the sword of secular power.

The influence of the *Passional* can be seen less directly in a woodcut from around 1525 by Hans Sebald Behem, *The Fall of the Papacy* (ill. 132).[26] On the right, the pope is toppled from his throne by arrows coming from the top left-hand corner, from the mouth of Christ. Each of these arrows, bearing a biblical text, represents the Word. Surrounding the pope is a crumbling building, which presumably signifies the papal Church collapsing under the attack of the Word, for some of the arrows strike the building itself. Behind the pope stand four cardinals, dismayed by his collapse; to the left, a large group of kneeling clergy attempt to hold up the papal throne by means of a long rope. They are aided by three standing figures, clearly princes who support the pope, for the two figures nearest the pope have some resemblance to Charles V and his brother Ferdinand. In the left background, a crowd of evangelical believers observe this scene, led by Luther in his doctor's cap and bearing a cross. Four of these figures hold open books, perhaps signifying the Bible, and one gestures towards the scene in the church. This may indicate that it is the preaching of the Word by Reformation preachers that has caused the collapse of the papacy.

131   Illustration in *Des Bapsts und der Pfaffen Badstub*
(J. Cammerlander, Strassburg, 1546)

132   Hans Sebald Behem, *The Fall of the Papacy*

The printed text clearly identifies the papacy with the Antichrist. Most of the thirteen arrows carry biblical quotations which describe the Antichrist: 'Many will come and say, I am the Christ' (Matthew 24.5); 'He sits in the temple and is adored' (2 Thess. 2.4); 'He proclaims himself to be God' (2 Thess. 2.4), and others. The blocks of written text correspond to the various figures: Christ, Christendom or the evangelical believers, the cardinals, the pope and the clergy. The princes are given no text, however, for they are silent, although both the pope and the clergy call upon them for support. The other texts make plain that the pope is the Antichrist: the cardinals call him an earthly god, while Christ and Christendom condemn him as an abomination. Links with Cranach's work appear in three features. An antithesis between Christ and the Antichrist is established by a diagonal line which connects them, along which flow the arrows and the rays emanating from the mouth of Christ. There is an implicit contrast between Christ's completed ascension into heaven, from where he speaks, and the fall of the Antichrist. Thirdly, there is the contrast between Christ and his followers, simple folk relying on the Word, and grouped behind the cross borne by Luther, and the pope, enthroned and surrounded by kneeling admirers clad in their rich robes of office. One feature does not appear to have come from the *Passional*, but to have been suggested by another of Behem's works, that in which Luther confronts the ungodly (see ill. 22). As in that case, this is a divine judgment against the papacy, so supplying the eschatological overtones found in the Antichrist legend.

Cranach's influence on the iconography of the pope—Antichrist was thus extensive and subtle, and can be traced in several other depictions which do not at first sight seem to resemble the *Passional* (see ills. 72, 73). This 'Wittenberg tradition', developed from Luther's writings, stressed the spiritual nature of the Antichrist, whose opposition to Christ was moral, spiritual and ultimately theological. Yet it was not the only means used by evangelical propaganda to discern the Antichrist. There were several other features of the legend which could be translated into visual signs and applied to the papacy. Some of these have been seen already in the discussion of popular culture. For example, the Antichrist was born of the Devil, or through the Devil's power. This suggested the depiction of the pope and his cardinals being born of a grinning she-devil (see ill. 64), or the pope being created by the Devil through black magic, in imitation of the divine creation of Adam (see ill. 65).[27] Another visual type presented the pope as the Devil himself, seen at its most lurid in the depiction of the pope as Wild Man (see ill. 104). An unusual version of this type was found cast on a great cannon captured from Protestant troops by imperial armies in the Schmalkaldic War (ill. 133), perhaps as a parody of the saints' images customarily cast on cannon in Catholic armies.[28]

Closely associated with the idea of the Antichrist was the notion of the world turned upside-down, for the Antichrist was the inversion of all that was Christian and godly. The world turned upside-down was a near universal theme in late-medieval culture, manifest in a variety of forms, if not always as a top-to-bottom inversion.[29] The German term *verkehrte Welt* captures more effectively the sense of a world topsy-turvy, inside out, inverted or reversed in which it occurs. Such 'symbolic inversion' did not necessarily have any eschatological or apocalyptic overtones, as with the Antichrist. It could simply refer to an inversion of a normal state of affairs, as in the case of play, where the seriousness of the mundane world is changed into frivolity.[30] In carnival we find an institutionalised form of such inversion, where the dignified is mocked, the elevated demeaned and order reduced to chaos. Carnival inverts social norms, social hierarchy and social order, so that it is completely a world turned upside-down.[31]

The theme of inversion is also an intrinsic part of Christianity. It is found throughout the Gospels in ideas such as the last shall be first and the first last, or he who humbles himself shall be exalted and he who exalts himself shall be humbled. Underlying such notions is a religious principle of inversion: the mundane, material world is an inversion of true reality, which is spiritual and eternal, opposed to the ephemeral and the material things to which men give their attention. The parable of Lazarus and Dives also exemplifies this prin-

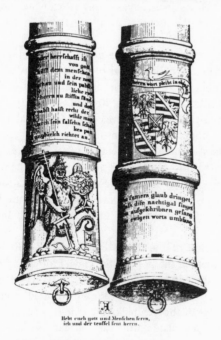

133   Illustration in F. Schweyger, *Chronik der Stadt Hall 1303–1572* (Schönherr 1867: 115)

ciple, interestingly enough one of the most popular New Testament parables of the later middle ages.[32] Here inversion could be used in a moralistic sense, as a form of compensatory justice. If moral relations were *verkehrt* in this life, in the next many would receive both their just rewards and fitting punishments. Associated with this sense of the *verkehrt* is the notion that the times are out of joint, and the moral order has been upturned. This was the link between monsters and portents and the disruption of the moral order that they signified. The monster and the portent were inversions of nature, signs of a disordered nature, indicating disorder in the moral world.[33]

A further variant of the theme can be found in the wheel of fortune and associated cyclical theories of history. The wheel of fortune involved a gradual turning of the wheel and the gradual completion of a cycle, but it also focussed on the inversion of diametrically opposed extremes. Thus it embodies an inversion of good and evil, of the noble and ignoble, and an upturning of the given order of rank, power and status. The stages of the turning wheel are only steps towards this total inversion of human affairs. Such symbolic inversion is also intrinsic to the notions of irony, parody and paradox, so that the use of the theme for propaganda was an obvious application of a cultural constant. A form such as the *Schandbild* relied on the notion of inversion for its effect, the person being attacked hanging upside down in some of them, or with an inverted coat of arms. This signified the inversion of his honour and the upturning of respect to contempt. This form of inversion is continually used, as we have seen, to attack the papacy. Awe is inverted to crude familiarity, dignity to indignity, religious respect to blasphemous contempt.[34]

We have seen this technique used in the woodcuts in which the *Landsknecht* defecates into the papal tiara (see ill. 59) or farts at the pope (see ill. 61). It was frequently used in pictures or medals which showed a cardinal–fool or a pope–fool (ill. 134). It forms the basis of the abuse directed at John Eck in the *verkehrt* version of his coat of arms, or of those of the pope. Again, the depiction of the clergy as excrement is an implicit inversion of the high to the base.[35] Like the light in the candleholder, they are not the light of the world, but its polluters. The scene in which women hunt monks and the clergy is another satiric reversal attacking clerical dignity.

Other propaganda works carried the principle beyond a reversal of respect and dignity to demonstrate a spiritual or mystical inversion or reversal. The depiction of the *Old and New Belief* was a brilliantly inventive use of the principle to show the papacy as the reverse of true belief. It also skilfully inverted the accusation that the evangelical movement represented innovation and unorthodoxy. The application of the Antichrist theme to the papacy was no less skilful, for it also showed the papacy as a world turned upside-down, an inversion of Christian belief. Cranach's *Passional* captured the notion of inversion, most notably in the last pair of woodcuts, by showing Christ ascending while the pope plummets to hell. The confrontation of Christ and

Belial (see ill. 130) also made use of the inversion technique, with the upend-
ing of the pope by a triumphant Christ.

Use of the world turned upside-down was, however, no mere technique. It
was also a firm conviction of the age that the world was *verkehrt*, that the
world was perverted or reversed, the times radically out of joint. This belief is
central to Sebastian Brant's perception that folly was the dominant characteristic of his time. Folly is a brutish inversion of man's spiritual nature, expressed
in the wheel of fortune depiction in *The Ship of Fools* (see ill. 90). Folly is
thus linked to theriomorphism as a form of world upside-down. Because men
have perverted their natures, they are changed into beasts. Thus a moral
inversion is perceived in an inversion of form.[36] The same kind of moral
inversion is found in a broadsheet from the early years of the Reformation,
which adapts a stock depiction of the inverted world to the purposes of evangelical propaganda. This often showed hares pursuing, capturing and roasting
human hunters and their dogs, a double inversion of hunter and hunted and
of meekness and aggression.

In our evangelical version (ill. 135) we see a stock depiction of a hunting
scene, but the roles of hunter and hunted are reversed; here the sheep are
hunting wolves. The wolves wear a papal tiara, a cardinal's hat and a bishop's
mitre, identifying them as the papal hierarchy. Two other wolves are depicted
as priests by stoles around their necks. They are herded towards a net where
they are captured or slain by the sheep. Leading the hunt are figures representing the Old and New Testaments, Moses, the symbolic figures of the four
Evangelists, Peter and Paul. Behind the net is the figure of Isaiah, whose
prophecy is wholly concerned with the turning upside-down of the world.
This 'godly hunt' is further identified by the figure emblazoned on the banner

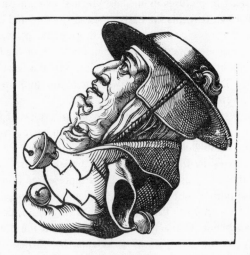

134   *Two-headed Cardinal—fool*, Munich Alte Pinakothek

Das yetz vil unkradts ist im land / das thuond die wölff in grawes gwand

Vnd ouch verwildet sind die schaaff / darum so volge die göttlich straff.

Des schöpffers aller creatur
habend acht by diser figur
Die nit erst nüwlich ist gedicht
doch was sy bdüt ietz beschicht
Als es got angesehen hat
das man sych uff die wölff verstat
Die inder gstalt in schäflis kleyd
zů verderbung der gantzen weyd
Darum so zeygt diß figur die
uff alle schäfly gottes die
Bißhär hie hand m...

sin wort / wie vor den wolffen gstaut
Uff das der hirt gewarnet werd
der die schäfly gottes uff erd
Solchs leeren die rechten warh:it
als sy vns Christus hat gesent
Daß sy aber nicht handglere
so harr es got also verkert
Das die schäfly ietz wüssen B...
was die heilig gschr...
M...

Wie sophistischer meisterschafft
logica mags ouch nit / das schafft
Aristoteles kan nüt meer
wider die Euangelisch leer
D3 geistlich (gnůt) recht ouch abgat
damit man vor gefochten hatt
So die waffen nit mögend ßhan
...ran

vnd niemant nüt vnd das sin grb
Tribt also sin gespey mit got
machet sinen namen zů spot
Das yetz leyder soul beschicht
Vil fuchsen legend schaffs kleyd an
wellend ouch christen namen han
Zeyg.d die gschrift mit hůbsch schin
...te Christus so bert
bar gewert
Finis

carried by one of the sheep-hunters, the risen Christ. In the clouds above, God the Father indicates this sign of the godly hunt.

The printed text provides a multiple layering of the reversal theme. First, although they appear in sheep's clothes, the clergy are really wolves. Second, they have not only devastated the flock, but they have also rendered them wild. The faithful have thus had their natures reversed. For this, the wolves have drawn upon themselves divine punishment, and are fittingly attacked by the very sheep they have turned to savagery. This seems to be an oblique reference to the fears of a war against the priests which were openly expressed during the early 1520s, and which was advocated by figures such as Ulrich von Hutten.[37] The same anticlerical feeling is expressed in the woodcuts depicting the hunting of the clergy, and it turns up in a *verkehrte Welt* depiction in which a monk and a priest are among those hunted and captured by the hares-turned-hunters.[38] Our example goes beyond anticlericalism, however, for it stresses that the world is disordered and morally *verkehrt* and so has called down divine judgment. This is executed by the faithful under the leadership of the Word, a clear reference to the evangelical movement, both as the result of the *verkehrte Welt* and as its corrective.

If the hunting scenes placed their main emphasis on moral inversion, other examples of *verkehrte Welt* stressed social inversion. The most striking depiction of the period is found in an illustration to a prognostic published in 1508 which predicted an upturning of the social order. The first chapter of this work speaks of an imminent great change in all estates of Christendom, encapsulated in a visual inversion of the most basic of Christian social relations of the middle ages, that between cleric and layman (ill. 136).[39] This shows a peasant celebrating mass at the altar, while a priest and a monk plough the fields outside. This was a radical inversion of the role of the priest who offered his prayers for the layman and mediated between God and man, and the peasant who supported the priest by the product of his labour. The drastic nature of the inversion is shown by a literal inversion of the church building in which the peasants say mass. This kind of social inversion is found running throughout evangelical propaganda, where the common man, the evangelical peasant or the poor stand for the supporters of Christ and the Gospel, while the clergy stand for its opponents (see ills. 22, 30, 33, 34, 76, 92). This forms the basis of much of the social critical content of evangelical propaganda.

However pervasive the notion of inversion or reversal throughout Reformation visual propaganda, the stock motifs of the world turned upside-down, as they appeared in the genre depictions with that name, found little direct use.[40] These joking improbabilities must have seemed slight and pallid in the face of the more serious inversions which evangelical propaganda produced. That God's representative on earth could be revealed as the Devil, as the inversion of the divine, was a reversal so radical that such stock motifs could scarcely do it justice. Indeed, the notion was so shocking that it could probably only be conceived in terms of a total and ultimate inversion of the world, the last days, the Antichrist and the dawn of the millennium. The full weight of the world turned upside-down in evangelical propaganda is, therefore, carried by apocalyptic motifs. These gave the identification of the pope as Antichrist an urgency and compulsion it would otherwise have lacked. The theme was most powerfully expressed in the vivid images of the Book of the Apocalypse, particularly in the apocalyptic beast.[41]

We have already seen some examples of the propagandist use of the apocalyptic beast in the satirical woodcut *The Seven-headed Papal Beast* (see ill. 75) and in the depiction of the pope as Wild Man (see ill. 104), which combined the beast with a figure from popular culture. However, the motif found its more appropriate use in illustrations to the Book of the Apocalypse. Here Cranach appears, once again, to have established an iconographical tradition, for the polemical use of the theme is first found in Cranach's woodcuts for Luther's translation of the New Testament, published in Wittenberg in September 1522.[42] The illustration for Apocalypse 11.1−8 shows the measuring of the temple and the two witnesses sent as prophets by God, who are devoured by the beast from the bottomless pit (ill. 137). The beast is crowned with a triple tiara to signify the papacy. The artist did not intend, however,

Das erſte Capitel von der vereede
rung aller ſtende der Chriſtenheyt/die mag bewert
werden auß den ſichtbarn zeychen des himels.

¶ Nach dem die menſchlich ſchwachheyt mag von der dick
en wolcken wegen der fleyſchlichen begirligkeyten/vnnd des
tieffen werfels der laſter/die verborgen maieſtet gottes nit er
kennen / noch die heymlichen/vnd von der ſundligkeyt abge
ſcheyden/ werck der natur begriffen / dem nach will ich den

136   Illustration in J. Grünpeck, *Spiegel der naturlichen himlischen und prophetischen sehungen* (W. Stöckel, Leipzig, 1522), BL 845.i.29, fol. A4 r

to identify the papacy by this one sign alone. The apocalyptic characterisation of the papacy is developed by various allusions in other illustrations. In the depictions of the two apocalyptic beasts, the seven-headed and the two-horned beasts, in chapter 13 the associations are less direct (ill. 138). Here, only the two-horned beast is linked to the papacy by giving it a monk's cowl. This beast, which 'makes the earth and its inhabitants worship the first (seven-headed) beast', thus equates the papacy with the seven-headed monster only obliquely. The motif of the papal tiara returns, however, in the depiction for chapter 16, showing the emptying of the bowls of wrath, one of which is emptied over the dragon seated on its throne. The dragon, similar to that depicted in illustration 137, wears the same papal tiara.[43]

Another apocalyptic association added to the papacy in the September New Testament was its equation with the whore of Babylon of Apocalypse 17, clad in purple and scarlet and holding a cup of abominations, who rides astride the seven-headed beast. Cranach also crowns this figure with a papal tiara (ill. 139), and the association is rounded off by depicting the destruction of Babylon in chapter 18 through a city which can be plainly recognised as Rome (ill. 140). Two well-known Roman landmarks, the Castel Santangelo and the Capitol, are shown among the collapsing buildings, and those who

137   Illustration to Apocalypse 11.1–8, in *Das Newe Testament Deutzsch*, trans. M. Luther (M. Lotter, Wittenberg, Sept. 1522), BL
138   Illustration to Apocalypse 13, in *Das Newe Testament Deutzsch* (Sept. 1522)

lament the fall of Babylon are depicted as 'Roman courtesans' – canonists and benefice-holders.[44]

The equation of the papacy with the whore of Babylon may have been suggested by the legend of Pope Joan, which enjoyed some popularity at the end of the middle ages. This told the story of how a woman became pope during the ninth century. Ghiberta, daughter of a citizen of Mainz, had a student as a lover. She learned Latin from him, and went with him to England in male disguise, where they both studied and took doctorates. The lover died and Ghiberta, now called Johannes, travelled to Rome, where she became a famous scholar and eventually a cardinal. On the death of Leo IV she was elected pope, and reigned for just over two years. In that time she took another lover and became pregnant, although she was able to disguise her condition underneath voluminous papal vestments. However, she unexpectedly gave birth near St John Lateran in the middle of a procession. Thereafter, no pope would pass in procession near this spot, and a special chair was created for papal elections, in which the new pope had to display his male genitalia in order to prevent a woman ever again being elected.[45]

This legend was mentioned frequently in the fifteenth and early sixteenth centuries: in Boccaccio's *On Famous Women*, which was published in a

139   Illustration to Apocalypse 17, in *Das Newe Testament Deutzsch* (Sept. 1522)
140   Illustration to Apocalypse 18, in *Das Newe Testament Deutzsch* (Sept. 1522)

popular translation in Germany in 1473; as the subject of a play written around 1480, where she is called Frau Jutta; and in two works by Thomas Murner, published in 1514 and 1517. Hans Sachs handled the theme in a song from 1532, and in a broadsheet, possibly the text of an original carnival play.[46] There were at least three woodcut broadsheets produced on the subject in the 1540s, showing the pope giving birth in the middle of a procession.[47] The appeal of the legend for Protestant propaganda was that it provided grounds to refute the papacy's claim to infallibility and to an unbroken succession. Since the legend was accepted as historically authentic, it was a piece of proof which Catholic authorities could not deny. The associations of sexual immorality also made it a splendid piece of anticlerical propaganda, and perhaps made the equation of the papacy with the whore of Babylon inevitable. There is no evidence of a link between the two in the September New Testament. The identification was most explicitly made in a picture book based on the Apocalypse by Martin Schrott, *On the Terrible Destruction and Fall of the Papacy*, published in the 1540s. The first illustration of this work shows the Babylonian whore seated on the seven-headed beast, giving the cup of abominations to the emperor and princes (ill. 141).

141   Illustration in M. Schrott, *Von der Erschrocklichen Zurstorung des Bapstums* (1550?), GNM 4° R1 1875b, fol. A5 v

She is clad in ceremonial papal vestments and papal tiara, while an inscription above her head reads 'Agnes, a woman from England, called John VII in the year 851' (Ghiberta was known as Agnes in certain versions of the legend).[48]

If Cranach's depiction of the Babylonian whore was not inspired by the Pope Joan legend, it may have suggested the connection to others. In any case, the visual attack on the papacy in the September New Testament is rather low key. Only six of the twenty-one illustrations single out the papacy. When it is used, the papal tiara is small and almost unobtrusive, and other papal references are not highlighted as sharply as some of the other examples of anti-papal visual polemic discussed above. The publishers were perhaps wary of arousing too much disapproval from authorities such as the emperor, for the fortunes of the infant Lutheran movement depended on the non-enforcement of the Edict of Worms. Indeed, in the next Wittenberg edition of Luther's New Testament, in December 1522, the triple tiara was cut away, leaving only a simple crown (see ill. 142). The other references to the papacy were possibly too indirect to be seen as offensive, and they remained.[49]

Other artists and publishers did not suffer from the same inhibitions, and Cranach's illustrations were quickly copied. The 1523 edition of Luther's New Testament, published by Thomas Wolff in Basel, with illustrations by Hans Holbein the Younger, used all the papal motifs from the September

142   Illustration to Apocalypse 17, in *Das Newe Testament Deutzsch*, trans. M. Luther (M. Lotter, Wittenberg, December 1522), BL

1522 edition.[50] The dragon threatening the witnesses and later seated on the throne has a papal tiara, as does the whore of Babylon, while the two Roman landmarks are included in the destruction of Babylon. The papal tiara is also a larger and more obtrusive item, and could scarcely be overlooked. By the time Luther issued his first complete translation of the Bible from Wittenberg in 1534, any reservations there about such visual labelling of the papacy had been set aside. The whore and the beast are now given very prominent tiaras (ills. 143–4). This greater licence in Wittenberg was influenced by the different position of the evangelical movement in 1534. By then, hopes of reconciling the emperor to the movement and of reversing Luther's condemnation at Worms were decidedly past. The newly formed Protestant movement had also developed a strong sense of persecution and a fear of physical attack by Catholic powers. This awareness of being a Church under attack is expressed at several points in the depictions of 1534, but most noticeably in that of the two witnesses attacked by the beast (see ill. 144). The two prophets are clad as evangelical preachers, and from their mouths issue tongues of flame, signifying that they speak with the inspiration of the Holy Spirit. The temple which forms the backdrop to the scene is the Castle Church of Wittenberg, so that the message was plain.[51]

The illustrations to the Apocalypse thus suggested several ways in which

143   Illustration to Apocalypse 17, in *Biblia*, trans.
M. Luther (H. Lufft, Wittenberg, 1534), BL

the papacy could be identified as the Antichrist. Perhaps the most popular of all, however, was the image of the beast, which appears in several forms in the Apocalypse. There is the dragon, the beast with two horns and the seven-headed beast, all of which were on occasion equated with the papacy. One of the more curious versions of this beast to be found in Reformation propaganda, however, was that of the three-headed beast, used frequently during the 1540s. One example resembles the woodcut in which Christ overcomes the warrior-pope. This shows the risen Christ trampling underfoot the apocalyptic beast, now with only three heads (ill. 145). In the right-hand background are the familiar themes of the crucifixion and the tomb guarded by three monks. The crucifix, however, is without the body of Christ and by implication the tomb is also empty, for the central figure is Christ risen in glory. The three heads of the beast characterise it in a more intricate fashion than in earlier iconography. One is the head of the pope, spewing out foul spirits, shown by their tonsures as monks, the 'demonic spirits performing signs' of Apocalypse 16.12. The second is the head of the Turk, recalling a common view of the time, which saw the Turk both as a sign of the last days and as identical with Gog and Magog, the hosts of Satan mentioned in Apocalypse 20.7.[52]

The third head, an angel with wings and a fair countenance, adds a new feature to Protestant polemical iconography. This refers to the Devil deceiving

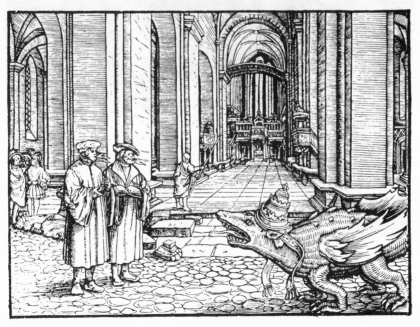

144   Illustration of Apocalypse 11.2–8, in *Biblia* (1534)

145   *Christ Defeats the Pope as Three-headed Beast*, Berlin

the unwary believer by appearing in the form of an angel. It was also a characteristic of the Antichrist that his fair appearance disguised his diabolical
origins.[53] Here the printed text relates it to the Interim, the religious settlement imposed on Protestant states after the emperor's victory in the first
Schmalkaldic War. This made some concessions to evangelical belief, but
imposed an essentially Catholic settlement. The Interim split the Protestant
movement badly, the strongest points of disagreement arising over the so-
called *adiaphora*, 'matters of indifference', which were not essential for
salvation and over which some concessions to Catholicism might be made.
The situation was further complicated by the appearance of a second 'Interim'.
The Albertine Elector of Saxony, granted the title for supporting the imperial
side in the Schmalkaldic War, had no wish to offend the emperor, nor to
alienate substantial numbers of Lutheran subjects. He produced for his lands
another settlement, labelled by its opponents the Leipzig Interim, which
made many concessions to the externals of Catholic practice, while attempting to preserve the core of evangelical doctrine. Much of the Roman rite of
the mass was restored, along with vestments, bells and traditional church
vessels.[54]

Such *adiaphora* were attacked by hard-line Protestants as matters which
merely concealed the Devil. The whole Interim was condemned as the work
of the Antichrist, and a concerted campaign was launched to show that the
Interim was but another aspect of the antichristian papacy.[55] This is the
origin of the third head in our illustration. The broadsheet is an attack on the
Interim, and seeks by this means to equate it with the pope, the Turk and the
Antichrist, of which all three are manifestations. The motif of the three-
headed beast was used in another attack on the Interim which combined
visual and oral propaganda (ill. 146). This shows a choir of monks and canons
singing a hymn of praise to the Interim. Perched on a column in the centre of
this illustration is the three-headed dragon, beside it stands a fool with cap
and bells, a sign that the Interim is fool's work. The printed text reminds the
reader of the long history of monastic abuse, with foolish singing, drinking
and gaming, all alluded to visually by the singing clergy. One drinks from a
giant beer mug, another holds a gaming-board. The label 'Interim' on the
frock of the canon to the left of the central music text recalls the stipulation
about the wearing of vestments, the same inscription on the beer mug, perhaps that it is fit only for drunkards. The music text is a parody set to the
tune of the hymn *Beatus vir*, with words given both in Latin and in German.
The German text stresses 'Happy is the man who trusts in God and does not
approve of the Interim, for it has the devil behind it.' The second part of this
strophe 'denn es hat den schalk hinter im' is a word-play on Interim, which
thus served as an oral reminder of the Protestant interpretation of the
settlement. The word *schalk* also has a double meaning, either 'fool' or
a synonym for the Devil.[56] Hence the fool in the depiction behind the

Interim, a figure which also made use of the association of folly with the diabolical.

Other broadsheets attacking the use of the alb, the mass-vestment required by the Interim, stressed the idea of the Devil behind it. One showed the Devil holding up the alb, another used the technique of the lift-up flap, similar to that used to reveal Alexander VI as Satan, which was lifted to show the Devil hidden behind the alb.[57] The use of the papal beast to attack the Interim is found in another parody hymn sheet (ill. 147).[58] This also uses the hymn *Beatus vir*, this time with parts for four singers laid out so that it could be placed on a table between them. In the centre is the figure of the pope—dragon,

146   Master BP, *Satire on the Interim*

holding a sword recalling the warrior-pope. This beast wears a cope bearing a demon's face, another attack on the Interim's stipulations about vestments. The vices of the clergy are alluded to by the dice which make up the cross on the papal tiara, and in the monk and nun who dance together between the texts labelled B and C. The counterpart to this pair are a monk and demon dancing together, the demon's serpent tail extending between his legs to suggest a penis. This demon is also a monk, for he carries a breviary in a pouch tied to his waist. The monk holds aloft a goblet in which is a small monk-puppet, probably an allusion to a fool-puppet, and so to the folly of monasticism and of the Interim. Each of the four musical parts has a figure representing a member of the Catholic clergy: a hermit, a canon, a cardinal and a monk. The hermit is attended by a demonic bird-dragon; the monk emits a stream of foul spirits, a sign of the apocalyptic beast; the cardinal has a raven clutching a flute; and the canon has been given a demon playing a portable organ while it strokes his cheek with a fox-brush. This unlikely quartet is conducted by the pope–dragon, thus revealing the kind of tune called by the Interim: it is the hymn of the Antichrist.

A more elaborate interpretation of the three-headed 'worm Interim' is found in a 1552 pamphlet, *The Holy Woman Saint Interim*. The titlepage (ill. 148) shows the three-headed dragon, with a demon's mouth on its stomach, spewing out brimstone. Its long serpent-like tail ends in a scorpion's sting. Its body is covered with scales, and it has one eagle's claw and one toad's foot.

147   *Hymn-sheet Parody on the Interim*

These features recall the Papal Ass, and the pamphlet interprets them in much the same fashion as Melanchthon had explained the bizarre characteristics of that beast. The intertwined necks of the three heads signify that the ungodly support one another in their diabolical work. The scorpion tail poisons Christians, who are signified by the clear stars around it. The eagle's claw is the power of the emperor, which supports the Interim, the toad's foot the godless form on which the papacy stands and goes forth. The written text also points out the resemblance to Cerberus, the three-headed guardian of hell, but the reader is left in no doubt about the apocalyptic nature of the beast. Its mother is the whore of Babylon, and for this reason one of its heads bears the whore's crown, the triple tiara. By this means it is identified as the Antichrist, and in the same way as the Antichrist, it was conceived through the agency of Satan. Its three heads also show it as the offspring of promiscuity, for they reveal that it had three fathers, which the pamphlet names as three authors of the Interim.[59]

By the middle of the sixteenth century, both the dragon—pope and the three-headed pope had become part of the visual vernacular of German Protestantism. Melchior Lorch used the latter in a work from 1555, showing the three-headed pope paying a *Landsknecht*.[60] In 1552 Peter Gottland used it in an engraving on the triumph of the New Faith over the Old. This adapts

148   Titlepage to *Die heilig frauw Sant Interim*
(M. Apiarius, Bern, 1552), BL

the iconography of St George and the dragon (ill. 149). It shows the infant Jesus in the role of St George, with triumphal banner, on horseback, defeating a three-headed dragon. The dragon's lair, identified as the papal Church, collapses, while a princess kneeling in the middle ground, a constituent element of St George iconography, is identified as the evangelical Church.[61]

The association of the pope with the Turk requires further comment, for this also linked the papacy to the Antichrist legend. In late-medieval tradition the mystical Antichrist could be discerned in heretics, bad Christians and un-believers. It was natural enough for an age plagued by incursions from the Turk to link him to the diabolical, most commonly with Gog and Magog, the hordes of Satan. The question of whether the Turk was the Antichrist or merely his servant was a pertinent question. Luther thought seriously about the problem, and evangelical theologians debated it.[62] If the theological answer was that the pope was the sole Antichrist, the triple-headed dragon seemed to settle the question the other way for visual polemic. The strongest conviction of the equation of the two can be seen in the woodcuts of Mathias Gerung, dating from the 1540s.[63] In one of these, Gerung depicts the pope and the Turk as demons seated in hell (ill. 150). On the right sits a devil above whom two small demons hold a papal tiara. He holds a papal key in one hand, in the other a royal crown, a bishop's mitre and a cardinal's hat. Attending

149   P. Gottland, *St George and the Dragon – Allegory of the Triumph of the New Faith over the Old* (1552), Dahlem

him are the three figures belonging to this headwear, perhaps receiving their positions from the demonic pope. On the left, the other devil is crowned by a turban held by two demons. The Turk—devil holds a crown and wields a sabre, and is attended by a Turk. The link between the two devils is shown by intertwining their tails.

Gerung returned to this theme in a woodcut in which Christ, above whom hover the Holy Spirit and God the Father, preaches to the faithful, while angels thrust the damned into hell. Here the pope and the Turk, both represented as apocalyptic beasts crowned respectively with the triple tiara and the turban, drag bands of their followers into hell (ill. 151). Behind these chained groups of the damned, left the Turks and right the Catholic clergy, two demonic musicians provide music for the scene.

Elsewhere, Gerung represented the pope as a lion and the Turk as a bear, attacking poor folk with swords.[64] Another of his woodcuts depicted the confrontation between the hordes of the pope and those of the Turk, while in the background the Christian faithful are gathered into the safety of the church. Here they are preached to by Christ, while Peter, Paul, Moses and St John stand guard outside.[65] However, Gerung came close to the iconography of the three-headed dragon in another work emphasising the similarity of the

150   M. Gerung, *The Pope and Turk as Demons Enthroned in Hell*, BM
151   M. Gerung, *The Pope and Turk as Demons Drag their Followers to Hell*, BM

pope and the Turk (ill. 152). The Turk and the pope are seated in a strange chariot, which is pulled in opposite directions by two sets of beasts. Those on the Turkish side seem to be strange demonic beasts, those on the papal side beasts associated with the Devil, the bear, the lion and the goat. The Turk admonishes his followers, warlike Turks armed with swords and pikes on which are spitted human limbs and heads. The pope also encourages his followers, whose weapons of war are the signs of Catholic cult, indulgences, the monstrance and the banners of processions. The followers of the papacy are thus equated with those of the Turk, the means of Catholic belief with the barbaric weapons and practices of the infidel. This equation is made more overt, however, in the form of the pope and the Turk, for both appear as two parts of one body joined at the waist, just as the three heads of the three-headed dragon form part of one beast. The Turk and pope thus form a two-headed beast, an apocalyptic monster. This apocalyptic overtone is confirmed by the divine hand clutching the sword of divine retribution in the clouds above, signifying the last days and the Last Judgment.[66]

The theme of the Antichrist thus had many variations and associations which, taken together, formed a complex visual code. This code was one of the most effective and lasting creations of evangelical propaganda. Its success depended as much on the exploitation of popular religious emotions as it did on polemical technique; it depended, in short, on a firmly held belief in the Antichrist and his relevance to the time. This figure was most compelling and

152   M. Gerung, *The Chariot of the Pope and the Turk*, BM

evocative within an apocalyptic framework, linked to the last days and the world turned upside-down. We have seen in an earlier chapter how an apocalyptic mood was reflected in interest in signs, wonders and prophecies. The evangelical movement took up and extended this sense of living in a *verkehrte Welt*, but this was only possible because that belief was already so firmly rooted in popular mentalities.[67] We can see this in the popular prophecies which appeared at the beginning of the Reformation and which, quite independently of it, highlighted the figure of the Antichrist.

A good example is Hans Virdung's *Practica on the Antichrist*, published sometime around the end of the first decade of the sixteenth century, which drew on the Sibylline prophecies, Methodius and Joachim, as well as on Virdung's astrological knowledge.[68] The work was provoked, Virdung tells us, by the obsession of his contemporaries with the Antichrist. Everyone speaks and writes about his coming, and Virdung was continually being asked, by noble and non-noble alike, to predict the date of the last days. According to Methodius, the Antichrist was to appear sometime between 1300 and 1569. Some had claimed that he would appear in 1300, in 1484 or in 1503, although all of these had been proved wrong. Many were now saying that he would reveal himself in 1528 or 1531 and be defeated after three years. Others claimed that Gog was born in 1501 and would lie hidden for fifteen years until 1517, when he would begin his brief reign. On astrological grounds Virdung calculated that the Antichrist and the last days were due sometime during the seventeenth or eighteenth centuries, thus conveniently locating these events in the distant future.

Virdung's work sufficiently attests the eschatological preoccupations of his contemporaries, who scanned popular prophecies for historical signs to confirm or deny their misgivings. This trend is also seen in a collection of extracts from some of the most popular prophecies, from the Sibyls, Bridget, Cyril, Joachim, Methodius and Brother Reinhart, which appeared in various editions in 1518, 1520, 1521, 1527 and 1530.[69] This brief compendium highlighted the prophecy common to many of these figures, that a holy man would appear to reform the Church and inaugurate a new reign in both spiritual and secular realms. In the earlier editions, the incursions of the Turks into Germany, as deeply as Cologne and the Rhine, were to herald a new reformation of all estates. A holy man preaching in France, Spain and Italy was also mentioned, but, although the later editions were 'updated' by arguing that the prophecies had been fulfilled by recent events, Luther was not taken to be this figure.[70] This perhaps attests to the orthodoxy of the compiler; certainly it is evidence of the mood of expectation which the evangelical movement found ready-formed on its appearance.

We have seen how evangelical propaganda tried to turn popular prophecy against the papacy, but it must be emphasised that this proved effective largely because the propagandists also believed such prophecies to be true.

Osiander is a useful example, since he seemed so cautious about popular prophecy in his edition of the *Wondrous Prophecy of the Papacy*. At the same time that he published this work, he also put into print a prophecy by St Hildegard that he had discovered alongside the Joachimite prophecy. This prophecy, he claimed, 'has begun its fulfilment in our day, and shall be brought to completion'.[71] In his preface Osiander runs through the whole range of divine signs and prophecies which the papacy has not heeded: the prophets, Christ, the Apostles, voices in the temples and in the air, signs in the heavens, battles in the clouds, madmen. All the signs given to Jerusalem have also been given to the papacy. There are biblical prophecies – Daniel 7–8, Zechariah 11, the Book of the Apocalypse, Matthew 24, 2 Thessalonians 2, 1 Timothy 4 and 2 Peter – all passages which Lutherans took to describe the nature and practices of the papacy.[72] Prophecies have also been produced, Osiander went on, by the papacy's own bishops, abbots, monks and nuns, by astronomers, by common rumour expressed in proverbs, by visions and by signs in the heavens. To remove any doubts of the weight he attached to these prophetic works, Osiander concludes his preface by mentioning that he has even more prophecies about the papacy which he cannot publish because they mention Nuremberg, and to avoid trouble they must be left alone.[73]

For evangelical believers such things were, of course, secondary. They certainly provided ample confirmation of their own awareness that the world was *verkehrt*, that the Antichrist was the cause of it, and that he was revealed in the papacy. Their ultimate standard of proof, however, was the Bible. This had important consequences for the contemporary apocalyptic mood. No matter how widespread such feelings or how popular these signs and prophecies were, they lacked some kind of authoritative confirmation. It could be found in two areas. First, they could be found to be in accord with Scripture and so confirmed by the Bible. Second, they could show their fulfilment in historical or contemporary events. It was the strength of the evangelical movement that it provided both simultaneously. In biblical terms, the Antichrist was shown to have been exposed and the imminence of his defeat proclaimed, the last great battle announced. In historical terms, he was identified in the guise of men and institutions – the clergy one encountered daily in the streets, named popes whose portraits were painted as manifestations of the Antichrist.[74] Important to all this was the visual dimension – the pope could be *seen* to be the Antichrist, the clergy *seen* as his servants.

What was involved here was the acting out of a real-life eschatological and apocalyptic drama. For this reason, depictions of scenes from the Apocalypse were peopled with contemporary places and persons. We have already seen the characterisation of Babylon as Rome in the depiction of Apocalypse 18 in the September 1522 New Testament (see ill. 140). In this edition contemporary identifications are numerous. Among those adoring the seven-headed and the two-horned beasts is Maximilian I (see ill. 138); those who receive the cup of abominations from the whore seated astride the beast include Charles V, his brother Ferdinand and Duke George of Saxony (see ill. 139). The illustration of the emptying of the bowls of wrath in Apocalypse 16 again includes Archduke Ferdinand, alongside him the mercenary leader Georg von Frondsberg (ill. 153). The four lion-horsemen of Apocalypse 9.17 include as the first and second riders Duke George of Saxony and Franz von Sickingen (ill. 154). Finally, the armies of heaven which thrust the apocalyptic beast into hell in Apocalypse 19.19–20 are led by Hutten and Sickingen; aided by the angel, these put to flight the host of the kings of the earth who serve the beast (ill. 155).[75]

This edition of the New Testament was published when the evangelical movement was perhaps near the peak of its eschatological fervour, and no other edition rivalled it in its contemporary identifications of apocalyptic events. Yet similar motifs returned in the 1534 Wittenberg edition of the complete Bible. The illustration of the lament over the fall of Babylon in Apocalypse 18 replaces landmarks from Rome (see ill. 140) with those from Worms, the scene of Luther's condemnation by the empire (ill. 156). More significantly, the illustration of Apocalypse 20.9, showing the hordes of Gog and Magog besieging the beloved city, depicts the Turks storming Vienna in

153   Illustration to Apocalypse 16, in *Das Newe Testament Deutzsch* (Sept. 1522)
154   Illustration to Apocalypse 9.17 in *Das Newe Testament Deutzsch* (Sept. 1522)

1529 (ill. 157).[76] Recalling the role assigned to the Turkish invasions in the popular prophecies, this shows how sensitive to apocalyptic signs evangelical believers still were in the early 1530s. Indeed, in the 1530 edition of the New Testament by Hans Lufft of Wittenberg, which used the same woodcut, the word 'Vienna' was inscribed on the woodcut to assist the identification.[77]

It is not to be expected that the average reader would have recognised all the individuals and places as easily as the propagandists intended, but the intention is undeniable. Luther added marginalia calling attention to contemporary events as exemplifications of the apocalyptic text.[78] There is no doubt about the perspective in which evangelical believers saw the events of the early Reformation. Propaganda about the Antichrist and the world turned upside-down was so successful because it communicated the Reformers' own sense of crisis and urgency. It could be seen both as a potent response to the prevailing mood and as providing an answer to it. It has been said that Luther's identification of the papacy with the Antichrist lowered the tension and anxiety associated with this figure.[79] Our discussion here contradicts that statement. Rather than lowering the tension, evangelical propaganda heightened it, and directed it onto the clergy and the papacy. It involved the evangelical believer in a cosmic struggle against absolute evil. The sense of an imminent crisis was present before the Reformation. The evangelical move-

155   Illustration to Apocalypse 19.19–20 in *Das Newe Testament Deutzsch* (Sept. 1522)

ment drew upon popular belief to involve the believer in a struggle intimately involved with that crisis, the final confrontation with the papal Antichrist and the world turned upside-down.

156   Illustration to Apocalypse 18, in *Biblia* (1534)

157   Illustration to Apocalypse 20.9 in *Biblia* (1534)

7

TEACHING THE GOSPEL:
PROPAGANDA AS INSTRUCTION

Two kinds of process were involved in the propaganda we have examined so far. One was largely negative, to denigrate papal belief and to present evangelical belief as its antithesis. The second looked backwards, presenting the Reformation through the familiar and the traditional, using the associations of popular culture and popular belief. It was no less important to establish the Reformation in more positive terms, as a movement with a distinct theological viewpoint and definite religious characteristics of its own. We shall now analyse how it set about this task.

The persistent catch-cry of the movement was the Word of God, its major task the revival of the Word in the religious life of the time. Its primary aim was thus to lead men to use biblical criteria in judging religious matters. We have seen earlier how such criteria were used to identify the enemies of the Gospel. The next step was to enable men to discern who were its advocates. A good example of how this step was taken can be seen in a 1532 broadsheet, *God's Complaint over his Vineyard* (ill. 158), with a woodcut by Erhard Schoen and printed text from Hans Sachs.[1]

The woodcut is structured as an antithesis, the scene being divided into an evangelical theme on the left, and a Catholic theme on the right. The Catholic part of the vineyard is cultivated by the pope and several monks. It brings forth as its fruit not grapes, but the objects of Catholic cult and devotion — rosaries, reliquaries, monstrances, images, indulgences, church organs (a sign of church music), censers and incense, church bells, mass-books and vestments, the signs of fasting (fish and pretzels) and holy water, signified by the kettle and asperger. Another form of 'fruit' consists of monks' cowls, nuns' habits, cardinals' hats and the berets of mass-priests. In the background centre, God the Father, identified by his crown and halo, sets about cleaning out the vineyard thus laid waste by 'human laws and doctrines'. He is assisted by angels, who uproot or cut down the dead branches and cast them into a fire. The monkish tillers of the garden are driven out, and a giant hound is chained at the gate of the vineyard to prevent their return.

On the left-hand side, an evangelical preacher instructs an assembled congregation with the words: 'Blessed are those who hear the Word of God, and keep it, and act according to it.' He indicates the crucified Christ, the true fruit of the vineyard. From the foot of the crucifix flows a stream watering the newly planted vines which bear real fruit. The stream is a sign of the saving waters of baptism, and the type of crucifix is taken over from pre-

Reformation popular devotion, where it was used to signify the saving blood of Christ in the Eucharist. In this type of crucifix, Christ is crucified on a winestock, and the stream springing from its foot usually signified the wine of communion. Here it has become a sign of the water of baptism, a Protestant reshaping of a traditional Catholic sign.[2]

This visual assembly is rounded off by the printed message, the poem by Hans Sachs and the various captions within and above the woodcut. The poem is in the form of a complaint, placed in the mouth of God the Father by means of biblical quotations and references. These point out that the vineyard is God's beloved people, laid waste by idolatry, referring to Jeremiah 12.1–2 and Isaiah 3.14. Another reference to Jeremiah 2.13 complains that God's people have left the living fountain of water for broken cisterns. This

158   Erhard Schoen, *God's Complaint over his Vineyard* (1532)

may be the reference intended visually by the monk on the left of God the Father who is digging a dry and empty well beside the fountain of living water which wells up beneath the crucifix. Those who should have cared for God's people have not given them pure water, but poisoned water, to drink. Moreover, wild beasts have been allowed to break into the vineyard and devour the fruit (Isaiah 56.9–10), while the watchmen are blind. Sachs expounds further the complaints made by God. Where divine prophets are not heeded, God will sit in judgment on the despoilers of his vineyard (Jeremiah 23), whose human laws and teachings have poisoned his commands. These Old Testament references are complemented by New Testament similes of the vineyard, in particular that in John 15.1, where every vine which does not bear fruit will be cut down and cast into the fire. This is made a major theme by the caption above the woodcut: 'Christ says: "Every plant which my heavenly father has not planted will be rooted up" ' (Matthew 15.13). Sachs completes his poem with other references to the vineyard: Luke 13.6–9; Matthew 21.1; Isaiah 5.1.

The broadsheet thus draws on an extended biblical metaphor, the vineyard of the Lord, and links it to an important sign from the New Testament, Christ the vine.[3] The addition of the preacher and the congregation creates a large assembly of signs with instructional purpose, which is given a biblical interpretation by Hans Sachs' text. In sum, it instructs the reader in biblical terms in the correct understanding of true and false religion. The only poorly integrated image is the hound at the gate of the vineyard, possibly a classical reference to Cerberus, the canine guardian of hell, thus alluding to the fate of those cast out of the Lord's vineyard. However, the overall significance of this work is its attempt to invest this assembly of signs with theological content.

The vineyard theme had been used before in Reformation propaganda, but not with the same effect, so that we may judge by the comparison the degree of innovation in Schoen's broadsheet. It appeared, for example, in a polemical work of 1524 by Thomas Stoer, *On the Christian Vineyard.*[4] The titlepage contained a woodcut from Hans Sebald Behem showing Christ and St Paul indicating with displeasure three goats devastating the vineyard. This woodcut had little polemical purpose and provided only an incidental illustration for the written text. Schoen's woodcut was more probably inspired by illustrations in a prognostic by Joseph Grunpeck. Following St Gregory, the Church was here illustrated as a vineyard (ill. 159), the depiction also showing Christ in the winepress, a popular means of representing the real presence of Christ's blood in the wine of the Eucharist. A further illustration in this work shows the vineyard of the Church being laid waste by the Turk, a motif which no doubt suggested Schoen's attack on the papacy as despoilers of the vineyard of the Lord.[5] Schoen's adaptation of the theme was taken further by Lucas Cranach the Younger in an oil painting in which the vineyard is divided by a hedge into two distinct halves, the left-hand section being laid waste by the Catholic clergy. At the entrance, the pope and his clergy demand payment from St Peter for their work. On the other side of the hedge, evangelical preachers carefully tend a flourishing garden. Many are recognisable as major reformers. Luther rakes the ground, Melanchthon draws water from a well, and Johann Forster empties a bucket onto the soil. Johann Bugenhagen is hoeing, and a figure kneeling to tend the vines is probably Justus Jonas. Others in the vineyard appear to be princes, and a family group of donors, possibly the princely family of Saxony, stand before its fence.[6]

Schoen's woodcut sounded the eschatological note, never far away in early Reformation propaganda, by showing God as judge, actively intervening in his vineyard. The monks being driven over the fence and the angel burning the weeds of papal belief seemed to indicate that the waste and rubble can be cleared and the entire vineyard saved from ruin. By contrast, the Cranach painting expresses a sense of resignation. The vineyard is now clearly divided, one part sealed off from the other. Meanwhile, the pope demands from St Peter his just reward, an echo, perhaps, of the biting satire *Julius Exclusus*, in which Julius II demands entry at the gates of heaven only to be rebuffed by St Peter.[7] Moreover, the painting lacks the predominant eschatological tone of the woodcut, and the latter's extensive theological references are left largely unstated. The vineyard has simply become a metaphor for the Church, and the instructional purpose of Schoen's work is wanting.

Another biblical image is employed in a broadsheet based on the parable in Matthew 7.24–7, *The House of the Wise and Unwise Man* (ill. 160).[8] The woodcut again uses the form of the antithesis, and here it is the house which signifies the Church. On the left is the house of the wise, the evangelical Christians, built on the firm rock of Christ. This is signified by the pillars of

159   Illustration in J. Grünpeck, *Spiegel der . . .
prophetischen sehungen* (1522), fol. Dii v

the house, formed by the Old and New Testaments and the paschal lamb, symbol of the risen Christ. Above, in heaven, the risen Christ himself promises peace to his Church, which is impervious to attack from the godless. The latter are signified by a cardinal with a papal bull to the left of it, and by a canon to the right, who threatens it with the pyre, which doubtless signifies burning as heretics. The Church is also literally threatened by a monk with a bow and arrow and a peasant with a sword. The latter is an interesting reversal of earlier connotations attached to armed peasants as supporters of the Gospel. Here it seems to allude to peasant unrest as a worldly threat to the Church, which it will nevertheless survive.

On the right is the house of the unwise, the Church of the godless, who are depicted largely as monks. It is built on the foundation of the Antichrist and the shaky pillars of Duns Scotus and Aquinas, the pillar representing the last being barely able to stand up. The seven-headed apocalyptic beast which rises up beneath the building is both the prop and the cause of the collapse of the ungodly Church. But no less effective in bringing about its collapse is the broad stream of the Word of God, which sweeps away its tottering pillars. Above, an angel proclaims that Babylon has fallen, echoing the apocalyptic note provided by the beast.

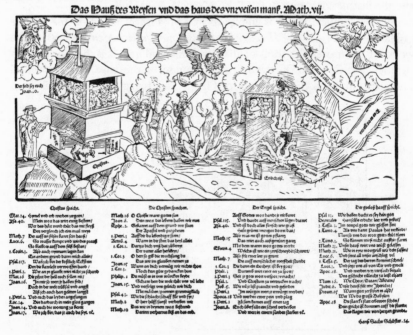

160   G. Pencz, *The House of the Wise and Unwise Man*
(1524), Berlin

This broadsheet uses a less complex biblical image than that of the vine-yard, but it is more creative in its visual message. The moral antithesis 'wise and unwise man' is presented through the two buildings, and so is transformed into the theological antithesis 'true and false Church'.[9] This contrast is fur-ther developed in the 'fundament' image – the opposing supports are Christ and the Bible versus the Antichrist and the purely human teaching of Scotus and Aquinas. This partly theological contrast is complemented by a more polemical antithesis based on the resilience of the true Church, a biblical sign through which it can be identified. The ungodly cannot oppose the Word of God, but the true Church can easily withstand the puny attacks of merely human opponents. The work is thus an exhortation to confidence in the new Church which operates at a double level of connotation. At the level of the signifier (the wise/unwise contrast) it connotes the wisdom of the true believer, which is true wisdom because it is assured of victory, an essentially moral point. At the level of the signified (the true Church/false Church con-trast), it connotes certainty of salvation, a theological point. Through this kind of chain of associations it strives to attain a level of theological com-munication, the visual signs being interrelated so that the connoted messages can also be shown to be linked.

This technique was used in an even more polished way to communicate two other central concepts of the new belief, those of the preacher and the evangelical community. An early example can be found in 1522, in the title-page of a work by Eberlin von Günzburg, *An Exhortation to the Christians of Augsburg* (ill. 161).[10] The woodcut, probably by Heinrich Satrapinus, shows a preacher addressing a crowd with the aid of a crucifix and an open book, doubtless the Bible. He preaches not from a pulpit but in the open air and, although his alb identifies him as a cleric, he is clearly a popular preacher operating outside the formal structure of the Church.[11] This woodcut, thought to represent Eberlin von Günzburg, may hark back to an earlier depiction of another popular preacher, the Drummer of Niklashausen, who was depicted in Schedel's *World Chronicle* preaching in similar circum-stances.[12] What is striking in this depiction is the way the congregation is represented as a body of actively participating believers.[13] This is signified by the hand gestures of members of the congregation who appear to be arguing with the preacher. Indeed, they are no body of wholly convinced evangelical believers, since the woman seated in the left foreground holds a rosary in her right hand. The suggestion of debate is carried also by the gestures of the preacher, who holds his arms spread wide apart, his right hand marking a place in the open book, as though to serve as a reference for discussion. Here, and in the following examples, we can see a skilful use of gestural codes to order the other signs in the woodcut and to convey the message.

A similar iconographical idea is found in the depiction of a sermon in the 1530 edition of Cicero's *De officiis*, published in Augsburg by Wolf Steiner (ill. 162).[14] The preacher stands in a simple pulpit, perhaps in the open air, although this is unclear. He holds the book closed beside him and gestures with two fingers towards his congregation. The hand gestures of the two men seated on blocks or boxes on the left again create the impression of a lively interchange, as does the hand gesture of the woman seated centre front. To her left, another woman holds her hands up in an attitude of pious attention. A standing figure visible between the heads of the two men seated on the left is perhaps a monk. In the background two other men approach the scene, apparently attracted by the lively discussion going around the pulpit.[15] The printed text beneath explains the purpose of the woodcut, that it is intended for the simple and unlearned. Those who cannot understand complicated doctrines should heed the simple message: love God, keep his commandments and do to your neighbour as you would have him do to you. This is the content of the 'brief sermon' delivered by the preacher.

The idea of debate and discussion during a sermon could be applied more fully for educational propaganda. We see this in a woodcut by Georg Pencz, *The Content of Two Sermons* (ill. 163), which appeared in Nuremberg sometime during the later 1520s. The theme of the sermon is now combined with the antithetical form, the woodcut space being divided into two halves by a pillar. Facing towards the centre from pulpits on the left and right are a preacher and a monk. They confront each other as though they were dis-

161   Titlepage to Eberlin von Günzburg, *Ain fraintlich trostliche vermanung* [P. Ulhart, Augsburg, 1522], BL

putants competing for the attention of the congregation. However, the congregation has already been divided into two groups. On the left, the evangelical
group listen attentively to the Word of God. On the right, the orthodox
believers tell their rosary beads, as though paying little heed to their preacher.
However, the evangelical congregation follows the words of its preacher
through the words of Scripture itself. This is signified by the group of women
sitting beneath the pulpit, two of whom have open the pages of a book,
doubtless the Bible, in which they are following the preacher's exposition of
his text. The evangelical group seems to come from a slightly lower level of
society than the orthodox. Both groups contain folk in burgher or artisan
dress, but the men at the back of the evangelical congregation wear hats
which perhaps identify them as simple artisans or peasants.

   The pictorial message is expressive but limited. It is certainly a disputation,
but one which the viewer is called upon to judge. This is stated in print by the
two lines of text beneath the dividing pillar: 'Judge herein, pious Christian,
which teaching is true.' Corresponding to this verbal appeal is a visual appeal,
represented by the figure who stands with arms outstretched beneath the
pillar. He probably represents the 'cryer', the wise man who summons the
viewer to judge the scene, his gesturing hands indicating approval of the one
and disapproval of the other.[16] Thus, there is no ambiguity about how the
viewer is to judge, but to grasp the content of the two sermons we must turn
to the printed text. This is indicated roughly in the lines above the woodcut,
which allude to the good and bad shepherds, the one who preaches the Word
from the mouth of God, the other who is interested only in exploiting the
sheep.

162   Illustration to Cicero, *De officiis* (W. Steiner,
Augsburg, 1530)

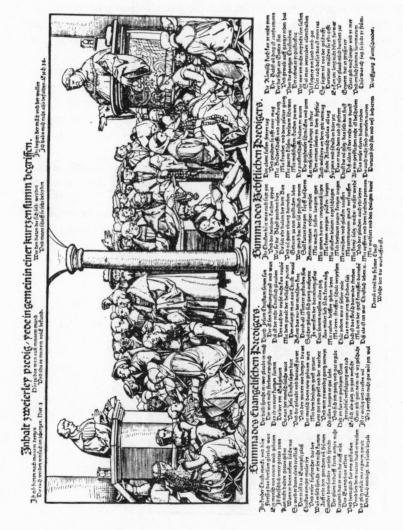

163   G. Pencz, *The Content of Two Sermons*

The main body of the printed text contains a summary of evangelical belief: sinful man's need of Christ as mediator, Christ's saving death, the necessity for salvation of belief in Christ, the new birth through faith which justifies before God, all of which is proclaimed in the Gospel. Orthodox belief is described by its chief characteristics: the pope as the spokesman of God whose commands are given under pain of the ban, good works, the monastic life, fasting, observances, ceremonies, consecrations, ringing of bells, organs, display of relics, the purchase of grace, begging, pilgrimages, feasts, confession, confraternities, the foundation of masses, the decoration of churches, purchasing indulgences and redeeming souls from purgatory by paying for masses. This lengthy enumeration is intended to call the reader's attention to the power of the new belief in its simplified message. It also shows how much more effective a visual representation could be than the written enumeration. Illustration 158 presented much the same enumeration of Catholic cult and belief through visual signs which were instantly apprehensible. For the unlettered it was far more effective in presenting the contrast between old and new belief than Pencz's work. This contrast between printed and visual texts is recalled by the rest of the Catholic preacher's words, which hark back to the *Passional Christi und Antichristi*. The pope's role is summarised through the mouth of the monk thus: he cannot err, all things must bow to him, he sits in the place of God and has power on earth over all spiritual matters. Whoever does not find favour with him will be expelled. The monk closes his sermon with a warning about the new heresy abroad in the land. Although the old belief has stood for many hundred years, the new belief seeks to make fools of our fathers.

This work seems to be less effective at teaching the content of the 'two sermons', and more successful in reminding men of a contrast with which they were already familiar. It was polemical rather than pedagogic. Yet it concentrated the viewer's attention on a central point of evangelical belief, the preaching of the Word, and on the dispute of the two faiths about it. It was a useful image, and was copied twice. It was used once as titlepage to a 1545 Latin work about the dispute between evangelical and papist religion. The second version is a single woodcut found by Derschau, perhaps intended for use in a broadsheet or titlepage (ill. 164). Except for minor changes, both woodcuts are alike, and one may have been copied from the other, although there is no doubt that Pencz's work was the model.[17] The sense of disputation he established so effectively is slightly impaired by the omission of the 'cryer', and to compensate for this both copies add words to the visual space. The evangelical preacher has the Latin words: 'This says the lord God'; the monk the words: 'Thus says the pope.'

Pencz's idea was taken up most effectively, however, by Lucas Cranach the Younger in a double broadsheet which combined the idea of two kinds of preaching with the visual representation of Catholic cult achieved by *God's*

Complaint over his Vineyard. It presented the 'difference between the true religion of Christ and the false idolatrous teaching of the Antichrist' (ills. 165–6). The work is divided into two opposing halves by a pillar in the centre. On the right is papal teaching. Here we find a grossly fat monk preaching without the aid of the Bible. His message, spelled out in print above his head, is that one may see here many ways to blessedness that are not heretical, and through which one may easily become blessed. The reader is then presented with a visual catalogue of Catholic practices which were listed only symbolically in the *Vineyard* woodcut.

In the background there is a procession around a church, praying to a saint, probably the local patron. Two pilgrims approaching from the right show that it is a pilgrimage church. In front of these two figures, a dying man stretched out on a table receives the cowl, so being given the certitude of dying within the privileged monastic Orders. Two monks lay the cowl upon him, while a nun sprinkles him with holy water, and intones the words: 'The cowl, the tonsure and the water aid you.' To the right of this group, a bishop consecrates a bell, while in front of him a solitary priest celebrates a private mass. Behind the priest, a group of monks consecrate an altar, assisted by a devil. Gathered around the pulpit, attending to the monk–preacher, is a crowd of Catholic clergy – cardinals, canons, monks and members of various religious Orders – and some lay folk beneath the pulpit beside the dividing pillar, barely recognisable by their headgear.

In the bottom right-hand corner sits the pope selling indulgences, assisted by a nun. On the table before him are coins on a large silver plate, and he handles another pile of coin. There is also a money sack on the table, similar to that seen in the satirical arms of the pope (see ill. 58). The pope holds up

164   Copy of Pencz, *Content of Two Sermons*

an indulgence, on which is written a version of the words said to have been used by Tetzel in his 1517 indulgence campaign: 'Because the coin rings, the souls to heaven springs.' Beside the table is a large money chest, and beside it lies a fat sack of coin, on which is written: 'This is shame and vice, wrung from your offerings.' Before the table, with another fat moneybag at his waist, is a stout monk clutching two chickens, perhaps an allusion to chickens paid as feudal dues or part of the clerical tithe. In the clouds above, God angrily rains down fire and brimstone upon this scene, while St Francis, recognisable by his monastic habit and stigmata, vainly intercedes for those below, showing the uselessness of the saints as mediators between man and God.

Unlike the Pencz woodcut, which was comparatively free from polemical language, this depiction is richly overlaid with emotive signs. The tone is set by the inscription on the bull held by the pope and its attack on the fiscal side of Catholic belief is driven home visually in all the signs surrounding the pope in that corner of the woodcut. This is surprising, given the late date of composition of the work, probably around 1547 or thereafter.[18] One might have expected that the attack on the money-making aspects of Catholicism had worn thin by then, especially as it was also recognised as an abuse by Catholic authorities. However, it is in keeping with the bitter polemical and satirical tone of the woodcut, and to heighten this satirical note, it draws on many of the popular cultural signs which we have discussed elsewhere.

Among these popular cultural signs we can note a devil blowing with a bellows into the ear of the monkish preacher, a version of the Devil's bagpipe or speaking-tube, which identifies the monk's message as diabolically inspired and of the Antichrist.[19] The diabolical theme is repeated by the figure who plays the central role in blessing the altar. This has spectacles, a bird's beak and claws, and wears a fool's cap. This link between folly and the Devil leads the reader to the theme of the Catholic clergy as fools. The monk holding the giant candle in the left foreground has been given a fool's cap for a cowl, while the monk behind the fat monk with the chickens has a carnival puppet peeping out of his cowl. The vices associated with folly have not been omitted. One is perhaps delicately alluded to in the nun who assists the pope with his sale of indulgences, but another is very evident in the shower of playing-cards and dice falling from the cowl of the monk to the right of the one with the candle. The coarse and overfed features of all the monks add to this impression, and another monastic vice, slyness and cunning, is signified by the figure to the left of the candle-bearer who is wearing a stole made wholly from fox-brushes.[20] Finally, there hangs over this entire representation of Catholic belief a sense of doom and desolation, connoted not only by the hail of fire and brimstone hurled down on it by God, but also by the hard and stony ground on which all of these scenes are set; an indirect allusion, perhaps, to the parable of the stony ground.

165   Lucas Cranach the Younger, *Two Kinds of Preaching –
the Evangelical*

166   Lucas Cranach the Younger, *Two Kinds of Preaching –
the Catholic*

Turning to the 'true religion of Christ', the starting-point for the reader is again the preacher. He is clearly recognisable as Luther, preaching from the open book of the Bible. He preaches not with his own words, but with those from the Acts of the Apostles, inscribed on the pulpit: all prophets attest this, that there is no other name in heaven than that of Christ. Luther is thus indirectly identified as a prophet, and in another revival of earlier Luther iconography, he is again given the sign of the inspiration of the Holy Spirit, the dove in the nimbus above him. His pointing fingers indicate the end of a banderole which leads into the heavens, a contrasting gesture to that of the monk opposite him, whose fingers point downwards, to the clergy assembled beneath his pulpit. Luther's gesture leads the reader along the textband, which says 'Behold the Lamb of God', to the paschal lamb and flag, the symbol of Christ as Saviour. The reader is led further along the textband to the figure of the crucified but risen Christ, through the text: 'I am the way.' This in turn leads up to God the Father as Lord of the world, holding the orb, over the words: 'There is only one mediator.' Additional text has been added in the space between Christ and God. The top text is placed in Christ's mouth: 'Holy Father, save them; I sacrificed myself for them with my wounds ... ' The bottom text reiterates this salvific message: 'If we sin we have an advocate before God, so let us turn in consolation to this means of grace.'

This series of theological messages is arranged like an arch, and sheltering beneath it is the church of evangelical believers. To the right, a crowd of lay-men listen to Luther preaching, among them a figure recognisable as a prince of Saxony. He is shown carrying a cross, signifying that this is the Elector John Frederick, imprisoned for his faith (in the Protestant interpretation of the matter) after losing the Schmalkaldic War of 1546–7.[21] To the left of this group are depicted the Protestant sacraments. In the foreground, communion is given under both kinds before an altar dominated by a crucifix, the sign of Christ's saving death. Beside this are inscribed the words which justify giving the cup to the laity: 'Drink all of you ... ' (Matthew 26.27). In the middle ground, centre, a baptism is conducted.

This is a very full picture, but in contrast to the depiction of 'false belief' it is well ordered and simple. It presents the essentials of Protestantism: preaching of the Word, Christ as the only mediator, through whose death sin is forgiven. This theological thought is then reflected in the sacramental means through which it is actualised in the community of believers, through baptism and the sacrament of the altar. There are some minor details of the entire work which are worthy of note. The adherents of Catholic belief are depicted predominantly as members of the Catholic clergy and hierarchy, those of Protestant belief as laity, most of whom seem to belong to the more prominent sections of society. More importantly, there is now no question of dispute, and the viewer is given no choice between two alternatives. The representatives of true and false belief do not stand confronting each other as disputants, but back to back without any interaction. This is also the intention of the heightened satirical and polemical tone of the right-hand woodcut. The overall message is that there is only one true belief through which one may be saved. Adherence to Catholic belief is not only diabolical folly, but also leads to damnation.

This message was not new, of course, and is found in evangelical propaganda from the beginning of the new religious movement. What is different about this example is the attempt to present a profile of a new institution, the Lutheran Church. Pedagogic propaganda for the Reformation can be seen to move through distinct stages. First, it attempted to show men the importance of using biblical criteria to judge matters of religion, especially, as we saw in chapter 3, to discern the difference between the old and the new belief. Second, it had to identify and communicate effectively the central doctrines of true belief. A third stage was to identify and characterise, not just two kinds of belief or preaching, but two different Churches. We have been examining this development in most of the examples in this chapter. However, this process enters an important new stage with the depiction of the Lutheran sacraments. These ritual ceremonies, more than any other, single out not just a set of doctrines or belief, but identify a Church as a community of acting believers. The propaganda thus takes its readers along the road to the institutionalisation of the new movement.

This can be seen most clearly in some further examples of educational propaganda. Another product of the Saxon school is a woodcut by Lucas Cranach the Younger (ill. 167). This is also in the form of an antithesis, but here the dividing line is formed by the figure of Luther himself.[22] He preaches from a pulpit which is adorned with the symbols of the four Evangelists, while the open book of the Bible lies before him. As in the Pencz woodcut, gestures suggest the antithesis. Luther's left hand is stretched out and turned downwards in a gesture of rejection towards the papal scene on his left. His right hand makes an indicative sign with two fingers, pointing to the crucified Christ. On his left, the pope and members of the Catholic hierarchy are devoured by the jaws of hell, attended by rejoicing demons, one of whom lays a small spiral of excrement on the top of the head of a nun, who is barely visible at the back of the crowd. Another demon kisses the pope's foot as he sinks back into hell.

To Luther's right, a group of evangelical Christians receive communion under both kinds from the hands of two Lutheran ministers. The crucified Christ and the lamb and flag on the altar are signs of the theological content of the sacrament. In this depiction it is interesting that those receiving the bread on one side of the altar are all women, while those receiving the cup on the other are all men. It is unclear whether there is any significance in this division of the sexes other than the artist's desire to create a balanced composition on the evangelical side of his work, in contrast to the disorder and confusion on the papal side. More noticeable is that the congregation are all high members of society. Indeed, in many of their features there is resemblance to the ducal family of Saxony. Most interesting of all is Luther's position in the composition. Depicted as the proclaimer of the Word of God, he has been placed in the role of cryer assumed by the greybeard in Pencz's woodcut. He has also, however, been placed in the position of judge, with the doomed on his left being rejected and cast into the flames, and the saved on the right being shown the clear means of salvation. This means of salvation, the crucified Christ, is also visible to the damned, but they chose to ignore it, looking to the pope or to each other. This is a further stage of institutionalisation, for we now see an ordered Church with an Establishment of its own, denoted by Luther as leader and the princely house of Saxony as its protector. Moreover, in Luther it has its first confessor. In the previous work, Luther appears as divinely inspired prophet; here he appears almost in the place of God, as divine judge or at least as the agent on earth of divine judgment.[23] We shall examine further evidence for this viewpoint shortly.

Another woodcut from the Cranach school also demonstrates the same phenomenon. Dating from around the middle of the sixteenth century, this shows two figures distributing communion in a church (ill. 168). They are identified by name as Luther on the left and Hus on the right. They are giving

167   Lucas Cranach the Younger, *Luther Preaching, with the Pope in the Jaws of Hell*

communion under both kinds to members, living and dead, of the house of Ernestine Saxony, all of whom are named. Receiving the sacraments in the foreground are the first two of the 'Lutheran' electors, Frederick the Wise kneeling on the right and John the Constant on the left. Behind Frederick the Wise is the next Elector, John Frederick, and his wife Sibylla of Cleves, behind the altar John Frederick II and two younger princes, Johann Wilhelm and a third John Frederick. In the centre of the altar stands a fountain representing the second of the Lutheran sacraments, baptism. The blood flowing from the side of the crucified Christ becomes a fountain of saving water, while the two basins of the fountain are supported by the intertwined roots of a large vine. The vine is a long-established motif, both for baptism and for Christ's salvific role when linked to the fountain, and also recalls the *Vineyard* woodcut which used the theme.[24] In the background left, we see a reference to a third sacrament accepted by Lutheranism, where Luther appears to be hearing confession from John Frederick.[25]

Such an illustration no longer seeks to characterise Lutheranism by its opposition to Catholicism, but presents it as a Church in its own right. However, there is also an implicit attempt to distinguish the Lutheran Church from other forms of evangelical belief. The emphasis on baptism found in this example and in the depiction of true and false belief by the younger Cranach (see ill. 165) clearly divided Lutheranism from Anabaptism, particularly in the latter case, by explicitly showing infant baptism.[26] It has also been argued that the depiction of the crucified Christ on the altar associated with the distribution of communion was intended to assert the doctrine of the real presence against Zwinglian belief.[27] If this was the case, the intention was

168   *Luther and Hus Distribute Communion*, GNM

rarely made explicit and it was certainly less evident to a reader than the other signs presented in these visual works.

One of the most noticeable features of the examples of attempts to educate through propaganda that have been studied so far is their low level of theological content. This was a particular difficulty for visual propaganda, for theological complexity was, perhaps, best presented through the spoken or written word. Iconographically, certain signs could become identified with certain doctrines, such as Christ in the winepress signifying the real presence (see ill. 159), or the fountain of grace indicating the saving power of baptism (see ill. 168). Cranach's depiction of true and false belief attempted to resolve this problem by providing a visual compendium of Reformation doctrine, although it still relied on the emotive power of anti-papal polemic. Further, Cranach's summary of Reformation belief was closer to a set of slogans than to a proper theology. Few works of visual propaganda were able to cope with the problem without falling back on idealised allegories or highly abstract symbols. Only a few did so with any degree of success.

The most interesting of these, which might be called 'theological broadsheets', has attracted little attention since it was republished by Derschau at the beginning of the nineteenth century. Although it lacks a title, its theological content enables us to entitle it *The Origin of Sin and Man's Justification before God* (ill. 169).[28] It is in the form of a *Bilderbogen* made up of six friezes, each broken up into four scenes, so that the entire work can be read like a comic strip. The artist is unknown, being identified only by the initials NG on the base of the pillar separating the first and second scenes of the last row. The style is similar to that of the Cranach school, probably from the early period of the Reformation. Each of the scenes contains banderoles labelling the figures depicted, so that the message can be easily read.

Reading along the first row, we first see the creation by God of Adam and Eve, Adam being labelled as Man, so that the subsequent progress of this figure throughout the strips represents Man's spiritual progress. The next scene shows Man breaching God's command by Original Sin. Accordingly, Man is bound by Disobedience in the third scene, and in the fourth is driven forth as a bound slave to Sin. Sin is here clad as a Wild Man, signifying man's unredeemed nature, so that Man is, so to speak, held captive by a part of himself. This sequence is typical of the whole series. Each set of four scenes forms in sequence a distinct theological message, and the entire series of six rows are intended to add up to a simplified theology of salvation. The theology is, of course, Pauline — the first row depicts the thought, expressed in Romans 5–6, that sin came into the world through one man and that man has thus become a slave to sin through this original act of disobedience.

In the second row, Man is tormented by Conscience and Despair. Here Man is clad in a monastic habit to signify his attempts to please God through works alone. In the second scene we see him tormented by Despair and

169   Monogrammist NG, *The Origin of Sin and Man's Justification*

brought by Sin and Eternal Death before the angry judgment of God, who is about to pierce him with the arrow of his displeasure. In the third scene, however, Man receives the freely given grace of God, symbolised by the dove of the Holy Spirit. Having cast off the monastic habit of works, Man now kneels naked before God. Disobedience, Sin and Eternal Death are thus overcome, blind Reason flees and Man's liberated Conscience soars up into the heavens. In the final scene, this overcoming of the demands of Good Works is depicted by showing Man felling Good Works, in the shape of a nun, with a club: Man no longer needs Good Works. The theme of Man being driven to desperation by his troubled conscience faced with sin and God's wrath is found in Luther's commentaries on Galatians and on 1 Corinthians 15.[29] Although there is no precise passage in Luther corresponding to the train of thought in this row, it is clearly influenced by Lutheran theology.

The third row develops this theme further, adding the role of the Law. First, Man stands between the demands of the Law, symbolised by the figure of Moses, and of Sin and Disobedience. In the next scene, Law brings Man to the recognition of Sin, which is seated on a throne holding Man as his bound slave. Again, this echoes Luther in his commentary on 1 Timothy 1.6.[30] In a reprise of the theme from the previous row, the third and fourth scenes show Man led by Eternal Death and pursued by the Wrath of God; this leads him to hell, whither he is driven by Despair, Conscience and Sin.

The first three rows could be taken to refer to the situation under the Law. The fourth row introduces the Incarnation, and thus the promise of salvation brought by Christ and the Gospel. The first scene represents the incarnation through the annunciation. The second shows Man torn between the teaching of Christ and the advice of Reason, blindfolded and blowing into Man's ear with a bellows. This figure embodies several of Luther's views on reason. Reason is blinded by the malice of the Devil, and here seems to play the role of a devil blowing evil into man's ear that we have seen before (see ills. 68, 81, 100, 166). Here, as elsewhere within this work, Reason is clad as a courtesan, recalling Luther's characterisation of reason as 'the Devil's bride ... the foremost whore the Devil has'.[31] The third scene continues this Lutheran emphasis, with Man led by Reason carrying the figure of Good Works towards a church. This is reminiscent of a religious procession, the figure of Good Works resembling a saint's statue. Again, there is the echo of Luther's view that a reason blinded by the Devil and ignorant of faith will glorify good works, and that the blindness of human reason is so incomprehensible that it can form no judgment about works.[32] The outcome of such futile efforts is shown in the fourth scene. The elusive figure of Good Works escapes the grasping hands of Man, who lies prostrate from his efforts. He is thus the more easily overtaken by Sin and Eternal Death.

The fifth row expands the theme of attempts to gain righteousness by good works. The first scene shows blind Reason, the Devil's whore, carrying a long spear, perhaps in allusion to sin as the Devil's spear.[33] The meaning of this scene is doubtless found in the second and third scenes, that Reason has driven man into attempting to gain righteousness through prayer to the saints, depicted in the second, or through fasting, the rosary or indulgences, in the third. In this row, as in the previous row, Man is again clad in a monastic habit to indicate his attempts to please God through works alone. Meanwhile, Man ignores the figure of the crucified Christ, shown through the open church window in the second scene. In the last scene of this row Man lies prostrate from the failure of these efforts, while he is judged by the Trinity in heaven.

The last row provides a solution to these troubles. First Christ takes upon himself Sin and the Devil, mounting the ladder to the cross with them as his burden, while St John the Baptist and the prophets indicate his saving action. By this means, in the second scene, Man is led up the ladder to heaven by the angel of Faith. At the top is the figure of Christ crucified, through whom one comes to the Father, seated in the clouds. In the final double scene Man is followed by Persecution and the Old Adam, who seek to hold him back or trip him up. However, Patience repells them and Man advances to the Gospel, assisted by Faith and Hope. The Gospel, in the form of an evangelical preacher, indicates that Man must pass through Bodily Death, but the way will lead to the Father in heaven. This extraordinarily rich composition thus reflects many of Luther's views on two kinds of righteousness, good works, the law, justification and reason. It works by dramatising the story of salvation through personified theological concepts, a stock iconographic device of the period.[34] We might ask, however, how effective this was as a pedagogic device. It scarcely seems likely to have communicated Lutheran theology to the uninitiated. The most effective use for such a work was to employ it as a teaching aid, as a means of expounding orally the main points of evangelical theology, which could be suitably dramatised and spelt out line by line by a preacher or teacher. This is an explanation made the more likely by its form as a *Bilderbogen*, which was used traditionally by the German ballad-singer or bench-singer to put his message across to a popular audience.[35]

We have evidence that this kind of technique was envisaged by Reformation propagandists from the pamphlet we discussed in chapter 1, *A Dialogue between a Christian and a Jew . . . concerning Christ the Cornerstone*. This work was based on the idea of using a woodcut illustration to expound the main points of evangelical belief. Although the work was published without the woodcut, the accompanying illustration can be identified (ill. 170), so that we can see how this expository technique was meant to work.[36] Each scene is numbered, thus providing an order in which the images are to be read. The number 1 is missing, but is clearly intended to be the figure of the crucified Christ in the centre of the composition. All the geometric lines of the composition converge to establish this, a point we shall

170   *Christ the Cornerstone*

return to later. The cross-beam of the crucifix forms the top side of a square which shows the crucified Christ as the foundation of both Old and New Testaments. At the four corners of this square are four figures representing the Old Testament; reading clockwise from the left-hand corner, David, Isaiah, Moses and Job. A smaller square set within this contains the symbols of the four Evangelists, representing the New Testament. Thus, the pamphlet exposition tells us, both Old and New Testaments agree with Christ. The Gospel shows what is commanded by Moses, David shows that no man can do anything of his own power and must rely on God. As foretold by Isaiah, God's grace is conferred through Christ, who is to bear the sins of the world.[37]

Outside the square are six further figures, one on either side and one at each corner. The three figures down the right-hand side of the crucifix (the left from the reader's viewpoint) are those who pointed the way to Christ. From top to bottom these are John the Baptist; Christ's mother Mary, who attests the power of God and shows Christ to be the only mediator; and St Peter, whose key signifies that Christ has conferred on him, through faith and love, the keys of heaven. St Peter also confirms in his epistle that all believers are a sacred priesthood. On Christ's left are three figures who foretold the Antichrist: from top to bottom, Daniel in the lions' den, St John the Evangelist and St Paul, whose sword stands for the Word as the sword of the spirit. These six figures represent the pillars of Christendom for all those who believe in Christ alone. The pamphlet commentary explicitly mentions here that the usual four pillars of the Church, Jerome, Ambrose, Augustine and Gregory, have been deliberately omitted: they are to be found in the ranks of pious Christians.[38]

The arrangement of these six figures leads the reader on to numbers 2 and 3. To Christ's right, prefaced, as it were, by those who pointed the way to Christ, is the true, the evangelical Church, all of whose members as depicted here indicate the crucified Christ. First, there is the Good Thief; beside him, in a pulpit, the 'evangelical preachers, such as Luther and others'; further down, an evangelical congregation, the 'Christian Church, unified without sects according to Christ's teaching, according to the clear Word of God'. Significantly, this group has been placed next to St Peter, who confirmed that all believers are a sacred priesthood. The mounted figure before the pulpit introduces an apocalyptic note. He is, the pamphlet tells us, the figure Faithful-and-True seated on a white horse, from Apocalypse 19.11. But whereas in the Apocalypse this figure stands for the Word of God who executes God's wrath, the pamphlet takes him to signify every pious ruler who receives the Gospel in his land or city and allows it to be preached.[39]

Opposed to this Church, on Christ's left, is the Church of false belief, the Church of the Antichrist. This is introduced by the prophetic figures who foretold the Antichrist (Daniel, John and Paul), and reinforced by the figure of the Babylonian whore astride the beast, holding aloft the cup of abominations. This figure corresponds to that of Faithful-and-True on the other side, and makes the contrast between the two Churches an eschatological confrontation. In this Church of the Antichrist there is the unrepentent thief, a preacher representing the 'indulgence preachers such as Eck, Emser and Cochleus', who mock, deride and despise Christ, and the crowd of papal clergy. These are labelled in the woodcut, in reference to John 15.2, as the barren branches to be cut off from the vine of Christ. The contrast between the two Churches is rounded off by that between light and darkness, signified by the sun and the moon.

This contrast is continued in the top triangular section of the woodcut, numbered 4 and 5. In the left-hand corner, with the number 4, Christ rises from the tomb, the candelabra perhaps signifying the Saviour as the light of the world. In the right-hand corner is a tomb, with a closed door guarded by an angel with a sword, doubtless signifying eternal death. The bottom triangle is more sub-divided. The number 6 indicates a closed door, possibly that of the evangelical Church, which is unyielding to the attacks on it by a demon with a long spear, which both woodcut and pamphlet tell us symbolises the usages of the papal Church.[40] On the other side, a demon holds open the portal of Satan, which the unjust will enter. The contrast now moves to the intersecting circles above and below that containing the crucified Christ. At the top, numbered 8, is the Holy Spirit, signifying grace; at the bottom, numbered with 9, the realm of the world or nature. This shows Adam and Eve forced to labour in the sweat of their brow, and Cain slaying Abel. The final contrast is that between God the Father, indicating the risen Christ on his right hand, numbered 10, and the mouth of hell, numbered 11, the fate of the unrighteous.[41]

Exposition of this illustration thus enables a reader to be taken through the content of the salvation message of the evangelical movement, explaining the various signs and relating them to Reformation doctrines. Central to the entire exposition is Christ's sacrificial death, which is emphasised by the geometric composition of the schema. The cross is the centre of the Old and the New Testaments. It is also the means through which divine grace flows down from the Father and the Holy Spirit, through the interlinked circles. It is also the point of conflict between the true and the false Churches, for the two triangles containing these overlap in the person of Christ, to whom even the false Church lays claim. Christ is thus the cornerstone on which belief is built, symbolised by the squares formed around him (fig. 1). This kind of geometric schema was used frequently in pre-Reformation representations of articles of faith, such as the sacraments and occasionally in the Pauper's Bible. It was thus a familiar technique for addressing the unlearned. Indeed, the advantages of the non-linear arrangement of the message can be seen very clearly in this example. Although the sequence of thought is indicated by the consecutive numbering, the images could be read in any order, as occurred in the pamphlet, where the Jew, the character to whom the woodcut is explained, simply picks out an image which strikes him as interesting, and asks to have it interpreted.[42] Once expounded, the visual image then served to recall the doctrine, a kind of evangelical adaption of 'the art of memory'.[43]

This work seems more effective than the intricate exposition of the doctrine of justification in the *Bilderbogen* by NG. It relies on a carefully structured use of some familiar antithetical images, but its success ultimately is

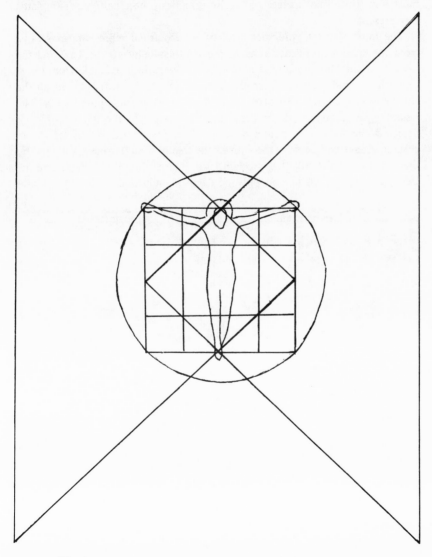

Fig. 1

dependent on the strong and simple sign of the crucified Christ, and the doctrinal significance with which this is imbued. Indeed, the crucifixion was perhaps the one image most consistently adapted by the Reformation as an expression of its characteristic doctrines. Earlier emphases on the crucifixion as a meditative, devotional image, or as an indication of an historical event, are supplanted by an allegorical representation which preaches visually the doctrine of the redemptive significance of the cross.[44] In almost all of the most powerful visual images of the Reformation, the crucifixion is in some way present.

The most effective and successful of the doctrinal representations came from the school of Lucas Cranach, the contrast between the Law and the Gospel, or the Old and New Testaments.[45] The earliest example from Lucas Cranach the Elder comes from the later 1520s (ill. 171). It is based on the antithesis, a form used so often throughout Reformation propaganda. The visual space is divided down the centre by a tree, to the left of which is depicted the Law as expounded in the Old Testament. In the left background, Adam and Eve eat the fruit of the tree of life after being tempted by the serpent. As a result of this original sin, man is the prey of death and the Devil, through which he can only be damned, indicated by the two figures

171   Lucas Cranach the Elder, *The Law and the Gospel*, BM

hounding Man into the jaws of hell. This is Man under the Law, signified by Moses holding the tables of the Ten Commandments, with other Old Testament prophets behind him. In the clouds above, Christ as Lord of the world sits judging man, with the sword and the lily in his ears. Two figures, Mary and John the Baptist, seek to intercede for sinful man, although in vain. The gloomy message of the Old Testament and the Law, which only condemn man, is also signified in the barren branches on the Old Testament side of the antithesis formed by the central tree.

In opposition to the hardness of the Law, the Gospel brings hope, signified by the blooming branches on the New Testament side of the tree. In the background is depicted, however, an Old Testament scene, the brazen serpent, the figure of Christ's saving death on the cross.[46] On the hill in the right background Mary receives the rays of heavenly grace, signifying the incarnation, further indicated by the angel bearing the cross down to her. To the left, another angel brings the news of the birth of the Saviour to the shepherds on the hills in Bethlehem. The main figures on this side depict the events through which the Gospel message is realised. The crucified Christ sheds his saving blood in a stream onto man. Through the agency of the Holy Spirit, the dove through which the stream passes, this becomes the saving water of baptism. Man has his attention called to the sacrificial death of Christ by the figure of John the Baptist. Beneath the crucifix is the paschal lamb, the symbol of Christ's victorious death, which is completed by his resurrection. This is depicted in the bottom right-hand corner, where Christ overcomes death and the apocalyptic beast, representing the Devil. This completes man's release from sin and death, neatly balancing the corresponding depiction on the far left.

This schema became one of the most popular themes of the Reformation, largely because it captured so effectively the gist of Luther's doctrine. Indeed, it seems to have been almost directly inspired by some of Luther's expositions on the theme of the Law and the Gospel, such as that in his commentary on Galatians.[47] It was a wholly biblical depiction and relied on signs accessible to every person of the time. Above all, it established a uniquely evangelical position, without reference to papal or Catholic teaching. It could be used purely as a visual representation, or supplied with appropriate biblical references, as in illustration 171. The Law is headed by a citation from Romans 1.18: 'The wrath of God is revealed from heaven against all ungodliness and wickedness of men.' The Gospel is headed by a verse of Isaiah 7.14, which shows the prophetic link between Old and New Testaments: 'The Lord himself will give you a sign. Behold, a young woman shall conceive and bear a son.' Beneath the depiction of the Law are quotations spelling out its significance (Romans 3.23; 1 Corinthians 15.56; Romans 4.15; Romans 3.20 and Matthew 11.13). The Gospel is likewise supplied with texts on faith (Romans 1.17 and 3.21 — both classic expressions of the basic Lutheran doctrine that the just live through faith), and expressing the hope of salvation (John 1.29; 1 Peter 1.2 and 1 Corinthians 15.55). The combination of scriptural texts and visual signs expressing their content made such a depiction the evangelical version of the Pauper's Bible.[48]

This became a popular theme with Cranach and his school, especially for altarpieces.[49] Artists from this school who used the theme included Melchior Sachs, Hans Brosamer and Peter Gottland.[50] More importantly, in terms of our main interest here, it formed a popular theme for titlepages. It was, for example, a natural choice for editions of the Bible and was used in the title-page of the 1541 Wittenberg Bible in Luther's translation.[51] This added a polemical note by showing the Devil wearing a cardinal's hat, and a monk and a pope writhing in the flames of hell. The schema was often slightly rearranged in these titlepages, as in that of the 1541 Wittenberg edition of the New Testament in Low German (ill. 172).[52] Here the brazen serpent is placed on the Old Testament side and the Adam and Eve depiction is moved into the middle ground as a counterpart to the risen Christ slaying death and the Devil. Thus, we move across from the serpent's victory over Adam and Eve to Christ's victory over the serpent in the shape of the beast.

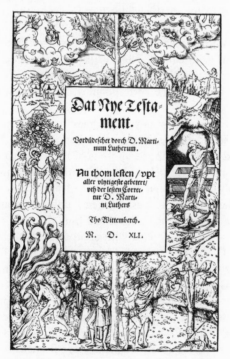

172   Titlepage to *Dat Nye Testament* (M. Lotter, Wittenberg, 1541), BM

Another version, used frequently in Wittenberg editions from 1537–46, has begun to reduce the schema to the dimensions of a decorative border (ill. 173).[53] The basic antithesis is still suggested by the withered and blooming sides of the tree in the centre. The Old Testament and the Law are indicated by God giving Moses the tablets of the Law in the top left-hand corner, beneath this the Fall, and Man pursued to hell by death and the Devil in the bottom left, while Moses and the prophets indicate the Ten Commandments. Reading down the right-hand Gospel side, we see the annunciation, the death of Christ, the lamb and flag and the risen Saviour conquering death and the Devil. The figure of man is not repeated on this side. John the Baptist merely looks across to man pursued by death and the Devil and indicates the crucified and risen Christ with two hand gestures, while Man looks back over his shoulder towards the saving teaching of the New Testament. Following Cranach's earlier model of this composition, the brazen serpent and the proclamation of the news of Christ's birth to the shepherds are squeezed in behind the figure of John the Baptist.

The pedagogic propaganda we have considered so far exemplifies two tendencies. It communicates the central doctrines of the Reformation, so

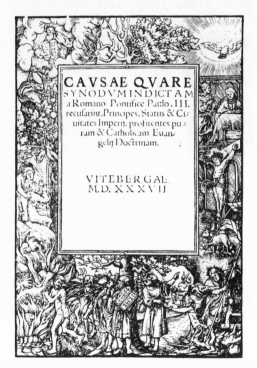

173   Titlepage to *Causae quare synodum indictam a Romano Pontifice Paulo III* (Wittenberg, 1537), BL

establishing the content of right belief, but alongside this it also seeks to establish a clear-cut notion of the true Church. This Church is identified by its defining characteristics. Besides biblical belief and doctrine, it consists of divine inspiration, preaching, the emphasis it places on Christ and his saving Word and the use of the sacraments (baptism, confession and the Lord's Supper). It defines the true Church essentially as the Lutheran Church, for the iconography draws clear lines between Lutheran belief and that of other evangelical groups. The emphasis on baptism, especially infant baptism, clearly distinguishes it from Anabaptist belief. Its stress on the real presence in the communion drew a clear dividing line between Lutheran and Zwinglian belief.[54] A final stage is the identification of a territorial Church, with its own tradition and its own confessors and saints. We can trace the development of this final stage through several woodcuts dating from the 1540s.

Some of these works take up the signs established in the early iconography of Luther. In a broadsheet published sometime after Luther's death in 1546 (ill. 174), we see a full-length depiction of Luther holding a crucifix. Blood streams from the hands of the crucified Christ, and above, the Holy Spirit shines on both Luther and the crucifix. Luther is thus identified as part of the work of saving grace. Behind Luther, at his feet, a goose reads in a book,

174   *Luther with Crucifix and a Goose*, Wickiana

signifying Hus and his demand to have the Bible placed in the hands of the laity.[55] The work thus expresses the part played by both Hus and Luther in the revival of the Bible and so of salvific doctrine. This is a counterpart, perhaps, to the depiction of Luther and Hus distributing communion, stressing their role in restoring the cup to the laity. We saw in chapter 2 that the idea of an evangelical tradition encompassing Luther and Hus was expressed at an early stage in the development of Luther iconography. How far this idea of an evangelical tradition could develop can be seen in a Czech broadsheet showing the stages of revival of the Gospel (ill. 175). This shows Wyclif kindling a spark in a tinder box, from which Hus takes a light. From Hus's taper Luther lights a larger light, which then becomes a large torch. From this torch the light and flame is passed on to Melanchthon. All this occurs under the divine inspiration of the Holy Spirit. This gradual revival and transference of the light echoes the Holbein woodcut on the light of the world. It also establishes both a clear history of the origins of the Reformation and a kind of apostolic succession among the founders of the evangelical movement.

This example is interesting, but others did not show its awareness of the international origins of the Reformation. Luther was more often seen in the context of the Saxon origins of the Reformation, no doubt reflecting the influence of the Cranach school of artists. Thus, a woodcut showing Luther and the Elector John Frederick kneeling before the crucified Christ (ill. 176) emphasises the Reformation's reliance on princely protection. Luther is commemorated as the man who taught the saving death of Christ, the Elector as the man responsible for furthering the revival of true belief.[56] This was a popular subject, with three woodcut versions and an etching.[57] The last bears an inscription spelling out the message of the woodcuts, that both men are

Kontrffektowé/Jana Wigleffa/Miſtra Jana Husſa/Doktora Martina
Luthera/a Filipa Melanthona.

IAN WIKLEF   M: IAN HVS   D:M: LVTER   F: MELANT:

175   *Wyclif, Hus, Luther and Melanchthon as Reformers*

united under the cross as those who have suffered for the sake of Christ. This kind of depiction has been labelled 'the Reformers and patrons of the Reformation', but it has hints of Protestant martyrology about it, and above all is analogous to the pre-Reformation devotional picture.[58]

The devotional purpose of such illustrations is stated clearly in a woodcut which also served as a book illustration, entitled *A Hymn, 'Preserve Us Lord, with Your Word'* (ill. 177). It depicts God the Father enthroned in glory, beside him the risen Christ thrusting the pope, the Turk and members of the Catholic hierarchy into hell. Standing to the left as witnesses of this scene are Luther, who indicates the risen Christ, and two princes, probably Frederick the Wise and John Frederick, as well as three reformers, Melanchthon, Hus and Caspar Cruciger. On the right stand the family of the house of Saxony, six women, one of whom is Sibylla of Cleves, wife of John Frederick, two children and an old man. The printed text contains a prayer in five verses, invoking the protection of Christ and the Holy Spirit against the danger of the Turk and the pope.[59]

This work is thus commemorative and devotional at the same time. It recalls the victory of true, evangelical belief over the unbelief of the papacy and the infidel, stating clearly that this is a work of God to which the Reformers and princes are witnesses. Luther, in particular, is the man who has pointed out this development, placing him in a near-prophetic position. The devotional intent is embodied in the prayer or hymn supplied with the visual text. Like the pre-Reformation devotional picture, it was intended to recall the work of God and so inspire to prayer.

The idea of the evangelical witnesses or confessors is taken a step further

176   *Luther and John Frederick before the Crucifix*, Berlin

by another type of depiction, which shows the baptism of Christ in the presence of the Reformers and protectors of the Gospel (ill. 178). On the right, Christ is baptised by John the Baptist, while God the Father sends the dove of the Holy Spirit to impart his blessing on the Saviour. On the left, this scene is witnessed by Luther, who indicates it with his left hand, and by John Frederick, Sibylla of Cleves and their three sons, who all kneel beside Luther. In the background is the identifiable outline of Wittenberg. The printed text instructs the reader that Christ is the only Son of God, and it is to him that one should turn in need, not to creatures or idols. Christ alone is Saviour through his death on the cross. Luther made this known from the small town of Wittenberg, and John Frederick confessed the same doctrine until his death, as did his family. From such a depiction the reader should see how one must live under the cross and be constant in belief in God's Word. This injunction, with which the text closes, recalls John Frederick's suffering for the Gospel through his imprisonment following the Schmalkaldic War, also alluded to in an earlier work (see ill. 165). Here, Luther is once again accorded a quasi-prophetic status, signified by his indicative gesture and the fact that he stands as a witness to the baptism of Christ, placing a protective hand on the shoulder of the prince.[60]

177   *A Hymn 'Preserve us Lord with your Word'*, Berlin

This work also appeared in a Latin version,[61] but the same theme was developed more elaborately in another large woodcut showing the baptism set before the walls of Nuremberg (ill. 179). This is a *Bilderbogen* of five blocks, the whole depiction thus having an impressive size suitable for formal public display. In the centre is the baptism scene, to the left a large group of the princes of Saxony and Brandenburg, who supported the Reformation during its first period of struggle to the end of the 1550s. The likenesses are very crude, and the artist has therefore added the names of the persons intended: the Elector Augustus, George Frederick, Margrave of Brandenburg, George the Pious, Margrave of Brandenburg, Margrave Albert of Brandenburg, John the Wise, Margrave of Brandenburg, the Elector Maurice of Saxony, John Frederick the Mittler, Heinrich of Saxony, George the Rich of Saxony, John the Constant and Frederick the Wise.[62]

The ranks of the Reformers contain some surprises. These are also labelled by the artist: Hus, Luther, Melanchthon, Justus Jonas, Caspar Cruciger, Johann Bugenhagen, Paul Eber, Johann Aepinus, Johann Forster, Georg Major, Johann Pfeffinger, Erasmus and Sebastian Fröschel. The inclusion of Erasmus among the Reformers is surprising, although it is by no means unique.[63] The debt of the evangelical movement to Erasmus' biblical scholarship was increasingly acknowledged by the 'second generation' of the Reformation.[64] The other Reformers all had close links to the Saxon Reformation and to Wittenberg. One or two had links with Nuremberg,[65] but the town outline of that city seems to have been included largely for its close connection with the Saxon Reformation from the beginning of the evangelical

178   *The Baptism of Christ before Wittenberg*

179   *The Baptism of Christ before Nuremberg*, Berlin

movement. This large illustration clearly served to commemorate the 'founding fathers' of the Reformation through its princely protectors and leading theologians. It also served a devotional and confessional purpose, for it is supplied with the text of the Creed, written in the boxes in the top left- and right-hand corners.

The baptism of Christ before the Reformers and evangelical princes was a popular theme of the middle years of the sixteenth century. Besides the versions already discussed, there was another woodcut showing four princes in armour and four Reformers before an outline of Nuremberg and an oil painting involving princes from the house of Brandenburg from 1556.[66] A more simplified version of the theme merely shows John Frederick and Luther kneeling to each side of the baptism depiction (ill. 180). The interpretation of this type of depiction is a matter of dispute. For Protestant commentators, they represent commemorative allegories of the origins of the Reformation.[67] The 1556 painting has been seen as an allegory of the religious peace of Augsburg. By emphasising baptism, the sacrament which was shared in common with Catholics, this is said to be an irenic gesture towards the idea of a wider Christian community.[68] This interpretation hardly seems to fit the various versions of the theme, especially its exclusive stress on the Saxon Reformation and Reformers. Moreover, the *cuius regio, eius religio* principle

180   *Luther and John Frederick as Witnesses of the Baptism of Christ*, Albertina

established in the Augsburg peace of 1555 is directly opposed to any such irenicism. The commemoration in these works of those princes who actively promoted Lutheranism as the sole faith in their territories seems to point in the opposite direction.

As has often been the case in the woodcuts we have examined, the baptism type fulfills several purposes at once. First, it is intended to make a theological point, to stress Christ as the chosen and only Saviour on whom men should rely. Here, it should be seen as an image complementing those of the crucified and the risen Christ, through which the evangelical movement sought to express its doctrinal content. Second, it commemorates the witnesses and confessors of the movement, although it is clearly conceived in a narrow Saxon perspective. It is close to the third purpose, which is devotional, to serve as an aid to prayer. This is shown by the inclusion of a prayer or hymn in some versions. Here it stood close to pre-Reformation devotional representation, the version featuring only Luther and John Frederick resembling in form a triptych altarpiece.[69] Finally, there is no doubt that it identifies a Church, an institution with ecclesiastical leaders and secular protectors. This tendency is clear in many earlier examples of pedagogic propaganda. Here the emphasis falls on a territorial Church, with both spiritual and secular heads.

One implication of such depictions placing historical figures in the framework of divine events is that the Reformation is on the way to producing its own hagiography, its own catalogue of saints, confessors and Church Fathers. The images of Luther which circulated from the beginning of the evangelical movement began the trend, and it was continued in those later works, such as illustration 167, which presented him as a divinely inspired prophet (see also ills. 165 and 174). Few other figures achieved this status, except Hus perhaps. However, the tendency to glorify the leaders of the Lutheran Church continued by placing them in divine situations, rather in the same fashion as patrons in pre-Reformation religious painting. Thus, a painting of the raising of Lazarus created as an epitaph for the Nordhausen Mayor Meienberg featured familiar figures of major Reformers (including Erasmus), a Last Supper in the castle church of Dessau included Reformers in the place of apostles, and a Last Supper depiction in the predella of an altar in Rheinsberg not only depicted Reformers as apostles, but gave them haloes as well.[70] With this kind of development, which takes place largely within the framework of church art, we pass out of the area of popular propaganda as it has been discussed in this book.

How successful was popular propaganda as a form of instruction? How far did it serve to identify a distinctive theological viewpoint for the Reformation? It certainly created a number of powerful images associated with the figure of Luther. Others were less distinctive — the emphasis on the crucified Christ was as much a part of Catholic visual representation, and could not be seen as any exclusively evangelical image. There was certainly the clear presentation of a distinctive Church, particularly in the portrayal of a territorial Church, seen in the group of depictions we have just examined. These were, however, more historical than theological in tone, and presupposed an existing allegiance to Lutheranism. The only widely successful theological depiction was the antithesis of the Law and the Gospel, attested to by the frequency of its use. That pedagogic propaganda produced so little that was positive, compared to the undeniable success of its anti-papal features, is significant for our overall assessment of visual propaganda. This will be the purpose of the last chapter.

8

THE RHETORIC OF THE IMAGE

The argument that has developed throughout this book has something of paradox about it. The Reformation was undeniably part of a movement from an image to a print culture, and was directed against popular culture and popular belief.[1] We have seen Reformation propaganda using, and thus accepting, popular culture; not breaking images but remaking them. The puzzle is even deeper: would not the advocates of the old order have attempted to marshal all the powerful emotive force attached to the images of the old belief in order to combat the new? Curiously, however, there was surprisingly little counter-propaganda from the side of orthodoxy. There seems to be little or no reason why the same weapons of popular propaganda could not be turned against the Reformation. Although there were a few attempts to do so, they rarely attained the creative brilliance of the evangelical propagandists.

Examples of anti-Lutheran broadsheets can be found from the very early days of the movement, perhaps as early as 1520 or 1521. One of these (ill. 181) depicts 'Luther's game of heresy', and seeks to associate Luther with vice and the Devil. It shows Luther brewing up a huge cooking-pot, assisted by three devils, while two others provide music for the scene. Luther is clad in his monastic habit, with a diabolical raven perched on his shoulder. From the pot arise the fumes of all kinds of vice — falsehood, unbelief, pride, envy, scandal, disobedience, contempt, haughtiness, lies, heresy, blasphemy, unchastity, fleshly freedom, disorder and disloyalty. Each of the figures depicted has been given a text. Luther's refers to what he ladles from the pot: 'I take out falsehood and deceit, I am ashamed of no evil.' The two devils supplying music express their glee at Luther's game, and the other devil who assists Luther at the pot states that he will mix gall and poison in the brew, for the simple man will not notice it. The four larger blocks of text serve as a commentary on the scene. As a simple man, the writer states, he could easily see what Luther was up to in 1520. Luther will produce only dissension, contempt of authority and bloodshed, a prophecy which the author hopes will prove false. In an attempt to capture the tone of popular prophecy, the author names himself the 'loyal Eckart', a prophetic figure from medieval epic who warns of impending disaster, and who in popular folklore warns of the coming of the wild horde.[2]

The sheet attempts to discredit Luther through several associations. First, he is linked to the Devil, perhaps the most distinct visual message. Next, he is

181   *Luther's Game of Hersey*

associated with vice, disunity and above all with social disturbance. Thirdly, popular prophecy and folklore were invoked to establish Luther as an ominous figure. Yet all these associations are carried largely by the printed text. Only the raven perched on Luther's shoulder might provide a visual link to the tradition of popular prophecy, alluding perhaps to the monk with the Devil on his shoulder, foretold in Lichtenberger's prophecy, who was to raise dissension in the Church. The text fails to exploit this feature, and the allusion to the figure of Eckart is left implicit. Nonetheless, this broadsheet appeared in a second edition, where Luther is now shown bearded, in plain allusion to his disguise as Junker George, adopted in the Wartburg in 1521. The raven has been replaced by a locust, but this second version is otherwise identical with the first. Some annotations have been added by a reader of the extant copy of this second edition. Luther is labelled with his name, the word 'devil' is written next to the locust, and the words 'pot of quarrels' on the cooking-pot.[3]

This broadsheet is typical of the limitations of the small quantity of anti-Lutheran visual propaganda that has survived. It relied heavily on the literacy of the reader and had an unimaginative visual message, usually associating Luther with the Devil. But even good ideas for propaganda were not fully exploited. A book illustration shows the 'statue of a heretic', with a figure atop a pedestal who is clearly intended to be Luther (ill. 182).[4] A winged demon blows into his ear with a bellows, thus showing him to be inspired by the Devil. Below are two devils about to drag him from his pedestal by means of a chain tied around his feet, so that he will fall into the flames of hellfire which lick around the pedestal base. This was a clever visual idea, neatly reminding those who idolised Luther that anyone set up on a pedestal could be toppled. It implied that he had been raised up by the Devil, and would be toppled by the Devil. The devil with the bellows might be seen as a reply to the motif of the dove by which Luther's divine inspiration was proclaimed by his followers. With all this potential, the illustration was completely wasted as popular propaganda. It appears as an illustration in a Latin work enumerating all the heretics since the beginnings of Christianity, and is tucked away on an inside page where it would hardly attract casual attention. Certainly, it was repeated on the last page of the work, but could not be expected to achieve its maximum effect from there.

A visual association between Luther and the Devil was used more successfully in the titlepage of a polemical work of 1535, accusing Luther of alliance with the Devil (ill. 183).[5] Luther wears his doctor's cap, and has his hand on the Bible, in imitation of the early depictions. He is clasping hands with a devil to his left, a sign of their concluded agreement. That this pact is sealed with Luther's hand on the Bible establishes its blasphemous nature.[6] The small demon whispering into Luther's ear signifies Luther's diabolical inspiration. The caption puns on the names Luther and Lucifer to show that both

have the same qualities. The rhymed text beneath the woodcut tells the reader
that no frivolity or joke is intended; the pamphlet tells the earnest truth,
attested by holy Scripture. This was an effective reply to similar works from
the evangelical side, at least by successfully linking Luther to the Devil and
citing Scripture as proof. Such examples of skilful popular presentation, however, are rare.

Another skilful work can be found in the titlepage of a pamphlet from
1529 by Johann Cochleus (ill. 184). Cochleus was one of Luther's most
voluble and able opponents, and has sense enough to issue this pamphlet in
German as well as Latin.[7] It exploits both the monster tradition and the
apocalyptic overtones of the seven-headed beast, confronting the reader with
'the seven-headed Luther'. As a visual image it is more precise than the evangelical use of the same theme, *The Seven-headed Papal Beast* (see ill. 75),
because it attempts to identify each of the seven heads as a different face of
Luther. Each head is labelled, although the labels do not always fit exactly
the head as depicted. Luther as doctor is represented by a head with a doctor's
cap, as Martin by the head of a monk, signifying St Martin, perhaps an ironic

Statua

hereti=
calis.

182   *Statua hereticalis*, Dahlem
183   Titlepage to P. Sylvius, *Luther und Lutzbers
eintrechtige vereinigung* (1535)

contrast with the true Catholic saint. The head labelled Luther is depicted as a Turk by a turban, therefore as an infidel. In the centre the label Ecclesiast reminds the reader that Luther was a priest, indeed one 'who preaches what the mob wishes to hear'. The fifth head represents him as a fanatic, hair standing wildly on end and surrounded by hornets. The sixth head is that of the Church Visitor, a new office reviving laws in the old fashion, as Cochleus puts it in the text, thus accusing Luther of setting himself up as a new pope. The last head is labelled Barabbas, the robber released by Pilate in place of Christ. However, the head depicted is that of a Wild Man, signified by his club. In parody of Luther iconography, the seven-headed figure wears a monk's habit and reads from a book, signifying that Luther has as many messages as he has heads.[8]

This illustration was effective propaganda, but by 1529 it was too little too late. The papacy had already been identified too successfully with the monstrous and with the beast of the Apocalypse by numerous works of evangelical propaganda. As a parody of Luther iconography, *The Seven-headed Luther* seems to be more a defensive reaction than an aggressive attack on Luther's heresy. It also failed to develop the apocalyptic overtones of the monster theme. Another variation of this image is found in the titlepage of a second work by Cochleus published in 1529, this time a two-headed Luther (ill. 185). The left head is labelled Palinodus, someone who sings a stock

184   *The Seven-headed Luther* (1529), BL
185   Titlepage to J. Cochleus, *Dialogus de bello contra Turcas, in Antilogias Lutheri* (1529), BL

refrain.[9] The right head is labelled as Luther, and is bearded in reminiscence of Luther as Junker George, but the addition of a club also makes it an allusion to the Wild Man. It is a titlepage to a Latin work, and with its limited layers of connotation demonstrates clearly the difference in polemical quality from evangelical propaganda.

The Wild Man allusion was one of the few popular cultural signs taken up by anti-Lutheran propaganda. There was also the occasional trick- or joke-depiction. In imitation of the cardinal–fool (see ill. 134), there was a Luther–fool, supplied with texts in German and Latin (ill. 186).[10] Another example, without text, resembled a trick postcard. Flaps could be turned over at both top and bottom in six steps to reveal a different figure. One began with a monk with a rosary, turned a flap to reveal a nun with a rosary, then a nun holding up her dress obscenely. The card was then reversed for the next sequence, showing with successive turns of the flaps a quack holding up a urine bottle, Luther holding the open Bible, and finally Luther holding up his habit obscenely.[11] Although clever and scurrilous, this had little clear polemical intent, and could be read as much as an attack on the Catholic clergy as on Luther. However it is typical of the tone of what often passed

186   *The Two-headed Luther–fool*, Worms Stadtbibliothek

for anti-Lutheran propaganda during the second half of the sixteenth and into the seventeenth century. It attacked Luther as immoral, a drunkard or degenerate. A good example is a broadsheet from the late sixteenth century (ill. 187), based on one of Hans Weiditz's grotesque depictions, *The Winesack*.[12] Luther is shown with a giant beer mug, his stomach so bloated that he must push it around in a wheelbarrow. On his back he carries a commode full of his followers, and in the barrow the books of his fellow heretics — Melanchthon, Zwingli, Oecolampadius and Calvin. Behind him trots Katherina von Bora, carrying on her back the Bible and a pannier. Clad as a nun, she bears their illegitimate child, *sola fide* or 'faith alone'.[13]

Perhaps the only extensive use of visual themes drawn from popular culture to be found in Catholic propaganda was made by Thomas Murner, in his *Great Lutheran Fool* of 1522.[14] This was written in verse, richly illustrated with woodcuts and reminiscent of a carnival play. It drew on all kinds of themes from popular culture and popular belief to satirise the followers of Luther. The chief follower is the Great Lutheran Fool, a giant fool who is stuffed with many lesser fools. They are in his head, his stomach, his ears, his boots and his wallet. In allusion to the old carnival custom of the *Narrenschneiden*, Murner seeks to extract all these fools, only here he uses exorcism. The work is rich in allusions to carnival, and Luther's followers are identified with the fool-puppets of carnival in both printed and visual text.

187   *Luther as Winesack*, Berlin

The development is purely comic, in the style of the carnival play. Murner exorcises the fools with nonsense formulae, lures them out by caterwauling and removes the fool Karsthans from the Great Fool's belly by means of a purge (ill. 188). Two others are crushed from the Great Fool in a winepress (ill. 189). Murner thus attempts to match the use of grotesque realism on the evangelical side, culminating at the end of his work where Luther is thrown down the privy (ill. 190).

One batch of fools who cannot wait to emerge from the body of the Great Fool are fifteen footsoldiers, a satire on the series of popular pamphlets by Eberlin von Günzburg, the *Fifteen Confederates*.[15] With a shrewd perception of contemporary social fears, Murner develops a long section in this part of his satire which attempts to associate Luther with the *Bundschuh*. Luther forms a league or *Bund*, the core of which is provided by the fifteen mercenaries. To these are added three riders, each bearing the *Bundschuh* on their shields. They elect Luther as their captain, who is then shown greasing a *Bundschuh* in expectation of a popular rebellion (ill. 191). Murner was here using a nicely calculated technique of guilt by association. Besides overtly identifying the evangelical movement with the symbol of peasant rebellion in

188   Illustration to T. Murner, *Von dem grossen Lutherischen Narren* (I. Grienninger, Strassburg, 1522), BL 11517.c.33, fol. Riii
189   *Von dem grossen Lutherischen Narren*, fol. Si

the generation before the Reformation, Murner also tried to identify Luther's supporters with the *Landsknechte*, men from the lowest level of society feared for their disorderliness and brutality. This charge was levelled most blatantly by depicting three haughty *Landsknechte* bearing banners emblazoned with the slogans of the evangelical movement, 'Gospel', 'Freedom' and 'Truth' (ills. 192–4).[16] In the written text supporters of the old Church attack this as a usurpation of the three slogans, while the visual text implies that the new Gospel and its freedom is that of the brigand.[17] However, Murner uses his knowledge of popular culture to go even beyond this. One *Landsknecht* newly returned from France, Brother Veit, decides not to join Luther's league. How can he swear by the saints if the Lutherans now regard them as useless? If the saints are turned out of the Church, to whom shall he turn in time of need?[18] Here Murner shows a shrewd propagandist sense. On the one hand, Luther's movement is rejected by someone from the lowest elements of society – his small and eccentric band is lower even than the *Landsknecht* Brother Veit. On the other, Murner appeals to the functionalist element in popular religion: if his saints be taken away from him, to whom shall the common man turn in distress?

Murner returns to the comic, carnivalesque theme in the last section of his

190   *Von dem grossen Lutherischen Narren*, fol. d3 v
191   *Von dem grossen Lutherischen Narren*, fol. T4 v

work. Luther and his band first attack a monastery, which is plundered, and then a castle defended by Murner in the form of a cat, the theriomorphic form through which Murner was attacked in evangelical propaganda.[19] The attackers are unable to capture the stronghold, but Murner strikes an agreement with Luther, whereby he will give up the castle in return for the hand of Luther's daughter. The Cat—Murner courts the daughter and marries her with great pomp, only to find on his wedding night that she has the pox. In good Lutheran fashion, Murner declares the wedding to be null and void. At the news of this affront to his family honour, Luther sickens and dies, without the benefit of the sacraments. To the accompaniment of caterwauling by Murner and a choir of 'cloister cats', he is interred in the privy, a carnivalesque consignment to hell. Finally, the Great Fool himself sickens and dies and Luther, inexplicably revived, contends with others for possession of his fool's cap.

Murner's work was undeniably a witty, satirical *tour de force*, but it is difficult to gauge its impact. In producing the book, the Strassburg printer of the first edition, Johann Grüninger, transgressed an earlier prohibition of scurrilous pamphlets. The Strassburg council ordered all stocks to be seized and burned, and copies already sold to be rounded up. A second edition

192   *Von dem grossen Lutherischen Narren*, fol. D4v
193   *Von dem grossen Lutherischen Narren*, fol. Pi v

appeared without place of publication, perhaps pieced together from parts of the confiscated edition, but it seems to have gained no wide circulation.[20] Murner had certainly tried to use themes and techniques similar to those found in evangelical propaganda. His knowledge of contemporary popular culture seems unrivalled, and he tried to blend this with a skilful use of wood-cut and rhyme. The work was perhaps too long – it runs to 4800 lines – and too untidy in structure to have been genuinely popular, even without the intervention of the Strassburg authorities. The *Great Lutheran Fool* nonetheless stands alone as the showpiece of Catholic counter-propaganda. In this regard it demonstrates the futility of the Catholic response – it was too meagre and too limited to have any large-scale or long-term impact.

The weight of propaganda, then, was overwhelmingly on the side of the Reformation. Was this just because the producers of propaganda sniffed the way the wind was blowing and shrewdly followed the popular trend? Or did they make the trend, as we have tacitly assumed throughout the discussion so far, by swinging popular opinion behind the new belief in and through their works? We have spoken throughout as though the propagandists stood outside the propaganda process. The artists and publishers responsible for broadsheet propaganda were not just seeking to manipulate public opinion, but also expressing their fervent conviction of the correctness of evangelical

194   *Von dem grossen Lutherischen Narren*, fol. P2 v

belief. This is indicated by the fact that most operated from the major centres of the Reformation in Germany — Wittenberg, Nuremberg, Strassburg, Augsburg and Magdeburg.

The most prolific source of propaganda was the Cranach school, operating from Wittenberg or Weimar. Lucas Cranach the Elder worked closely with Luther in the production of numerous works, often following Luther's instructions as to their content. His evangelical fervour and that of his son, Lucas the Younger, is undoubted and the two created a school of Reformation propaganda which extended over half a century.[21] Other artists associated with the Cranachs who produced works examined in this book were Melchior Sachs, Hans Brosamer, Jacob Lucius and the Masters IR, BP, H and AF. The Cranach school was the origin of a Lutheran orthodoxy in its pedagogic propaganda, creating a picture of an Established Church under the aegis of the territorial prince, as well as being largely responsible for the iconographic idealisation of Luther which presented him as the German prophet. There is no question that this school set out to force public opinion along the road to religious reform, in much the same way as Wittenberg itself became the inspirational centre of the new movement.

The same kind of commitment is evident in the work of the propagandists active in Nuremberg, a city with the closest ties to Wittenberg. Active in the first generation, during the 1520s and 1530s, were the brothers Hans Sebald Behem and Barthold Behem, Georg Pencz, Erhard Schoen and Peter Fletner. From the 1540s onwards there were the publishers Hans Glaser and Stefan Hamer, and artists such as Peter Gottland, Melchior Lorch, Hans Weigel, Virgil Solis and Hans Adam. Spanning both of these 'generations', with his prolific literary output, was Hans Sachs, who supplied the verses for so many broadsheets discussed above.[22] At a superficial glance it might be said that Wittenberg supplied the doctrinal inspiration for evangelical propaganda, while Nuremberg supplied popular culture and carnival. As we have seen in a work such as the *Depiction of the Papacy*, a wholly characteristic product of Wittenberg, the traditions of popular culture and popular belief were a no less integral part of the Saxon school. There is, however, a grain of sociological truth in the observation. Nuremberg artists stood closer to the common man than the court artists of the Cranach school, with its factory-like production and princely commissions.[23] The Nuremberg artists lived closer to the bread-line, and more independently of the city magistrates. They were more socially aware, more inclined to follow their own inclinations, less susceptible to any evangelical orthodoxy. They often operated against the disapproval, or at least under the critical scrutiny, of the magistrates. Many found themselves in trouble with the authorities because of over-vigorous propaganda, and in some cases, most notably with Pencz and the brothers Behem, such dissent could become almost revolutionary.[24] For these men, propaganda seems to have been an expression of their desire to convert others to their own kind of

commitment at any cost. They spoke to them from a common cultural background, drawing on and adapting creatively the traditions in which they had
been trained as artists.

Other centres stood far behind these two in their production of propaganda. Strassburg owes its reputation for visual propaganda predominantly to
the work of Hans Baldung Grien, although Hans Weiditz and Hieronymus
Resch were also active there during the first two decades of the Reformation.
From the late 1560s Tobias Stimmer revived this earlier tradition. Augsburg
also stood well behind Nuremberg, with Leonhard Beck, Hans Weiditz and
the Master HS. Magdeburg came to the fore during the age of the Interim,
with Pangratius Kempff responsible for many of the items traceable there.[25]
The Magdeburg contribution epitomises the intentions of popular propaganda — it was part of an active struggle for the Gospel, an attempt to influence the course of events by visual polemic.

There is, however, an important difference between what we have called
the two 'generations'. During the 1520s and 1530s the propagandists were
working out symbols of attachment to the Gospel and of aversion to the
papacy, and techniques of conveying these to their readers. By the 1540s
many of these were established as part of the visual vernacular, part of the
tradition presupposed by younger artists. Two figures who epitomise this
younger generation are Melchior Lorch and Mathias Gerung. Both were
artists of great skill and fiery evangelical fervour, who grew up with an inbred
hatred of the papacy.[26] They had seen it as nothing other than brutally and
remorselessly antichristian, and they took as their starting-point the visual
signs of the papal Antichrist. For this reason, perhaps, they were able to go
further than their elders and produce works of remarkable savagery, such as
The Pope as Wild Man, or Gerung's fierce allegories equating the pope with
the Turk. In their own works they attest the success of visual propaganda for
the Reformation in forming a new generation of adherents. The propagandists
set in motion the process of winning support for the Gospel, but they were
themselves part of that process.

In the last half a dozen chapters we have been analysing this propaganda
process. It can now be summed up in its totality as follows: At the beginning
there was an attempt to identify Luther as a holy man, and his cause as a holy
cause. In particular, he was to be identified with the furtherance of true
Christianity, and his opponents with its antithesis. To delineate more clearly
the choice between the new beliefs and the old, there was an attempt to construct a new language and new symbols of attachment to evangelical ideals.
These were not created *ex vacuo*, but through adapting language and emotive
signs deeply embedded in the culture and belief of those brought up in the
old faith. Some of these were derived from the movement's very source of
inspiration, Scripture itself. Others were part of a penumbra of popular ideas
about which the advocates of religious revival themselves had very ambivalent

feelings, deeply rooted popular beliefs and apprehensions aroused by the eschatological mood of the age. This ambivalence was in part resolved by attempting to educate their supporters in the characteristic doctrines of the movement, and by attempting to impart a sense of institutional solidarity. This stage of the process is akin to the routinisation of charisma, identifying the movement as a Church, with its own traditions, leaders and heritage.

If we can regard this as an adequate description of the development of popular propaganda for the Reformation, how are we to assess it as a process? How does it work, and how does it exercise its effect? To explore this further we could start with the most observable feature of the works we have described, the presentation of a simple black-and-white contrast between the opposing views. This depends on reducing the complex issues involved in the Reformation to a number of discrete and easily identifiable symbols. This is a process of simplification, but it is also a process of reification, embodying abstract theological issues in concrete form.[27] In particular, the contrast between the old and new belief is embodied in persons, in the contrast between Luther and the pope, between Christ and the pope, between the preacher and the monk or priest, between two kinds of worshipping communities. The use of visual symbols encourages and assists this process. The diabolical nature of the papacy, its metaphysical status as the Antichrist are concretised in visual depiction, as is the divinely sanctioned character of the evangelical movement. The reification thus occurs at both poles of opinion; both that which is approved and that which is disapproved are presented in terms of visual stereotypes. These stereotypes are structurally linked. The demonisation of the opponents of evangelical belief is accompanied by the sanctification of its advocates.[28] Thus, for propaganda purposes, the images of the true and the false Church are inseparable. If Luther and the patrons of the Reformation are invested with charismatic authority, the pope and his supporters are supplied with anti-charisma. This structural relationship is found, as we have seen in chapter 3, in the construction of individual works, but it also runs as a *Leitmotiv* throughout the entire body of evangelical propaganda. It explains why the image of the Antichrist-pope is accompanied by the image of Luther, the saint and prophet, or, more precisely, the exemplary Christian: the one was incomplete without the other.

The structural character of propaganda points also to one of its primary qualities, namely, that it is ideological in nature. By this is meant that it provides an explanation of the world and its condition.[29] This occurs in two ways. Either a particular issue or situation is shown to have universal significance, or a mundane matter is shown to be of transcendent import. The first is exemplified in the struggle against the Interim, shown to be part of the total struggle against the Antichrist. The second is seen in the confrontations between Luther and the ecclesiastical hierarchy (see ill. 20 or ill. 22), which are shown to have eschatological significance. At another level, social grievance is incorporated into the struggles of the evangelical movement, by claiming that the solution to social oppression is theological, that it occurs on a metaphysical plane (see ills. 22, 93).

Here, propaganda is involved in the creation or perpetuation of myth, most noticeable in the attempt to assimilate the struggle against the old belief to the myth of the Antichrist and its eschatological themes.[30] More remarkably, it creates new myths, sacred narratives about origins and transformations.[31] This is evident in the accounts given in various works about the origins of the papacy or the monks (see ills. 63–5), or in the exposure of the papacy as diabolical. This myth-making process is also contained in, indeed, as we have argued above, it is structurally linked to, the accounts of the origins of the Reformation itself. *The Triumph of Truth* (see ill. 46), or the various works linking Luther and Hus have this character. As in myth, the historical status of the narrative is less important than its symbolic truth, seen in the depiction of Luther kindling the fire of faith before the pope and his cardinals (see ill. 14).[32] Propaganda as myth is thus a form of symbolic communication − it creates a structure of meanings in which individuals can relate to one another and through which they seem to realise their ultimate purpose. As we have shown in the realms both of popular culture and of popular belief, this structure of meanings is created by taking over the experience of the past and supplying it with a new context. This both integrates the past with the present and provides an overarching explanation of present events.[33] This explanation is total, both because of its all-embracing scope and because it claims universal validity.

How is this new structure of meaning created? We have argued that evangelical propaganda depends on codes drawn from common experience. Using these codes, it takes over existing signs but shows different ways of decoding them. In the process, however, these signs come to have quite different meanings. There are two important transformations or shifts of coding in the signs used by evangelical propaganda. One is the transformation of connotation into denotation, that is, the secondary or implied significations of a term become its primary significations, and describe it exhaustively.[34] For example, monks no longer denote a class of religious persons, who may have connotations of irreligious or immoral life, as in *The Abbot on the Ice* (see ill. 26). They are now essentially an irreligious group, indeed, in *The Origins of the Monks* (see ill. 63) an anti-religious group.

A second kind of transformation is that from simple signification to a second-order system of signs, to metalanguage. This means that the signs of one system are used as the signifiers in another.[35] Thus the signs involved in the image of Luther as holy man are assumed as signifiers in the system which presents the opposition of true and false belief. To read the message of a woodcut like ill. 167, where Luther indicates the Lutheran sacraments and the fate of the papacy, one must assume a number of sign systems, all supplying signifiers for this particular assembly of signs. Both of these trans-formations involve a process of adaptation. In the first, more elaborate codes are narrowed by restricting the range of signification; in the second, a simple code has become more complex by acquiring a new plane of expression.[36]

The process of adaptation was by no means a simple procedure, however, because of the multivocality of many of the symbols used in visual propa-ganda. A visual sign could be invested with several simultaneous meanings, so that there was always a possibility of an ambiguous reading of its message.[37] We have seen numerous examples where this was the case. Although some possible meanings were automatically excluded by the new codes established in visual propaganda, there still remained a wide area in which a message could be decoded in ways other than those intended by the propagandists. To this extent visual propaganda alone was ill-suited to establish any new ortho-doxy, or to convey doctrines. The ambiguity inherent in the visual image could, of course, be resolved by the use of image plus text, with the latter supplying an unambiguous reading. The text can be seen as fulfilling two functions, anchorage and relay.[38] In anchorage, the linguistic text directs the reader in how to read the visual image, steering him towards the message intended by the propagandist. In relay, linguistic text and visual image stand in a complementary relationship, both forming an integral part of the overall assembly. The words are fragments of the total message, which is realised at the level of the 'story' told by the particular work. An example of this kind of combination can be seen on the various sheets of the *Depiction of the Papacy*.

All of this adds up to the creation of a 'rhetoric of the image', a structured system for conveying the intended meaning of visual propaganda.[39] The tech-nicalities of the semiological process are less important than the cultural phenomenon involved. The creators of evangelical propaganda, functioning as mediators of the new ideas, draw on different kinds of shared cultural experi-ence described in some detail in the chapters above. They take for granted as part of this experience a number of lexicons of visual signs from which they construct their means of persuasion.[40] It is this rhetorical power which is described in Luther's praise of the use of images in anti-papal polemic, that 'the common man is now so broadly informed and advanced in understanding that the clergy are worthless, as has been shown all too well in numerous songs, sayings and satires which one depicts on all kinds of sheets, and even through monks and priests on playing cards, that one is nauseous whenever one sees or hears a cleric'.[41] He was no less enthusiastic about its power of instruction, 'above all for the sake of children and the simple folk, who are more easily moved by pictures and images to recall divine history than through mere words or doctrines'.[42]

The aim of popular propaganda was 'to instruct the common man', and we must now consider the last and most important theme in this chapter, how

the common man was by this means to be won to the Gospel. We might use-
fully consider several models of how this might have occurred. Perhaps the
model most entertained by historians, whether explicitly or implicitly, has
been that of the individual conversion, a qualitatively different awareness of
religious experience found to be personally liberating.[43] This model we might
label 'the tower experience', after Luther's description of his own conversion
or discovery of Pauline justification. There are certainly numerous testi-
monies from the Reformation period that this was common enough among
those inspired by revived evangelical fervour. Whether we can assume that it
was the most common way in which support was won for the evangelical
movement among the broad masses cannot be considered here in any detail.
Considered from the viewpoint of popular propaganda, it does not seem to be
the kind of experience evoked or stimulated by the works under discussion.
Rather, they often presuppose some kind of conversion to have already
occurred or seek to make the reader more susceptible to such an experience.
This seems to be how Luther understood the role of visual representation. It
served as a reminder of the content of Scripture, and to facilitate its exposition
to the common man, but the real work of conversion, in Luther's view, was
carried out by preaching, reading and reading aloud the Bible.[44]

If we can state categorically that popular propaganda itself does not pro-
voke any 'tower experience', we must nonetheless consider the kinds of
susceptibility it might arouse in readers which might lead in this direction. An
observable feature of propaganda is that it simultaneously creates and eases
tensions.[45] It creates them by its function of evoking polarised stereotypes
and by channelling fears and apprehensions against distinct persons and
objects. It eases them by identifying the causes of apprehension and providing
a comprehensive ideological explanation and solution. This is best exemplified
through the myth of the Antichrist, where the anxiety associated with this
figure was alleviated by locating it in the papacy. At the same time the struggle
against the Antichrist became the more intense by being directed largely
against the papacy, and this in turn intensified the antipapal struggle.[46] A
similar phenomenon can be seen in Lutheran attitudes towards the Devil —
the area of demonic activity is narrowed and made more personalised, but for
all that is the more intense.[47] Psychologically this is close to the conversion
experience, with its easing of spiritual tensions but intensification of commitment, at the same time liberating and exacting. Here, popular propaganda
could be seen as preparing its readers for the experience of conversion, providing the shock of revelation about the old religion, and arousing hostility
towards it in the subsequent disillusionment of the disenchanted believer.

This provides a second model, closely linked to the question of images,
and which might be labelled the 'exorcism' model. Exorcism operates by
identifying and naming the demonic powers in possession of a person or
object, challenging them to manifest themselves, and bidding them to depart,

all through more or less established ritual formulae.[48] The same kind of process was involved in iconoclasm and the desacralisation of images. The numinous or magical power inherent in images was named and dispelled, either by breaking the image or by profaning it, the process labelled in an earlier chapter 'ritual desacralisation'. This depended both on fear of the image and on release from this fear. Thereafter the image was exorcised, a matter of indifference. This is attested to by Luther, who spoke of the fear struck in his heart by the image of Christ as an angry judge, but for whom images were subsequently religiously neutral.[49] For Luther such images were 'exorcised' by his own conversion experience, but he perceived that for iconoclasts the exorcism was achieved in and through their attack on the images, something he regarded as no less superstitious.[50] In the same way, however, the papacy and the old belief were exorcised in and through popular propaganda, through means described in the chapters above. The exorcism, however, was closer to that of the iconoclasts than to that of Luther, for it led not to indifference, but to aversion and disgust.[51]

The third model follows from this, that of 'negative assimilation' to the new movement.[52] In this model, the common man is convinced of the rightness of the evangelical cause by its opposition to and exposure of religious abuses. This is the effect of the anticlerical and antipapal thrust of so much of the popular propaganda, which we examined in some detail in chapter 3. The papacy and the papal clergy are exposed as the opponents of true religion, but they also oppose Luther, Luther's cause and the evangelical movement. The conclusion to be drawn was unavoidable – all who care about true religion must support the new movement. Nonetheless, this still evoked a more negative kind of allegiance. It relied on exploiting pre-Reformation anticlericalism, with its elements of social grievance and popular scepticism of institutionalised religion. There is considerable evidence that this kind of negative assimilation was involved in much of the popular appeal of the new movement.

A fourth model could be labelled 'ideological assimilation'.[53] In this model, propaganda claims allegiance from its readers through the ideological coherence it provides. Either it shows that disparate events or issues have universal purpose and meaning, which can be discovered only through the evangelical movement, or else it seeks to show that universal events are embodied in the movement and its cause. As example of the first is the way in which social grievance is shown as having spiritual roots and that it can only be alleviated by recourse to the Gospel. This is essentially the message of *The Poor Common Ass* (see ill. 93). The second is seen in the identification of the evangelical movement as part of the decisive and cosmic struggle against the Antichrist. In particular, in its exploitation of the theme of the world turned upside-down, it sought to concentrate in the movement the stream of eschatological feeling and chiliasm of the later middle ages. Osiander's use of the

Wondrous Prophecy of the Papacy is the best evidence of this kind of appeal.

A fifth model is that of 'cultural assimilation', where the propaganda seeks to align the Reformation with a particular kind of cultural allegiance, and so to trigger off a deeply rooted cultural response.[54] The prime example of this tendency is the appeal to the 'common man', identifying the common man with the evangelical Christian, most specifically in the shape of the evangelical peasant.[55] Here, a noticeable change occurs in the cultural appeal of evangelical propaganda, as it changes its stress on the role of the evangelical peasant to one on the role of the evangelical burgher, seen clearly in the social characterisation of the believing community in several works by the Cranachs (see ills. 165, 167).[56] More generally, propaganda use of the notion of community itself demonstrates the nature of cultural assimilation. The classic argument of Bernd Moeller explained the appeal of the Reformation in the German imperial cities along such lines.[57] By emphasising the mutual dependence of all members of the community on one another for salvation, and the notion of the Church as embodied *par excellence* in the civic community, the Reformation found an affinity with a whole outlook and way of life with which it could be shown to be more in harmony than the old religion. This emphasis is also found on a broader front in the propaganda we have examined. The concept of the Church as largely the clergy and the ecclesiastical hierarchy is rejected as false. Instead, an appeal is made to the experience of community, the basic functional unit of sixteenth-century society. This was perhaps the experience with the deepest cultural resonances for men of the age, and it was here that propaganda directed its most potent appeal. In place of the papal Church, the Church of the clergy, it set the image of the small believing community, an actively devout body gathered around its preacher.

The last model for consideration can be called 'incitement to action'. According to Jacques Ellul, this is the major aim of all propaganda – not just to change opinions, but to move people to action.[58] It can even be suggested that it was, in many cases, incitement to action which preceded change of opinion.[59] Once committed through action to some positive stance, the way is open to wider assimilation of the views propounded by the propaganda. Incitement to action occurs in popular propaganda in numerous ways, both direct and indirect. Most directly, there is the depiction of positive action in support of the Gospel, whether in the figure of the evangelical peasant wielding his flail against its opponents (see ill. 76), or that of the common man rebuking the clergy (see ill. 30), or even in the advocacy of an anticlerical war. More indirectly, it incites to imitation in the demeanment and humiliation of the clergy and the papacy. The link between propaganda and incitement to action was held by civic authorities to be self-evident, and they regarded 'scandalous pictures' as a cause of disturbance.[60]

It would be misleading, of course, to speak as though propaganda concentrated only on winning new recruits to its cause. It served also to arouse fervour and sustain morale among the converted, and to undermine that of the enemy. These models, however, are no less applicable to such uses, and could be exemplified in the Reformation propaganda of the 1540s onwards, which was less a matter of establishing an evangelical movement, and more of consolidating it. More importantly, we must bear in mind that they are only ideal types, and that one or several may have been involved in any single case. The most significant was 'incitement to action', for a change of opinion without some positive action accompanying it was of dubious value in furthering the Reformation in any of its stages.

This raises the question of effectiveness. As we stated at the outset, the most reliable test of this is to be found in behaviour, in how far people put into practice the lessons learned from their propaganda reading. A proper study of this subject would require use of a wider range of sources outside the propaganda examined here. It would be similar in kind, perhaps, to that by Gerald Strauss on the effectiveness of Lutheran educational ideals in 'indoctrinating the young'.[61] Internal to propaganda, we can find some limited indications of effectiveness. These show that effectiveness is a complex matter, and by no means a simple question of a one-way working on an audience. We can see this clearly if we distinguish between three 'moments' of effectiveness, characterised by their orientation towards the past, the present and the future.

First, we have seen that Reformation propaganda was highly successful in exploiting the heritage of the past, in using numerous traditional images from popular culture and popular belief. Second, it was remarkably 'present-oriented' in catching the mood of its time. In many areas, it echoed shrewdly the common opinion about social grievance, concern with injustice, anti-clericalism, lay desires to control one's own salvation and the demand for a more spiritual, less sacerdotal Church. Here it was effective in focussing and sharpening perceptions and in inciting to action. We have found this attested also from outside the propaganda by those occasions on which propaganda imagery was matched by historical events. Third, it built for the future by creating not only single images, but also a visual vernacular which became the cultural heritage of later generations. This was both a positive and a negative achievement, typified by the images of Luther the German prophet and of the Antichrist-pope.

As far as we can tell from the present study, Reformation popular propaganda did not measure up to its own ideals of effectiveness. Its total impact was constrained by this triangle of forces. It did not produce the powerful new symbols of allegiance which might have created a new 'symbolic universe' distinctly different from that of the old faith. Its 'symbolic universe', rather, was a combination of the three moments of past, present and future, in which the future-oriented, creative impulses were limited by the other two. For example, the image of Luther the German prophet created a tradition of 'Luther myth' which extended into the nineteenth century, but this tradition was no more than a refurbished, Protestant version of the traditional saint's life.[62] An example of the orientation towards the present was the propaganda emphasis on eschatology and the *verkehrte Welt*, which gave it immediacy and relevance at a time of social and spiritual crisis. Yet it was an emphasis which could not be sustained without running the risk of trivialising the theme and of distracting from the task of dealing with the mundane demands of less elevated problems. Perhaps the absence of good pedagogic propaganda is not unconnected with this feature: Reformation propaganda was too preoccupied with proclaiming the end of the world to show men how to live pious lives within it.

Another way to view the question would perhaps be to consider that popular propaganda was too much a product of popular mentalities to be able to transcend them. Relevant here is the criticism of Lutheranism made by more radical varieties of Reformation, which saw it making too many compromises with the old, 'superstitious' religion. Significantly, there is little of the popular propaganda surveyed here that came from the Zwinglian or radical traditions. Clearly, this was because of the hostility of these traditions to images, compared with the qualified acceptance of them in the Lutheran tradition. This alone probably ensured that the visual propaganda of the first half-century of the Reformation would be overwhelmingly Lutheran. The Zwinglian–radical critique of Lutheran compromises with superstition was an accurate enough assessment, for Lutheranism did make a qualified acceptance of popular culture, with all of its visual elements, which in turn put a characteristic stamp on its popular propaganda. It is this stamping of Lutheran propaganda with popular culture that makes it such a good source for the study of popular mentalities. This leads us to even broader questions about the success or failure of the Reformation itself. As Gerald Strauss has pointed out, the Reformation, despite its undoubted achievements, failed signally to create a new kind of devout Christian among the popular masses.[63] One could not argue that this failure was the failure of its popular propaganda; rather the popular propaganda is symptomatic of the wider failure. Thus, questions about the effectiveness of popular propaganda along these lines lead to wider questions about the nature of the Reformation itself.

Finally, we hope that this study has established the value to the historian of visual evidence. There are many other studies to be pursued in the field: Reformation popular propaganda in France and the Netherlands, that of the Counter-Reformation, the depiction of social conflict in visual evidence, what visual evidence can tell us about early modern rural and urban culture to name but a few. We may conclude with a reflection on the appropriateness of the methodology used in this book to investigate visual propaganda. As we hope to have shown, the sixteenth century was highly sensitised to signs, systems of signs and the many ways of reading them. Well before modern linguists invented the discipline, they were practising a basic semiology. The reasons for this were given by Luther himself, who realised that the visual image was one of the most powerful means of communication of his day. It is impossible, he wrote, for men not to make images of things, and it is therefore a human tendency to conceive of all things in signs, for 'without images we can neither think nor understand anything'.[64] Here he called attention to a first principle of the study of popular mentalities; in this book we have but followed his sound advice.

Appendix

DEPICTIONS OF LUTHER IN THE 1520s

The following catalogue lists the various printed depictions of Luther traceable for the 1520s, with all variations and modifications, and the different editions in which they appeared, including engravings and single-sheet woodcuts. It is more comprehensive than the excellent listing of Ficker 1934 in showing printers and editions wherever possible, and in analysing the frequency of use of different types of depiction. It has been compiled from Ficker 1920, 1924 and 1934; Hagelstange 1907; Schottenloher 1912; Stuhlfauth 1921b; Zimmermann 1927; and from my own research undertaken for this book. It is unlikely that it is exhaustive, since this will only be possible with a complete bibliography of all German printed works of the 1520s, soon to be published by the Special Research Programme of the University of Tübingen.

This catalogue has been organised as follows: all single portraits are listed first, subdivided into those depicting Luther as a monk with tonsure (nos. 1–21), and those showing him in a doctor's cap (nos. 22–6). The next small group are those where he appears in decorative borders on titlepages (nos. 27–9). The third category covers all other depictions where Luther appears with other figures, first those in which he is the main actor in the scene (nos. 30–43), then those where he is a secondary figure (nos. 44–8). Finally, there is a small group of Luther as knight (*Junker Jörg*), commemorating his period in the Wartburg in 1521 (nos. 49–52).

Significantly different versions of a single depiction have been given a separate number, while minor variations are catalogued as sub-divisions within a number. Tables 1 and 2 provide analyses by type and publisher. Bibliography and locations are provided wherever possible.

1a Luther as monk with large tonsure, facing r., Latin inscr. (1520). Engraving by Cranach. *Bibl.* Ficker 1934: no. 6. *Locn.* Dahlem, GNM K 868

1b Trial copy of 1a. Engraving (1520). *Bibl.* Ficker 1934; no. 5.

2   Luther as monk before niche, facing r., l. hand on breast, book visible, Latin inscr. Engraving by Hans Cranach (?) (1520). *Bibl.* Ficker 1934: no. 7. *Locn.* Munich Graph. Samml.

3   Copy of no. 2, facing r., no inscr., finger on book. Woodcut (1520). *Bibl.* Ficker 1934: no. 10.

   i   *Von der Babilonischen gefengknuss der Kirchen* (J. Nadler, Ausburg, 1520). *Bibl.* Dommer 1888: 213, no. 2B; WA vol. 6, 491d.

   ii Luther, *Grund und Ursach aller Artikel* (J. Nadler, Augsburg, 1520). *Locn.* BL 3905.ee.64, STC 542.

4a Copy of no. 2, facing l., no. inscr., finger on book. Woodcut (1520?)

   i   *Von der Babylonischen gefengknuss der Kirchen* [J. Schott, Strassburg, 1520] . *Bibl.* Dommer 1888: no. 170; WA vol. 6, 490a. *Locn.* GNM R1 1960.

   ii Another edition, slightly different. *Bibl.* WA vol. 6, 491c.

   iii *Hel. Eobani Hessi in Martini Lutheri laudem defensionem Elegias* (J. Preuss, Strassburg, 1521). *Bibl.* Ficker 1934: no. 8; Dommer 1888: 213, no. 2?

4b The same as no. 4a, but with four-line Latin inscr. Woodcut.

   i   *De captivitate Babylonica ecclesiae* [J. Schott, Strassburg, 1520] . *Bibl.* Ficker 1934: no. 9; WA vol. 6, 489c. *Locn.* BL 697.h.21, STC 549.

   ii   *De captivitate Babylonica Ecclesiae* [Augsburg, 1520?]. *Bibl.* WA vol. 6, 489D. *Locn.* BL 3906.dd.6(6), STC 549.

5   Copy of no. 2, facing l., but no finger on book. Coloured woodcut (1521), issued by J. Preuss, Strassburg? *Bibl.* Ficker 1934: no. 11.

6   Copy of no. 2, facing l., but no finger on book, four-line Latin inscr. Woodcut.
   i   *De captivitate Babylonica ecclesiae* [A. Petri, Basel, 1520?]. *Bibl.* Ficker 1934: no. 13; WA vol. 6, 489E. *Locn.* BL 3905.ee.133, STC 549.
   ii   Luther and Hutten as *Christianae libertatis propugnatores* (A. Petri, Basel, 1521). *Bibl.* Ficker 1934: no. 14.
   iii   With portrait of Hutten, issued by A. Cratander, Basel (1521). *Bibl.* Ficker 1934: no. 12.

7a   Luther as monk before niche, facing l., book open with three lines visible, but hands not visible. Woodcut, dated in top r. corner (1520).
   i   *Von der Babylonischen gefengknuss* (S. Otmar, Augsburg). *Bibl.* Ficker 1934: no. 16; WA vol. 6, 491d.
   ii   *Passio oder das leiden unsers herren Jhesu Christi: gepredigt durch Doctor Martini Luther* [S. Otmar, Augsburg], (1522). *Bibl.* Dommer 1888: no. 282; WA vol. 10/iii, xx.
   iii   *Funf schöner Christlicher Sermon gepredigt durch Doctor Martini Luther zu Wittenberg* [S. Otmar, Augsburg], (1523). *Bibl.* Dommer 1888: no. 404.
   iv   *Ein sermon von dem weltlichen recht unnd Schwerdt: durch Doctor Martini Luther zu Wittenberg* [H. Hergot, Nuremberg]. *Bibl.* Hagelstange 1907: 104.
   v   A variant of the above, without further information on place or printer. *Bibl.* Ficker 1934: no. 18.
   vi   Another variant, a later edition, with year date top r. corner damaged. *Bibl.* Ficker 1934: no. 17.

7b   The same as no. 7a, with inscr. at bottom of portrait and twelve-line German text, issued with portrait of Hutten by Otmar, Augsburg (1520). Woodcut. *Bibl.* Ficker 1934: no. 15.

8   The same as no. 7a, with a block added with dove above Luther, Latin inscr. Coloured woodcut (1520). *Bibl.* Ficker 1934: no. 65. *Locn.* BM 1903-4-8-21.

9a   Luther as monk in niche with decorated pillars, facing l., both hands holding half-open book. Dated on l. and r. pillars 15 – 20. Latin inscr. with date 1521. Woodcut.
   i   *Doctor Martini Luthers offentliche verhör zu Worms* (S. Grimm, Augsburg, 1521). *Bibl.* Ficker 1934: no. 20; Hagelstange 1907: 103.
   ii   *Doctor Martini Luthers antwort auf Pfintztag, den 18. tag Aprilis im 1521* (S. Grimm, Augsburg, 1521). *Bibl.* Ficker 1934: no. 19; Hagelstange 1907: 102.
   iii   Luther, *Von dem Eelichen Leben* (S. Grimm, Augsburg, 1523), fol. Div. *Bibl.* Hagelstange 1907: 104; WA vol. 10/ii, 270.
   iv   Luther, *Sermon von unrechten Mammon* (S. Grimm, Augsburg, 1522). *Bibl.* Schottenloher 1912: 222. *Locn.* BL 3905.d.39, STC 566.
   v   Another variant, without further details of place or printer. *Bibl.* Ficker 1934: no. 21.

9b   The same as no. 9a, without text. Woodcut.
   i   *Doctor Mar. Luthers Passio durch Marcellum beschrieben* (S. Grimm, Augsburg, 1521). *Bibl.* Hagelstange 1907: 103; Ficker 1934: no. 22.
   ii   Another variant, under the portrait in large letters *D. Marth Luth.*, without further information on place or printer. *Bibl.* Ficker 1934: no. 23.

10 Luther as monk in niche with pillars, facing l., r. index finger points to half-open book, finger of other hand on book, seven-line German inscr., *Ich bin der Luther* . . . Woodcut (1520). *Bibl.* Ficker 1934: no. 24.

11a Luther as monk, facing l., without niche, r. hand on breast, half-open book. Woodcut. Used for *On Applas von Rom kan man wol selig werden* [M. Ramminger, Augsburg, 1520]. *Locn.* BL C37.e.49, STC 756.

11b The same as no. 11a, with white space left top r. (for dove?). (1520), Nuremberg? *Bibl.* Ficker 1934: no. 27.

12a Copy of no. 11a, by Hans Baldung Grien, with dove of Holy Spirit and large nimbus around Luther's head. *Bibl.* Ficker 1934: no. 67.

    i   *Handlung so mit doctor Martin Luther auf dem Reichstag zu Worms ergangen ist* (J. Schott, Strassburg 1521). *Bibl.* Dommer 1888: 117, no. 225.

    ii   *Acta et res gestae D. Martini Lutheri in Comitiis Principum Vuormaciae* (J. Schott, Strassburg, 1521). *Bibl.* Dommer 1888: 121, no. 231.

    iii   Luther, *Von der Beycht* (J. Preuss, Strassburg, 1522). *Bibl.* Dommer 1888: 135, no. 258; WA vol. 8, 135L.

    iv   Luther, *XIII Predig* (J. Schott, Strassburg, 1523). *Bibl.* Dommer 1888; 208, no. 402; WA vol. 10/iii, xviii.

    v   Luther, *XVII Predig* (J. Schott, Strassburg, 1523). *Bibl.* Dommer 1888; 209; WA vol. 10/iii, xvii.

    vi   Luther, *Postille* (1521). *Bibl.* Schottenloher 1912: 224, note 1.

    vii   Luther, *22 Predigten. Bibl.* as for vi above.

    viii Luther, *Antwort auf das überchristlich Buch Bock Emsers. Bibl.* WA vol. 7, 617B.

    ix   M. Stiefel, *Von der Christformigen Lehre Luthers* (J. Schott, Strassburg, 1522). *Bibl.* as for vi above.

12b The same as no. 12a, with *Biblia* along top of book. Single-sheet woodcut. *Bibl.* Hagelstange 1907: 106.

13 Luther as monk, facing l., r. hand on breast, l. hand leafing in open book. Above him a dove, with large nimbus. Engraving. J. Hopfer, Augsburg (*c.* 1520–3). *Bibl.* Bartsch 1866: vol. 8, 522, no. 64. *Locn.* GNM K 763.

14 Tondo with Luther as monk, facing l., r. hand on breast, l. hand leafing in book, above him a dove, Latin inscr. in circular frame: *Martinus Luther Evangelicae Doctor.* Woodcut, attributed to Erhard Schoen. *Bibl.* Ficker 1934: no. 68; Röttinger 1925: no. 93.

15 Tondo set in richly decorated square, Luther as monk, facing l., head and shoulders. Woodcut. *Bibl.* Ficker 1934: no. 28. *Locn.* Dahlem.

16 Luther as monk, facing r., head and shoulders, behind suggestions of a niche, top r. a dove, bottom l. and r. initials D. – M.L. Woodcut. Used in Luther, *Umme wat sake unde stucke des Pawestes unde siner yunger boke verbrant syn* [Halberstadt?], (1520). *Bibl.* Ficker 1934: no. 66; WA vol. 7, 156M. *Locn.* UB Rostock.

17 Luther as monk, facing r., head and shoulders, crude with little resemblance. Woodcut. Used in J. Eberlein von Günzburg, *History Jacob Propsts* (A. Farckel, Colmar, 1521). *Bibl.* Ficker 1934: no. 29.

18 Luther as monk, three-quarter length, facing half-r., holding book to l. hand side, poor resemblance. Woodcut. *Bibl.* Ficker 1934: no. 35.

    i   M. Stiefel, *Von der Christfermigen leer M. Luthers* [P. Ulhart, Augsburg, 1522?]. *Locn.* BL 3905.d.101, STC 832.

    ii   M. Stiefel, *Von der christförmigen leer M. Luthers* [J. Schott, Strassburg, 1522?]. *Locn.* BL 3906.f.115, STC 832.

iii   Another edition [J. Schott, Strassburg, 1525?]. *Locn.* BL 3906.b.96, STC 832.

19a   Luther as monk, full length, directly facing reader, holding book across front with l. hand. Woodcut, Hans Baldung Grien?

i   *Passio D. Martins Luther, oder seyn lydung durch Marcellum beschriben* [J. Preuss, Strassburg, 1521]. *Bibl.* Ficker 1935: no. 31.

ii   Single-sheet woodcut, with Latin text around four sides: *Lutherus passus est/ sub papistis/ resurrexit in/ pectoribus christianis. Bibl.* Ficker 1934: no. 32. *Locn.* Dahlem 632-24 (9).

19b   The same, placed above a demonic beast on all fours in monk's habit. Woodcut. *Bibl.* Ficker 1934: no. 99.

i   M. Gnidius, *Defensio Christianorum de cruce id est Lutheranorum* [J. Schott, Strassburg, 1521]. *Locn.* BL C38.f.38, STC 362.

ii   *Murnarus Leviathan* [J. Schott, Strassburg, 1521]. fol. Dii. *Locn.* GNM R1 1002a, no. 3.

iii   Another variant, with only slight differences. *Bibl.* Ficker 1934: no. 100.

20   Luther as monk, full length, directly facing reader, holding book at angle on r. Used with matching portrait of Hutten as knight with half-drawn sword. Woodcut. *Bibl.* Ficker 1934: nos. 33–4. Used in Hutten, *Gespräch buchlein* [J. Schott, Strassburg, 1521], titlepage and at end. *Locn.* BL 3905.ccc.118, STC 426.

21   Luther as monk, full-length, half turned r., both hands gesturing as though speaking. Poor resemblance. Woodcut. *Bibl.* Ficker 1934: no. 37.

i   *Das Hauptstuck des ewigen und newen Testaments* (J. Nadler, Augsburg, 1522). *Locn.* BL 697.h.2(10), STC 554.

ii   *Von der Freiheit eines Christenmenschen* (J. Preuss, Strassburg). *Bibl.* Schottenloher 1912: 225.

22   Tondo with Luther in doctor's cap and gown, facing r., r. hand in speaker's gesture, circular Latin inscr., lettering reversed, at bottom Luther's heraldic rose. Woodcut. *Bibl.* Ficker 1934: no. 4. Used in Luther, *Ein Sermon geprediget tzu Leipssgk ... im xviiii Jar* (W. Stockel, Leipzig, 1519). *Locn.* GNM R1 1952 postinc.; Coburg Landesbibl. Sig. 57, 322.

23a   Luther in doctor's cap, profile, facing l. Latin inscr., Cranach signet. Engraving (1521). *Bibl.* Ficker 1934: no. 48.

23b   The same, with background filled in with lateral strokes. Engraving (1521). *Bibl.* Ficker 1934: no. 49.

24   Luther in doctor's cap, profile, facing r. with large nimbus, German inscr. Engraving by Daniel Hopfer (1523). *Bibl.* Ficker 1934: no. 55.

25   Luther in doctor's cap, profile, facing l. in tondo formed by wreath, set in richly decorated framework, at top initials D.M.L., at bottom initials of Albrecht Altdorfer. Engraving (1522). *Bibl.* Ficker 1934: no. 57; Bartsch 1866: vol. 8, 83, no. 61.

26   Luther in doctor's cap as evangelist, seated at desk facing r. on which is a crucifix; above Luther, who has a large nimbus, a dove. By Hans Sebald Behem? Woodcut. *Bibl.* Ficker 1934: no. 71.

i   Single sheet woodcut complained of by Aleander, 1521. *Bibl.* Schottenloher 1912: 225.

ii   *Das new Testament Deutsch* (H. Hergot, Nuremberg, 1524). *Bibl.* WA Bibel vol. 2, 305.

iii   *Das new Testament deutsch* (H. Hergot, Nuremberg, 1525). *Bibl.* WA Bibel vol. 2, 369.

iv   *Das new Testament teutsch* (H. Hergot, Nuremberg, 1526). *Bibl.* WA Bibel vol. 2, 402.

27   Luther as monk in doctor's cap, in title border, facing slightly r., full-length, holding book in l. hand, on r. of title. On the other side, St Paul with sword. Woodcut. *Bibl.* Ficker 1934: no. 92.

    i   Luther, *Von der Beycht* (W. Köphel, Strassburg, 1522). *Bibl.* WA vol. 8, 134D.

    ii   Luther, *Von Kauffshandlung und wucher* (W. Köphel, Strassburg, 1525). *Bibl.* Schottenloher 1912: 231.

28   Luther as monk in doctor's cap, in title border, on pedestal on r. of title, facing r., book under l. arm, r. hand indicates risen Christ on l. Beneath Luther his arms, beneath Christ the *arma Christi*. Woodcut. *Bibl.* Ficker 1934: no. 93. Used in Luther, *Wider die hymelischen propheten* (W. Kopfel, Strassburg, 1525). *Bibl.* Schottenloher 1912: 231.

29   Luther as monk with tonsure, in title border top l. corner, head and shoulders, facing slightly r., with dove and nimbus. Beneath Luther, Hutten, St Peter, St Paul. Woodcut. Used in Luther, *Eyn Sermon up dat Evangelion van dem Ryken manne und armen Lasaro Luce am xvi.* (Erfurt, 1523). *Bibl.* Ficker 1934: no. 69; Dommer 1888: 175, no. 332a.

30   Luther as monk with tonsure, writing at desk, above him dove and nimbus, messenger enters with spear and letter. Woodcut. Reverse of titlepage to Luther, *Von Anbeten des Sacraments* in Czech. (1523). *Bibl.* Ficker 1934: no. 70.

31   Luther as monk in doctor's cap, writing at desk, devil in winged hat enters through door l., with spear and letter. Woodcut. Used in *Absag oder vhed schrifft Des Hellischen Furstenn Lucifers, Doctor Martin Lüther ietzt zü gesandt* (1524). *Bibl.* Clemen 1907: vol. 3, 362.

32   Luther as monk in doctor's cap, seated l. at desk, above him initials M.L., devil enters through door with spear and letter. Used in *Absag brieff des Fursten dyser welt etc. wider Martinum Luther* (H. Höltzel, Nuremberg, 1524). *Bibl.* Schottenloher 1912: 228.

33   Luther as monk, same figure as no. 21, r. side of picture, confronts emperor, cardinal and clergy. Used in *Doctor Martini Luthers offentliche verher zu Worms* [J. Nadler, Augsburg, 1521]. *Locn.* BL 3906.f.112(1), STC 581.

34   Luther as monk, full-length, facing r. from l.-hand side, with hand on breast, holding book in left, confronts pope, cardinal, bishop, monk r. Used in *Ain anzaigung wie D. Martinus Luther Zu Wurms auff dem Reichs tag eingefaren* (M. Ramminger, Augsburg, 1521). *Bibl.* Schottenloher 1912: 226.

35   Luther fans the flames of Scripture before the pope and his cardinals.

    i   *Ein Tragedia oder Spill: gehalten in dem kunigklichen Sal zu Pariss* (H. Hergot, Nuremberg, 1524). *Bibl.* Schottenloher 1912: 228.

    ii   *Ein unterred des Bapsts und seiner cardinelen wie im zu thun sey.* *Bibl.* Schottenloher 1912: 227.

36   Luther as monk, full-length, similar to no. 21, on r. facing to l., arguing with imperial official, at rear emperor and electors. Used in *Doctor Martini Luthers offenliche Verhör zu Worms in Reichs tag* (M. Ramminger, Augsburg, 1521). *Bibl.* Schottenloher 1912: 225.

37   Luther as monk, full-length, facing l., with book in l. hand, greets two nobles, above him the morning star. Only crude likeness. Used in *In diesem tractetlin sind hubsche leider new gemacht* (J. Preuss, Strassburg, 1523). *Bibl.* Ficker 1934: no. 101.

38   Luther as monk in doctor's cap, on one knee, holding cross, contends with pope

and his supporters. Woodcut. Titlepage to *Die Luterisch Strebkatz* [P. Schoffer, Worms, 1524]. *Bibl.* Ficker 1934: no. 107. *Locn.* BL 3906.h.72, STC 581.

39   Luther in doctor's cap, in profile, full length, indicating crucified Christ in sheep-fold with l. hand, while pope and cardinal in shape of wolves ravage the flock. In background, SS Peter and Paul. *Bibl.* Wäscher 1955: vol. 1, 14.

40   Luther in doctor's cap stands beside crucified Christ in sheepfold, outside John Hus. Woodcut broadsheet (*c.* 1520–30?). *Locn.* Dahlem 37-1889.

41   Luther in doctor's cap confronts the ungodly, who complain of his doctrine. Above Christ as judge. Woodcut broadsheet by H.S. Behem, text by Hans Sachs (*c.* 1524?). *Bibl.* Ficker 1934: no. 59; Geisberg 1923: no. 222.

42   Luther in doctor's cap leads the faithful from Egyptian darkness. Woodcut broad-sheet by monogrammist H (1524). *Bibl.* Ficker 1934: no. 102; Geisberg 1923: no. 927.

43   Luther as monk with tonsure, as German Hercules. Woodcut broadsheet by H. Holbein the Younger (1523). *Bibl.* Ficker 1934: no. 97. *Locn.* Zurich.

44   Luther as monk with tonsure, holding bowling ball of Scripture, with pope, cardinals, clergy, Hutten, emperor. Only crude resemblance. Woodcut. Titlepage to *Kögel spil gebracttiziert auss yeczigen zwytracht des glaubens* [M. Ramminger, Augsburg] (1522). *Locn.* BL 11517.ee.6, STC 467.

45   Luther as monk in doctor's cap, with Hutten and Reuchlin as *Patron. libertatis*, opposing the *conciliabulum malignantium*. Woodcut. Titlepage to *History von den vier ketzer prediger zu Bern* (J. Preuss, Strassburg, 1521). *Bibl.* Ficker 1934: no. 98.

46   Luther in doctor's cap distributes Bible to unwilling clergy as bread from the 'divine mill'. Woodcut. Titlepage to *Dyss hand zwen schwytzer purer gemacht* [M. Ramminger, Augsburg, 1521]. *Locn.* BL 11517.c.58 (1), STC 845.

47   Luther as monk with tonsure, indicating the risen Christ, in bottom r. corner of depiction of the 'old belief', with figures representing the Old and New Testa-ments. Woodcut. Titlepage to *Vom alten und nuen Gott, Glauben und ler* (A. Petri, Basel, 1521). *Locn.* BL 3906.cc.78, STC 645.

48   Luther as monk in doctor's cap, walking at wheel of Christ's wagon in the 'Tri-umph of Truth'. Woodcut illustration in *Triumphus veritatis. Sick der warheyt* [1524]. *Bibl.* Ficker 1934: no. 105; Schade 1856: vol. 2, 196–7. *Locn.* GNM HB 10931.

49   Luther as knight, facing half-l. l. hand on sword hilt, r. hand gestures as if speak-ing. Woodcut by H.S. Behem (1522). *Bibl.* Ficker 1934: no. 76.

50   Luther as knight, head and shoulders, half turned r., inscr. *Image Martini Lutheri*. Woodcut by Cranach (1522). *Bibl.* Ficker 1934: no. 78.

51   The same as above, with Latin verses. (1522). *Bibl.* Ficker 1934: no. 79.

52   A copy of no. 50. *Bibl.* Ficker 1934: no. 80.

Table 1 *Analysis by types*

	Single portraits (1–26)		Title-borders (27–29)		Illustrations (30–48)		Totals	
	a	b	a	b	a	b	a	b
as monk	21	58	1	1	9	10	31	69
as doctor	5	9	2	3	10	10	17	22
as monk/saint	6	13	1	1	1	1	8	15
as doctor/saint	2	5	–	–	–	–	2	5
with Bible – monk	23	52	–	–	2	2	25	54
with Bible – doctor	3	3	–	–	3	3	6	6

a　versions　　b　editions

Table 2 *Analysis by publishers*

	Portraits		Title-borders		Illus-trations		Totals		
	m	d	m	d	m	d	m	d	
1 Strassburg									
J. Schott	9						9		9
J. Preuss	9				1	1	10	1	11
W. Köpfel				3				3	3
							19	4	23
2 Augsburg									
S. Grimm	5						5		5
S. Otmar	5						5		5
J. Nadler	4					1	4	1	5
M. Ramminger	1				3	1	4	1	5
P. Ulhart	1						1		1
Unknown	1						1		1
							20	2	22
3 Basel									
A. Petri	2				1		3		3
A. Cratander	1						1		1
							4		4
4 Nuremberg									
H. Hergot	1	3			1		2	3	5
H. Höltzel						1		1	1
							2	4	6
5 Colmar – A. Farckel	1						1		1
6 Leipzig – W. Stöckel		1						1	1
7 Worms – P. Schöffer						1		1	1
8 Erfurt – unknown				1			1		1
9 North German	1						1		1
	41	4	1	3	6	5	48	12	60

m   Luther as monk   d   Luther as doctor

NOTES

1 Printing, prints and propaganda

1   The only extensive examination of Reformation visual propaganda is Grisar and Heege 1921, but it is marred by its polemical anti-Protestantism and by its attempts to trace as much of the propaganda as possible back to Luther. Nonetheless, it made a valuable contribution in mapping out much of the field. Better, but brief, is Scharfe 1951, which circulated only in a typescript edition. A more recent study by Zschelletzschky 1975 discusses Reformation propaganda in a wider study of three artists. There has been no study of the quality of Coupe 1966 (on the seventeenth century), although iconographical features of Reformation propaganda have been the object of some excellent shorter works: Saxl 1957; Hoffmann 1978. Christensen 1979 was not available before completing this book.

2   See Dickens 1974: ch. 5; Eisenstein 1971 and 1979: ch. 4; Febvre and Martin 1976: ch. 8; Holborn 1942; Moeller 1979.

3   Diehl 1912: 65–73, 429–58; Loescher 1925: 11.

4   Goody and Watt 1968: 36.

5   Engelsing 1973: 11.

6   Aston 1977: 347; Goody and Watt 1968: 40.

7   Engelsing 1973: 32.

8   *Ibid.*: 26.

9   *Ibid.*: 22; Aston 1977: 348.

10   McLuhan 1973: 64–5.

11   Ivins 1969: 61.

12   Engelsing 1973: 22–3.

13   Kriss-Rettenbach 1963: 24; Huizinga 1955: 166–7; Febvre 1947: 471.

14   Huizinga 1955: 157.

15   Meyer 1938.

16   *Ibid.*: 235–6.

17   Kriss-Rettenbach 1963: 72–3.

18   *Ibid.*: 78–96.

19   *Ibid.*: 73; Spamer 1930: 36–7.

20   Meyer 1938: 251; Andreas 1959: 168.

21   Andreas 1959: 252 on Cusa; Kolve 1966: 6; Engelsing 1973: 23–4 for German examples.

22   McLuhan 1973: 184; Ivins 1969: 2–4.

23   Andreas 1959: 172; Hind 1963: 76; Spamer 1930: 27, 38, 42.

24   On bestsellers, see Engelsing 1973: 19; on pilgrimage tokens, see Theobald 1936: 76.

25   On the Emser broadsheet, see WA Briefwechsel, vol. 2, 268; on reuse of blocks, see Hind 1963: 280, 284; Schmidt 1962: 98.

26   Eisenstein 1968: 30–1 stressed the importance of realising that the Reformation message was delivered to a hearing public.

27   *Diss biechlin zaygt an die weyssagung von zukunfftiger betrubnuss* (H. Schön-
       sperger, Augsburg, 1522), fol. Aii r.
28   Schade 1956: vol. 3, 128.
29   Zschelletzschky 1975: 24.
30   *Ein Gespräch zwischen einem Christen und Juden . . . den Eckstein Christum
       betreffend* (1524), in Clemen 1907: vol. 1, 375–422.
31   See the copies in BL 1226.b.14; 4372.e.29(1).
32   Engelsing 1973: 23; Ivins 1969: 47.
33   On this process in general, see Burke 1978: ch. 4.
34   See, for example, Gravier 1942, who is aware of the value of visual evidence,
       but relegates his brief notes on the thirty-one illustrations to an appendix
       (293–8). One of the missed opportunities of the splendidly illustrated Laube
       et al. 1974 is its failure to provide any explanations for its numerous illus-
       trations. A notable exception in providing some explanation for his illustrations
       is Hillerbrand 1964.
35   One of the most important collections in Zurich has survived only by this
       means, see Wickiana 1975.
36   Derschau 1808.
37   Geisberg 1923.
38   Geisberg 1930.
39   By 1929 it was necessary to publish a separate catalogue to enable single sheets
       to be located; see Schmidt 1929.
40   Strauss 1974 and 1975.
41   Meuche 1976.
42   The following collections were consulted: Berlin-Dahlem, Kupferstichkabinett;
       Berlin Staatsbibliothek, Handschriftenabteilung; Coburg, Schlossmuseum,
       Kupferstichkabinett; London, British Museum, Print Room; Gotha, Schloss-
       museum, Kupferstichkabinett; Munich, Alte Pinakothek, Kupferstichkabinett;
       Munich, Staatliche Graphische Sammlung; Nuremberg, Germanisches National
       Museum; Zurich Staatsbibliothek. Extensive use has also been made of the
       photographic collection of the Warburg Institute, London. I was unable to use
       the collection of the Albertina, Vienna when carrying out research for this
       book, but its holdings have been accounted for in published collections.
43   For British Library, see STC. Collections also used were those in the Univer-
       sitätsbibliothek Göttingen, Bayerische Staatsbibliothek Munich and the
       Germanisches Nationalmuseum, Nuremberg.
44   This is a weakness in the methodology of Moeller 1979, as it is in many recent
       studies of Reformation pamphlets – see Tompert 1978 for an overview –
       which are regarded as constituting 'public opinion', so that analysis of their
       content is taken to reflect what people at large thought of the Reformation.
       More useful are Balzer 1973 and Schütte 1973, who attempt to investigate the
       propaganda *process*. Both works suffer, however, from poor knowledge of
       historical detail, so that their central contention, the interrelation of literary
       production and social situation, remains inadequately proven.
45   This outline owes much to the discussion in Berger and Luckmann 1971:
       110–46.
46   A similar discussion, with different terminology, in Balzer 1973: 16–27; the
       terms 'amplification' and 'reinforcement' are taken from Eisenstein 1968: 27.
47   Clemen 1907: vol. 1, 23–50.
48   A feature observed by several studies of Reformation propaganda: Böckmann
       1944: Uhrig 1936.

49	Schofield 1968: 314.
50	Beringer 1946: 108.
51	Strauss 1975: vol. 1, 1.
52	Zschelletzschky 1975.
53	Panofsky 1970: 51–8.
54	Saussure 1966: 13–15; Barthes 1967: 9–10.
55	Barthes 1967: 58–9.
56	For example, he may be dressed according to western or Byzantine style, holding a martyr's palm or shown in scenes from his martyrdom; he may be on horseback or on foot; in courtly dress or in armour; in chainmail or in a tunic; holding a lance, sword or shield; with or without a cloak or helmet; with a banner bearing the oblong 'cross of St George'; with or without the dragon, or the princess; in a free landscape or indoors; with other saints such as St Michael or as a defender of the Virgin; see Kirschbaum 1968: vol. 6, 365–90.
57	Gombrich 1960: 99.
58	Baticle 1973: 37–8.

2 Images of Luther 1519–25

1	See appendix, 'Depictions of Luther in the 1520s'.
2	Appendix, no. 28.
3	Ficker 1920: 5; Schottenloher 1912: 221; also Dommer 1888: 213, no. 1 (this copy is no longer traceable in Hamburg).
4	The suggestion of Schottenloher 1912: 221; Ficker 1920: ill. 15 reproduces one such medallion, which shows on the reverse a phoenix rising from the ashes.
5	Appendix no. 1a.
6	Ficker 1920: 3.
7	On these terms of C.S. Pierce, see Wollen 1974: 122.
8	These figures based on analysis of appendix, nos. 2–21.
9	Appendix, table 1.
10	Appendix, nos. 22–6.
11	*Schutzred und christenlich antwort ains erbern liebhabers gottlicher warheit der hailigen geschrifft* ... [S. Otmar, Augsburg] (1520), fol. B4r, BL 3906.cc.76, STC 581.
12	For the original version of ill. 8, see appendix no. 7; copies of this original are located in GNM H4885 and in BM; see Dodgson 1911: 319, no. 126.
13	Kirschbaum 1968: vol. 4, 243; Künstle 1926: vol. 1, 21.
14	See *Acta et res gestae ... in comitis principum Wormaciae* (J. Schott, Strassburg, 1521), Dahlem Catalogue 1967: 16, no. 4.
15	Appendix, no. 26.
16	It continued after Luther's death, for example, in Wolf Stuber's depiction of Luther as St Jerome, GNM P2783. Similar is the depiction of Luther as the Evangelist Matthew in Hans Lufft's 1530 edition of Luther's New Testament, see Schramm 1923: ill. 190.
17	See Hans Wallser, *Ain Bericht Wie Doctor Martini Luther von ersten hinder sollichen schwären handel kummen sey* (1521), fol. Biir, BL 11517.cc.32, STC 904. Laux Gemigger, *Zu lob dem Luther und eren der gantzen Christenhait* [Strassburg, 1520], fol. Ai v, BL 11515.b.24, STC 337. For detailed discussion of the pamphlets on Luther, see Korsgen-Wiedeburg 1976: 153–77; Lienhard 1978.

18   'so reden warlich die pauren ... sagen überlaut, Luther sei an prophet gottes', *Klag und antwort von Lutherischen und Bebstlichen pfaffen uber die Reformacion so neulich zu Regenspurg* (1524) in Schade 1856: vol. 3, 156; *Schutzred und christenlich ains erbern liebhabers gottlicher warheit* [S. Otmar, Augsburg], 1520, fol. Cir, BL 3906.cc.76, STC 581.

19   Gemigger, *Zu lob dem Luther*, fol. Ai v.

20   *Dialogus zwischen Petro und eynem Bawrn* (M. Buchfürer, Erfurt, 1523), fol. Aiii r, BL 1347.a.14 (14), STC 829.

21   Philadelphus Regius, *Von Lutherischen wunderzaychenn* [M. Ramminger, Augsburg, 1524], fol. Bii v, BL 3906.cc.91, STC 728. On the depiction of contemporary personages in apocalyptic situations, see Schmidt 1962: 93–8.

22   On these prophecies, Reeves 1969: 333–46; on these as applied to Luther I have drawn profitably on Preuss 1933. Unfortunately no attention is paid to the early years of the Reformation in an otherwise excellent handbook: Brückner 1975.

23   Haug Marschalck, *Von dem weyt erschollen Namen Luther: Was er bedeut und wie er wirt missbraucht* [S. Otmar, Augsburg], 1523, fol. Aii v, BL 3837.aa.44, STC 595.

24   Marschalck, *Namen Lutheri*, fol. Aiii v.

25   Preuss 1906: 12.

26   *Doctor Mar. Luthers Passio durch Marcellum beschrieben* [S. Grimm, Augsburg, 1521], STC 594; *Ain schöner newer Passion* [M. Ramminger, Augsburg, 1521], STC 677; the text reprinted in Schade 1856: vol. 2, 108–13, and in English in Bainton 1963: 54–8; see also Clemen 1903: vol. 3, 9–20.

27   H. von Kettenbach, *Ein practica practiciert auss der heylgen Bibel* [G. Erlinger, Bamberg], 1523, in Clemen 1907: vol. 2, 192.

28   Dahlem 632–24 (9); Appendix, no. 19a (ii).

29   See Bainton 1963: 59; for a wider discussion of medieval typology in Reformation propaganda, see ch. 3 and Hoffmann 1978: 189–210.

30   Cited in Preuss 1933: 41.

31   *Ibid.*: 41.

32   Kalkoff 1886: 34, 133.

33   *Ibid.*: 52.

34   Hampe 1904, vol. 1: 205.

35   Götze 1902.

36   Clemen 1907, vol. 2: 30.

37   *Ibid.* vol. 1, 143; *Eyn gesprech zwyschen vyer Personen ... von der Walfart ym Grimmetal* (M. Maler, Erfurt, 1523).

38   Barthes 1967: 58.

39   *Absag oder vhed schrifft, Des hellischen Fürstenn Lucifers, Doctor Martin Luther ietzt zu gesandt*, Clemen 1907: vol. 3, 363; *Absag brieff des Fursten dyser welt ... wider Martinum Luther*, see Schottenloher 1912: 228, ill. 7.

40   The stance recalls the apocalyptic vision of the Virgin standing above the moon attacked by the seven-headed beast, a divinely given sign of victory. I am grateful to Keith Moxey for pointing out the similarity.

41   *Kögel spil gebracttiziert auss yeczigen zwytracht des glaubens* [M. Ramminger, Augsburg, 1522], STC 467; titlepage reproduced in Clemen 1907: vol. 3, 239.

42   For a useful analysis of this broadsheet, see Zschelletzschky 1975: 230–4.

43   On this work see Burckhardt-Biedemann 1905: 38–44; Baumgarten 1904: 249–55; Hoffmann 1978: 204; on the popularity of the Hercules theme with humanists see Panofsky 1930: pt 2.

44   Dodgson 1902: 136, no. A140.
45   Kalkoff 1886: 52.
46   I have omitted discussion of one other image, Luther as knight (*Junker Jörg*);
        see appendix nos. 49—52, which did not find any propaganda use in the 1520s.
47   Weber 1964: 358.
48   Weber 1965: 46.
49   *Ibid.*: ch. 4.
50   Worsley 1968: 285—97 points out that charisma, in Weber's sense, describes
        more a subjective perception by the followers of a charismatic figure than
        their objective sociological relations. He rightly argues that charisma is too
        limited a concept to analyse the *social* relationships involved. For the reasons
        given in ch. 1, this study is concerned more with ideological than with social
        relations, which must form the subject of a separate study.

3 Enemies of the Gospel

1   Hoffmann 1978: 195 sees in this work a satirical reference to the thirst of
        Samson after he had slain a thousand men with the jawbone of an ass (Judges
        15.14—18).
2   Examples of the theme in Bartsch 1808: vol. 8, 413 (monk and nun surprised
        in a field by a soldier); Dahlem 611—24 (monk and nun as lovers); Passavant
        1860: vol. 2, no. 48 ('I' in alphabet formed by monk and nun embracing),
        no. 235 (monk and nun in bacchic feast). A number of other examples in
        Fuchs 1902: 36.
3   This has the ring of a proverb, but I have been unable to trace any from the
        time on which it may be based.
4   There is a similar depiction in the Albertina; see Schreiber 1926: vol. 4, no.
        1982, reproduced in Brückner 1969: no. 23.
5   See Bächthold-Stäubli 1927· vol. 2, 796; vol. 7, 427—9. Hans Sachs. 1524
        broadsheet on *The Twelve Pure and Impure Birds* lists the raven as a sign of
        fleshy blindness, and the magpie as a sign of being blinded by human teaching;
        See Geisberg 1923: no. 1194; Strauss 1974: no. 1139. Both birds as depicted
        in Sachs' broadsheet resemble those here, so that either could be intended.
6   Henze 1912: 143; Geisberg 1923: no. 1164; Strauss 1974: no. 1111.
7   On complaints over the economic activity of nuns in Cologne in 1525, see
        Holtschmidt 1907: 83, articles 27—9; and in Worms 1523—33 against the
        Ricardi convent, see Stadtarchiv Worms 1893, fols. 106—8.
8   See Grimm 1854: vol. 5, 1121. Murner also used the term 'to carve spoons' in
        Von dem grossen Lutherischen Narren, to indicate doing something insignifi-
        cant but still useful; see Merker 1918: 345, lines 1053—4.
9   Latendorf 1876: no. 264; Grimm 1854: vol. 5, 1120 also mentions that *Löffel*
        can mean fool.
10   Wander 1867: vol. 1, 38.
11   See Grimm 1854: vol. 1, 184.
12   The X on the book may indicate the Roman figure ten in reference to the Ten
        Commandments; see the same figure on a breviary cover held by a figure in
        the Michelfeld Tapestry (ill. 107); and Fraenger 1955: 201.
13   Here I have followed Zschelletzschky 1975: 223—4.
14   Zschelletzschky 1975: 222—4 seems unaware of this interpretation.
15   I have been unable to discover the significance of the clenched hand with a
        nail held by the monk bottom left.

16   This woodcut thus provides a good example of what Hoffmann 1978: 190–1 calls *typologische Exemplarik*, the use of biblical types as incitement to piety through imitation; see also Auerbach 1953.

17   Saxl 1957: 277–85, esp. 279–81, is sceptical of how far Holbein reflects the spirit of Luther, placing him closer to Erasmian humanism, but he does not bring out fully the evangelical themes in his analysis of this work.

18   This woodcut was also used in an 'evangelical calender' by Johannes Copp; see Götzinger 1865.

19   These themes are taken up in the pamphlet's text: the blind are those who do not accept the Word of God; such are those learned men from whom the scholars of Wittenberg had to rescue the Gospel; such men are supported by the sweat and toil of 'the poor common working man'; see *Ein Spiegel der Blinden* [A. Petri, Basel], (1523): esp. fols. A4, A5v.

20   On this image in general, see Leger 1959.

21   See Beitz 1921; Stuhlfauth 1920: 200–2; Zschelletzschky 1975: 250–4.

22   Zschelletzschky 1975: 250 interprets this as a reference to the cup for the laity, 'since the days of the Hussites the battle sign of the anti-Roman opposition'. Without further evidence, this seems to be an arbitrary reading, especially as it does not explain why the figure places his hand on the ladder. The use of the chalice seems more akin to its use in ills. 22, 91 to indicate a mass-priest.

23   Zschelletzschky 1975: 254 does not discuss the background scenes, so ignoring the references to the crucified Christ, which make this woodcut very different from Behem's in its indirect allusion to Lutheran doctrine.

24   Wander 1867: vol. 1, 1017–8.

25   U. Rhegius, *Wie man die falschen propheten erkennen* (Anders Goldbeck, Brunswick, 1539).

26   Turner 1978: 248–9.

4 Popular culture

1   Studies of 'popular culture' are at an early stage, and there is considerable dispute about definition; for useful discussion of the problems, see Barbu 1976; Burke 1976; and in more detail Burke 1978.

2   Thompson 1965: 147–52, 'Inns'.

3   Barbu 1976: 43.

4   See Bakhtin 1968: 6–7; Thompson 1973.

5   See Geertz 1975: 72 characterising the approach of Thomas 1973.

6   Mandrou 1975: 26.

7   Thomas 1973: 29–30.

8   See Lefebvre 1968: 66–7. Sebastian Brant and Sebastian Franck saw carnival as a survival of ancient paganism (*ibid.*: 29); for Lollard criticism even of religious plays, see Kolve 1966: 5, 10, 21.

9   Huizinga 1970: ch. 1; Kolve 1966: 10–21 has a similar discussion in the context of Corpus Christi drama. See also Caillois 1967 and Ehrmann 1968 for other views on play, the latter critical of Huizinga.

10   *Die Lutherisch Strebkatz* [P. Schöffer, Worms, 1524], STC 581; for the text, Schade 1856: vol. 3, 112–35 and explanatory notes 255–61; also Clemen 1904 for a different version of the game.

11   Clemen 1907: vol. 1, 53–83. A sketch in the margin of GNM 14535 shows Luther and Calvin, who is clad as a fool, pulling the Strebkatz with their teeth.

12 For these identifications, see Schade 1856: vol. 3, 258–60, and below p. 74.
13 Bakhtin 1968: 19–20.
14 On mock tournaments, Moser 1967: 156, 159–61; see the illustration in Drescher 1908: fol. 3.
15 See Gaignebet 1972.
16 Moser 1967: 168–9, 173. On the Wild Man, see Bernheimer 1952; Hamburg Catalogue 1967.
17 GNM Kap. 1010, HZ 4, reproduced in Zink 1968: no. 117; for a similar cartoon by Cranach, see Rosenberg 1960: no. 59.
18 See Geisberg 1923: no. 632; Strauss 1974: vol. 2, 598.
19 Falk 1923.
20 Moser 1967: 156.
21 *Triumphis Capnionis*, in Eleutherius Bizenius *Joannis Reuchlin encomium* [T. Anshelm, Hagenau, 1518], Dahlem 354–10.
22 Stuhlfauth 1921a.
23 Similar identifications to those in the *Lutheran Strebkatz*, see below, p. 75.
24 In the woodcut incorrectly given as John 10.
25 On the solemn entry, see that of Charles V into Augsburg, for example: Sach 1891: 220–24; on the Palm procession, Schiller 1966: vol. 2, 18, and Kirschbaum 1968: vol. 3, 365.
26 Röttinger 1916: 37. For Maximilian's triumphal arch, see Kürth 1927: 273.
27 On *Philautiae*, see Radice 1971: 73; on *Narrenschneiden*, see Merker 1918: 46.
28 On carnival in general, see the following publications of the *Tübinger Arbeitskreis für Fasnachtsforschung*: 1964; *Dörfliche Fasnacht* 1966; *Masken* 1967. See also Lefebvre 1968: 23–76; Bakhtin 1968; Burke 1978: ch. 7.
29 On the *Schembartlauf*, see Drescher 1908; Roller 1965; Sumberg 1941.
30 Moser 1967: 136; Lefebvre 1968: 25.
31 Moser, *ibid.*
32 Moser 1964: 26.
33 Moser 1967: 180–3.
34 Moser 1964: 28; Moser 1955: 169.
35 Klersch 1961: 32.
36 Moser 1967: 176.
37 *Ibid.*: 147, 163.
38 On links between Reformation and carnival, Scribner 1978, where twenty-four cases are analysed.
39 Merker 1918: 46.
40 Drescher 1908: 13; Sumberg 1941: 148, 223 (fig. 38).
41 P. Rhegius, *Von Lutherischen wunderzaychenn* [M. Ramminger, Augsburg, 1524], fol. Ciii v and fol. Bii v.
42 Stadtarchiv Ulm, *Ulmensien* 5314, fol. 20r.
43 Kuck 1896: 1.
44 See Bächthold-Stäubli 1927: vol. 2, 1261: *Fastnacht begraben*.
45 Zschelletzschky 1975: 259–62 overlooks the carnival theme.
46 On carnival tableaux in Nuremberg, see Sumberg 1941: ch. 7. Zschelletzschky 1975: 262 interprets the tree as a maypole, but there were similar trees in Nuremberg carnival floats: see the 'hell' for 1518 in Sumberg 1941: 226, fig. 49.
47 Sumberg 1941: 57, 84–6.
48 *Ibid.*: 220, fig. 14.
49 Moser 1967: 168; Perlbach *et al.* 1875: 137. One could see here an attack on

monks (= women) as transvestites, or perhaps an inversion of the kind involved in Cranach's scene of women hunting monks.

50   Drescher 1908: ix.

51   Roller 1965: 140; Sumberg 1941: 107–8.

52   Pfeiffer 1968: Ratsverlass 361; Drescher 1908: x.

53   Drescher 1908: x, 3.

54   Hampe 1904: vol. 1, nos. 1339 (Luther with the dove); 1378, 1380–1 (the 1523 prohibitions); 1444, 1454–5, 1459–60 (the 1524 prohibitions); 1576, 1789, 1929, 2111, 2339, 2680, 3010, 3157 (those for 1527–49).

55   Moser 1967: 170–76; for examples of pig and goat masks, see Sumberg 1941: 219, figs. 21, 23. See also Walzer 1967: 218–82.

56   These are explained in the *Lutheran Strebkatz*, Schade 1856: vol. 2, 114–17, which called them metamorphoses: the men have become so like the beasts that they have turned into them. On Lemp, *ibid.*, 125. These animal masks are also found in a pamphlet of 1522, *Eyn kurtz anred zu allen missgunstigen Doctor Luthers* (J. Nadler, Augsburg), reprinted in Schade (190–5) without the illustration. This shows Emser as a goat, Murner as a cat, Wedel as a sow, and an ass in Dominican habit, who is not identified, playing a fiddle. The introduction explaining the animal masks is taken over from the concluding page of *Murnarus Leviathan*, STC 637; see Schade 1856: vol. 2, 350.

57   Huizinga 1970: 165; on medieval animal allegories, see Schmidtke 1968. A characteristic of typological works using animal allegories, Schmidtke (81) says, is the linking of text and pictorial representation, a model clearly followed by Reformation propaganda.

58   Schade 1856: vol. 2, 116, 129, 133.

59   Bernheimer 1952: 57–61 on the links between carnival masks and demons.

60   Lepp 1908: 135.

61   Lefebvre 1968: 82 (bagpipes); for the ass on the lyre, see Radice 1971: 99.

62   Fuchs 1902: 35.

63   Laube *et al.* 1974: 168.

64   *Das Wolfgesang* [P. Ulhart, Augsburg], in Schade 1856: vol. 3, 1–35, 221–8. Schade (238) dates it as 1520.

65   *Eyn gesprech Brüder Heinrich von Kettenbach mit aim frommen alte mutterlein von Ulm*, in Clemen 1907: vol. 2, 72.

66   Grimm 1854: vol. 4, 1/i, 352.

67   Grisar and Heege 1921: vol. 3, 57.

68   Strauss 1974: vol. 4, no. 1534; Geisberg 1923: no. 1578.

69   Hupp 1930.

70   Edgerton 1972: 87, 91.

71   Kalkoff 1886: 178, mentioned also in an anonymous report from Worms in 1521: Kalkoff 1898: 55.

72   Schottenloher 1922: 64.

73   Brückner 1966: esp. 118–315 argues against the *Bildzauber* interpretation, seeing *Schandbilder* as relying on legal notions of honour; for the undoubted role of image-magic in the 'popular tradition', see Kieckhefer 1976: 50–3.

74   Grisar and Heege 1921: vol. 4, 14–57 on this work, and WA vol. 54, 346–73. It was also circulated in single sheets – see the edition in BL 562*.f.28.

75   Hupp 1930: *passim*.

76   Grisar and Heege 1921: vol. 4, 22–4, 26 identifies the two cardinals. That the third is intended to be Cochleus (26) is implausible, for Cochleus was never a

cardinal. Grisar and Heege perhaps overlooked the third cardinal's hat tied to the gallows beam; however, I have been unable to identify the figure.

77   Hupp 1930: 5–8.

78   Judas sometimes features in *Scheltbriefe* and *Schandbilder*, see Hupp 1930: 60, 79.

79   Hupp 1930: 8, although this often had a sexual connotation lacking in Reformation propaganda: the animals were often she-animals, the seal often in the form of a penis.

80   Grisar and Heege 1921: vol. 4, 24–5.

81   *Landsknechte* were regarded as the lowest level of society, see Radbruch 1961: 9, thus heightening the insult.

82   Bakhtin 1968: 19–21.

83   Grisar and Heege 1921: vol. 4, 30–2.

84   Bächthold-Stäubli 1927: vol. 3, 328–30 on *Gebärde*. The two cardinals are again Albert of Brandenburg and Otto Truchsess. The pope is Paul III, the Farnese pope, identified by the lilies on the canopy. This also identifies the pope intended in the ass on the bagpipe, for there is a lily on the tip of the tiara; see Grisar and Heege 1921: vol. 4, 22, 32. The Belvedere was also a papal building in Rome, adding another layer of allusion to the term *Belvedere zeigen*.

85   On this aspect, see Davis 1973: 81–3.

86   For an instance where this was done to episcopal letters, see Deppermann 1979: 87.

87   Grisar and Heege 1921: vol. 3, 37–40.

88   Bächthold-Stäubli 1927: vol. 1, 93.

89   For a similar version of the 'origins of the monks' in a 1523 broadsheet which includes the defecation theme, but not the gallows, see Laube *et al.* 1974: 168.

90   Grisar and Heege 1921: vol. 4, 33–4.

91   Bakhtin 1968: 192–4.

92   *Ibid.*: 265–6.

93   See Sumberg 1941: 220, fig. 24; Moser 1967: 175.

94   Matthias Gerung produced a similar work in 1546; see Strauss 1975: vol. 1, 268, no. 14.

95   P. Gengenbach, *Diss ist ein iemerliche clag uber die Todten fresser* [M. Ramminger, Augsburg, 1522], STC 472.

96   Grisar and Heege 1921: vol. 4, 17 insist that the pope is arising from hell.

97   For 'images in syntagma', see Baticle 1973: 29.

98   These features are discussed with respect to carnival in Scribner 1978: 319–22.

5 Popular belief

1   Important questions about the nature of popular belief are raised by Davis 1974: esp. 311–12, and Delumeau 1977: esp. chaps, 3–4. On popular belief as behaviour, see important studies by Finucane 1977; Trexler 1972 and 1974; Obelkevich 1979.

2   On these statues, see Huizinga 1955: 157.

3   On the liminal, see Turner 1978: ch. 1 and 249–50.

4   On processions, see Trexler 1974: 221–3; Phythian-Adams 1972: 74–6; Toussaert 1963: 245–7.

5   For a similar cod-piece, see Sebald Behem's *Der Nasentantz zu Gumpelsbrunn*, in Geisberg 1923: no. 262.

6   For further description of these and other carnival incidents, see Scribner 1978.

7   M. Luther, *Ain Sermon von der beschneydung am newen Jarstag* [H. Steiner, Augsburg, 1524], fol. Aiii v: 'Sitzt det Bapst an Christus stet in der kirchen und leuchtet wie dreck in der latern.' This was perhaps a common colloquialism — it is found again in an attack on Catholics in Magdeburg by the preachers Johann Fritzehans and Erhard Weissensee, see Kawerau 1894: 231.

8   On the two thieves, see Kirschbaum, 1968: vol. 4, 56–8; Schmitt 1937: vol. 4, 83–7; Réau 1956: vol. 2/ii, 492.

9   On the *Judaslied*, see Erk and Böhme 1894: 670, nos. 1963–4.

10   The taking of the bad thief's soul by the Devil was a stock feature of the iconography, see Réau 1956: vol. 2/ii, 492.

11   On the *arma Christi*, see Künstle 1926: vol. 1, 488; Kirschbaum 1968: vol. 1, 183–7; Réau 1956: vol. 2/ii, 508. (Réau points out that despite its heraldic character it was an essentially popular motif); Schiller 1966: vol. 2, 189–97; Berliner 1955.

12   On the mass of St Gregory, see Künstle 1926: vol. 1, 487–8; Kirschbaum 1968: vol. 2, 199; Réau 1956: vol. 3/iii, 614; Schiller 1966: vol. 2, 226–8, who points out that because the doctrine of purgatory was said to be traceable back to Gregory, the mass of St Gregory became a special devotional image before which a worshipper could obtain pardon to shorten time in purgatory.

13   For editions of this work, see Dahlem Catalogue 1967: 74, no. 104.

14   A less evident reading, not explicitly suggested in the broadsheet, could be taken from the fact that the mass of St Gregory was mostly depicted as a papal mass. The papal beast could thus reveal the mass as worship of the Antichrist, for which it was merely a mask.

15   On the host mill, Kirschbaum 1968: vol. 3, 289; Réau 1956: vol. 2/ii, 420. For a depiction of Christ in the winepress, see ill. 159; see also A. Thomas 1936 and Weckwerth 1960.

16   Hegg 1954; Stuhlfauth 1940: 241–3.

17   On the mill as secular image, see Henkel and Schöne 1967: 1453–70.

18   For a similar notion of 'images of transumption', see Coupe 1966: vol. 1, 159.

19   This work has been little commented upon, except to link it to earlier mill depictions; see Andresen 1864: vol. 3, no. 99; Coupe 1966: vol. 1, 159; Dahlem Catalogue 1967: 69, no. 97.

20   On ship imagery, see Kirschbaum 1968: vol. 4, 61–7; Vetter 1969; Vetter 1971.

21   GNM Kaps. 1335, HB 14595; see also Geiler von Kaisersberg, *Das schiff des Heils uss geleget nach der figur die I. von Eck gemacht hat* (I. Grüninger, Strassburg, 1512), BL 691.g.14; 555.d.2. Both of these editions contain this sheet between fols. 17 and 19, so that it could be sold separately; 691.g.14 is the same as the Nuremberg single sheet; 555.d.2. has the pages on the dorsal of the woodcut blank.

22   J. Grunpeck, *Speculum naturalis coelestis et propheticae visionis* (G. Stuchs, Nuremberg, 1508), fol. A6v; also in the German edition, *Spiegel der naturlichen himlischen und prophetischen Sehungen* (G. Stuchs, Nuremberg, 1508), fol. A5v.

23   J. Grunpeck, *Spiegel der naturlichen himlischen und prophetischen Sehungen* (W. Stöckel, Leipzig, 1522).

24   Johann Copp, *Was auff diss dreyundtzweyntzigist und tzum teyl vierundtzweyntzigist iar des hymmels lauff kunfftig sein* (W. Stöckel, Leipzig, [1523]), fol. Bii v.

25 Kirschbaum 1968: vol. 4, 144–5; Réau 1956: vol. 2/ii, 733; Kretzenbacher 1958.
26 Peuckert 1948.
27 On the wheel of fortune, see Doren 1922: Wackernagel 1872; Weinhold 1892.
28 Bartsch 1854: no. 2529; Andreas 1959: 189 (wheel turned by death); Doren 1922: Tafel 2 (corpse in grave).
29 See Harms 1972, whose identification of Reinecke Fuchs–pope as the Antichrist is ingenious but not wholly convincing.
30 On this titlepage, see Schottenloher 1922: 112 and Hoyer and Rudiger 1975: 120–1.
31 Zschelletzschky 1975: 72 does not give a full analysis; for more extended discussion, see Hoffmann 1978: 196–203, who stresses the difficulty of interpretation, especially the discrepancy between the picture and the Hans Sachs' text.
32 On astrology and associated beliefs, see Bezold 1892; Hellmann 1914; Hess 1911; Strauss 1926; Thorndike 1934: ch. 58; Warburg 1919.
33 On eclipses and conjunctions, see Hellmann 1914; for Copp's work, n. 24 above, the warning of the 1523 eclipse on fol. Aiii v.
34 Hellmann 1914: 9–11.
35 On the 1524 conjunction, see Thorndike 1941: ch. 11; Hellmann 1914: 12–15, for the editions 16, 23. Despite its tenuous argument that astrology was a cause of the German Peasant War, Friedrich 1864 is still a valuable discussion about the links between astrology and religious and social discontent.
36 On the Reynmann prognostic, see Warburg 1919: 31–3; on great conjunctions, see Hellmann 1914: 8; on influence of various planets, see Strauss 1926: 20–36, 67–8; on sounds of pipe and drum, see Bächthold-Stäubli 1927: vol. 6, 1576, vol. 8, 1171.
37 On Brant, see Wuttke 1976b: esp. 150–1.
38 Koegler 1907: 411–16. The original indicated by Koegler is Wickiana PAS II/9, 14. For other pamphlets on these 'heavenly lights', see Hellmann 1914: 14–15, 64–7.
39 On comets, see Thorndike 1934: ch. 57; Hess 1910: 301–3.
40 On this work, the original of which I have been unable to trace, see Röttinger 1925: 205, no. 307. It is reprinted in Jäckel 1975: 484 and in Laube *et al.* 1974: 271 without bibliographical details. Hillerbrand 1967: 99 republishes it, misreading Aries for Capricorn.
41 C. Lycosthenes, *Prodigiorium ac ostentorum chronicon* (H. Petri, Basel, 1557).
42 C. Lycosthenes, *Wunderwerck oder Gottes unergrundtliches vorbilden*, trans. J. Heroldt (H. Petri, Basel, 1557), fols. A5v–A8v.
43 *Ibid.* fol. A5v.
44 Klingner 1912: 92–100, esp. 95.
45 Wuttke 1976a, and more generally Wuttke 1974.
46 Holländer 1921: 318, fig. 182.
47 *Ibid.*: 312, fig. 176.
48 For the most noncommittal depiction in a broadsheet with the minimum of text, see Geisberg 1923: no. 1592; Strauss 1974: no. 1549. This version, which is in Gotha, seems to have been overlooked by WA vol. 11, 357–61 and Grisar and Heege 1921: vol. 3, 17, who mention only two non-Reformation works on the Monk Calf.
49 See WA vol. 11, 375.
50 See *ibid.*, 361, which gives Munich as location.

51   For this version, located in Wickiana, see Koegler 1907.
52   For the various editions, see WA vol. 11, 361–3. The edition used here is that by J. Rhau, Wittenberg, 1523.
53   For Luther's interpretation, see WA vol. 11, 380–85.
54   Lange 1891, whose comprehensive discussion provides the basis for all subsequent discussion of this monster and its uses in Reformation propaganda.
55   Cited Grisar and Heege 1921: vol. 3, 5.
56   For Melanchthon's interpretation, see WA vol. 11, 375–9.
57   For these editions, see *ibid.*, 361–5.
58   For the further influence of the *Papstesel*, see Lange 1891: 92–3; Warburg 1919: 50–51.
59   Lascault 1973: 294–5.
60   See above p. 74.
61   Lascault 1973: 118, 209.
62   Lycosthenes, *Wunderwerck*, 362. Related to this thought is the MS note written inside the rear cover of a collection of pamphlets bound together some time during the 1540s (BL 3906.d.81), which records that Pope Sergius II was the first pope to change his given name, because he felt ashamed of the nickname bestowed upon him as a result of his bestial life – Pigsnout (*Osporci* or *sawrüssel*).
63   See *Eyn kurtze anred zu allen missgunstigen Doctor Luthers* (1522), in Schade 1856: vol. 2, 190–5, esp. 190: Luther's enemies are turned into beasts *durch ein betriegung, so si inen selbst gemacht haben, durch eines teufels zuthun und zauberei.*
64   P. Gengenbach, *Wie der Haillig Vatter Bapst Adrianus eingeritten ist* (M. Ramminger, Augsburg, 1522).
65   Fuchs 1902: 62.
66   Usually reprinted in connection with Reformation polemic, there are no such tendencies in the text of this broadsheet, and it was probably more of an expression of pre-Reformation anti-papalism. It tells of Alexander VI striking a bargain with the Devil to obtain the papacy, and then being surprised one day to find the Devil seated on the papal throne, claiming himself to be pope. The copy in Dahlem has a French text, perhaps indicating its origins in pre-Reformation French antipapalism.
67   Described in Grisar and Heege 1921: vol. 4, 68–70, but without full explanation of the Wild Man theme.
68   On the Wild Man, see Bernheimer 1952: esp. 64–6; Hamburg Catalogue 1967: esp. x.
69   Lascault 1973: 49–51.
70   Emphasised by Lycosthenes, and by Grunpeck's 1502 work *Prodigiorum ostentorum et monstrorum*; see Lascault 1973: 323–5.
71   On St Bridget (Birgitta, Brigitta), Buchberger 1930: vol. 2, 364–6; Galling 1957: vol. 1, 1300. On the role of popular prophecy in the fifteenth century, see Reeves 1969: 553 for numerous references to Bridget, 560 to Hildegard.
72   See, for example, *Diss biechlin zeygt an die weyssagung von zukunfftigen betrubnuss . . . Sant Birgitta, Sanct Sybilla, Sant Gregorius, Sant Hilgart, Sant Joachim. Und wirt genannt die Burde der Welt* (H. Schönsperger, Augsburg, 1522); *Sant Hildegarten Weissagung, uber die Papisten und genanten Geystlichen* [Andreas Formschneider, Nuremberg], (1527), which appeared in two 1527 editions, BL 3905.e.98 and 3906.f.49; *Practica ausgezogen von Sybilla, Brigitta, Cirilli, Joachim, Methodii und Bruder Reinhard . . . vormals getruckt*

	im 18. Jar (n.p., 1521), in Munich Staatsbibliothek 4° Astr. P510-42. It also saw numerous editions: besides the 1518 edition referred to in the title, there were editions in 1520 (BL 1608/648), 1521 from J. Fabri, Speyer (BL 1608/734(1)), and 1527 (Munich Staatsbibliothek 4° Astr. 225–21).
73	On these cases, see Andreas 1959: 175–7.
74	*Bruder Claus* [P. Wagner, Nuremberg, 1490], BL IA.8022.
75	The discussion follows Grisar and Heege 1921: vol. 3, 44–56, with minor additions.
76	Grisar and Heege 1921: vol. 3, 51–2.
77	Reeves 1969: 359, 446, citing Bataillon 1937: 58–60.
78	*Ein gesichte Bruder Clausen ynn Schweytz und seine deutunge* (N. Schirlentz, Wittenberg, 1528), reprinted in WA vol. 26, 125–36.
79	*Ibid.*, fols. B3r–B4r.
80	On the two editions of Luther's interpretation, which appeared in Wittenberg and Nuremberg, see Grisar and Heege 1921: vol. 3, 56. The two broadsheets, only one of which is mentioned by Grisar and Heege, are GNM HB 2844 and Wickiana PAS II/2-3 (see also PAS II/7-16).
81	For an extended discussion of the work, see Fraenger 1955.
82	*Eyn wunderliche Weyssagung von dem Bapstum* (H. Guldenmundt, Nuremberg, 1527), a facsimile edition in Ritter 1923. Osiander was obsessed by the apocalyptic theme earlier, when he wrote the 1524 *Nürnberger Ratschlag* to justify the introduction of the Reformation in Nuremberg, devoting a lengthy section of the work to the apocalyptic themes of the Antichrist; see Müller 1975: 352–71. I am grateful to Lyndal Roper for calling my attention to this.
83	Reeves 1969: 452–4.
84	*Eyn wunderliche Weyssagung*, fol. Aii.
85	This is left in no doubt by another work published in 1527 by Osiander, *Sant Hildegardten Weissagung*, which he found with the Joachimite prophecy. He issued it in two editions (BL. 3905.e.98 and 3906.f.49), stated in the preface that he regarded it as a true prophecy, and concluded with the comment that there were many others he could publish, were it not politically indiscreet: fol. Bii r.
86	On these changes, see Warburg 1919: 47–9.

6 Antichrist and the world turned upside-down

1	On the Antichrist, see Bousset 1896; Musper 1970; Preuss 1906; Wadstein 1896; Rauh 1973.
2	Preuss 1906: 10–11. Much the same summary can be found in the most common version from the end of the fifteenth century, *Compendium de vita antichristi* (n.p., 1505?), BL 3834.aa.1.
3	Preuss 1906: 13, 15; on the Antichrist as an article of faith, asserted during a fifteenth-century disputation in Erfurt, 43.
4	On these problems, Musper 1970: 15; Wadstein 1896: 133–6.
5	On Antichrist in plays, see Aichele 1974: 27–50; Preuss 1906: 28–33; in blockbooks, Kelchner 1891: 2–3; in popular prophecies, Wadstein 1896: 34–5, 40–2, and the strongest expression of the belief in H. Virdung, *Practica von dem Entcrist* (n.p. & d.), Munich Staatsbibliothek Exeg. 4° 491, which Wadstein dates as *c.* 1508–16; on Brant and Geiler, see Wadstein 1896: 99; on Gengenbach, see Preuss 1906: 33; for editions of the *Compendium de vita antichristi*, see STC 213.

6   Preuss 1906: 44–64.
7   See Kawerau 1895; Grisar and Heege 1921: vol. 1, 1–59; WA vol. 9, 677–715.
       On the *Passional* as devotional genre, see Buchberger 1930: vol. 8, 143; WA
       vol. 9, 687; Fleming 1973.
8   Luther's views on the Donation expressed in *An der christlichen Adel*, WA vol.
       6, 434, lines 25–7; on its relation to his views of the Antichrist, 386.
9   On kissing the pope's foot as a sign of his high authority, see Wirth 1963:
       175–221, esp. 178–9: the custom began with Constantine, and its significance
       was set out fully in 1498 by Polydore Vergil. Luther felt especially strongly
       about Frederick Barbarossa kissing the papal foot in 1177, when he was
       released from excommunication: 181. For Luther's expressed views on the
       subject in *An der christlichen Adel*, see WA vol. 6, 433, lines 26–8; 435, lines
       25–7.
10   On use of the ban for temporal advantage, see WA vol. 6, 455.
11   On 'German fools', see Luther, *Von dem Papsthum zu Rom* (1520), WA vol.
       6, 288, line 30; 289, line 7.
12   On the contrast between Christ going afoot and the pope's massive retinue, see
       WA vol. 6, 420; on the pope being carried by bearers: 436, lines 10–12.
13   On the breaking of oaths, see WA vol. 7, 174; and see vol. 6, 453.
14   On the 'riding pope', see Träger 1970.
15   On not regarding the laity as part of the Church, see Vetter 1969: 20 for
       depictions of the ship of the Church where the laity are omitted.
16   For Luther's similar views, *De captivitate Babylonica*, WA vol. 6, 537; *Warum
       des Papstes und seine Jünger Bücher von D. Martin Luther verbrannt sind*
       (1520), WA vol. 7, 172–4, 177–9.
17   H. Schedel, *Buch der Chroniken* (A. Koberger, Nuremberg, 1493), fol. cclix.
18   Another example of adaptation of popular devotional forms discussed in
       ch. 5.
19   Borchardt 1971: 117–19, 241, 245.
20   On editions of the *Passional*, including seventeenth-century French editions,
       see WA vol. 9, 690–700.
21   Spamer 1930: 36–7.
22   Coupe 1966: vol. 1, 212.
23   Berlin YA 364.
24   Berlin YA 397.
25   *Des Papsts und der Pfaffen Badstub* (J. Cammerlander, Strassburg, 1546); for
       the Gerung woodcut, see Strauss 1975, vol. 1, 305, no. 50.
26   Berlin YA 273; and see Geisberg 1930: vol. 4, 5.
27   For Luther's views of the diabolical origins of the pope-Antichrist, see Preuss
       1906: 157.
28   Schönherr 1867: 115.
29   Curtius 1953: 94–8.
30   Babcock 1978 covers a wide range of such inversions; see especially Kunzle
       1978.
31   Bakhtin 1968: 11.
32   Mühlmann 1961: 308–12, 333–5; on Lazarus and Dives, see Boase 1972:
       28–35, 45.
33   Lascault 1973: 51, 189, 194, 248–50.
34   On inversion of awe, Bakhtin 1968: 7, 19.
35   *Ibid.*: 19–21, 147.
36   Lefebvre 1968: 88–90.

37   On fears of a *Pfaffenkrieg*, see especially the prognostic by J. Copp, *Was auff diss dreyundtzweyntsigsten . . . jer* (W. Stöckel, Leipzig, [1523]), esp. fol. bi, a warning Copp says he also gave in 1521 and 1522, fol. Aiii v.

38   Schlossmuseum Gotha, 205, reproduced in Zschelletzschky 1975: 358.

39   J. Grunpeck, *Spiegel der naturlichen himlischen und prophetischen Sehungen* (G. Stuchs, Nuremberg, 1508), fol. Aiii r. A Latin edition, also by Stuchs of Nuremberg the same year, has the same illustration on fol. Aiii v.

40   For world-upside-down depictions, see Kunzle 1978.

41   Peuckert 1948: 544–9; more generally Ball 1975; Bauckham 1978; Firth 1979; McGinn 1979.

42   Schmidt 1962: 93–112; Griser and Heege 1921: vol. 2, 2–14.

43   The triple tiara, as a symbol of papal power, indeed since 1400 taken to symbolise the power of the pope on earth, in heaven and in hell, Merker 1918: 329, embodied a central point of identification with the beast, the claim to secular power.

44   Schmidt 1962: 109; and see the same identifications used in the *Papal Ass*, ill. 98.

45   Völker 1977, esp. the bibliography on 124–5.

46   *Ibid.*: 21–37; Röttinger 1927: 80.

47   GNM HB 2828; Munich Staatl. Graph. Samml. no. 178924, also in BM C 296 (Rhine part); Berlin YA 271 (left-hand half only).

48   M. Schrott, *Von der Erschrocklichen Zurstorung . . . dess . . . Bapstums* (n.p. & d), BL 11501.k.20, STC 673. Preuss 1906: 69 calls attention to the use of the legend in a Hussite work, in which the election of the female pope is contrasted to that of the apostle Matthew (Acts 1.23).

49   Grisar and Heege 1921: vol. 2, 9–10; Schmidt 1962: 98 in rebutting the notion that these illustrations were intended as *Kampfbilder* emphasises the low-key references to the papacy.

50   Schmidt 1962: 122–7.

51   *Ibid.*: 210; Luther himself left no doubts about this identification, noting in the margin of the corresponding passage (Apoc. 11.2–8): *Das sind alle rechte frume Prediger, die das Wort rein erhalten, zu trost den Christen*, in *Biblia* (Hans Lufft, Wittenberg, 1534), fol. cxci.

52   Luther's marginal comment to Apoc. 20, on Gog, reads: *Das sind die Turcken*, *Biblia* (1534), fol. cxcviii v; on the general identification, see Peuckert 1948: 164–71.

53   Preuss 1906: 18.

54   On the Interim, see Franz and Rössler 1958: 451; on the Leipzig Interim, see Herrmann 1962.

55   For a substantial list of some of the ballads and mock hymns attacking the Interim, see Weller 1862.

56   Grimm 1854: vol. 8, 2070, 2072–3.

57   Strauss 1975: vol. 2, 507, no. 10.

58   See Wolf 1925 for the first mention of this work; also Funck 1934. Up to 1934 the sheet was located in the Königliche Preussische Staatsbibliothek Berlin, but it disappeared or was destroyed subsequently, since it cannot now be traced in either of the successor institutions to this body, the Stiftung Preussischer Kulturbesitz, West Berlin, or the Deutsche Staatsbibliothek, DDR-Berlin.

59   *Die heilig frauw Sant Interim* ([M. Apiarius] Bern, 1552), BL 11517.de.2 (2).

60   Passavant 1860: vol. 4, 182, no. 28; Bartsch 1808: vol. 9, 500, no. 1; this

work is located in BM C47* (Melchior Lorch), vol. 1, 1865-7-9-95. The image of the three-headed beast was later used again for Lutheran polemic against Calvinism, the three heads now being the pope, the Turk and Calvin; see Preuss 1906: 244.

61   The struggle against the Interim is also referred to in this work, for in the background is a silhouette of Magdeburg, which was in the forefront of opposition to the Interim, see Dahlem Catalogue 1967: 98.

62   Preuss 1906: 171–5.

63   On Gerung, see Wagner 1896 and Dodgson 1908.

64   Strauss 1975: vol. 1, 312, no. 57.

65   *Ibid.*: vol. 1, 287, no. 32.

66   The parallel with Savonarola's vision of the hand with the sword hanging over Florence is striking; see Weinstein 1970: 175 and the illustration facing p. 227. The sword was a human agency of divine wrath, in the case of Florence, Charles VIII; here perhaps the pope and the Turk?

67   Preuss 1906: 140 makes the same point by stating that the popularity of the Antichrist legend was not created by the *Passional*, but that Cranach's work relied on this popularity for its success.

68   H. Virdung, *Practica von dem Entcrist* (n.d. & p.).

69   *Practica ausgezogen von Sybilla, Brigitta, Cirilli* ... (n.p., 1521), Munich Staatsbibliothek 4° Astr. P 510–42. The 1518 edition is implied in the title of the 1521 edition; the [1520] edition published in Speyer is in BL 1608/648; another 1521 edition published by J. Fabri, Speyer is in BL 1608/734(1); an edition dated 1527 is in Munich Staatsbibliothek 4° Astr. 225–21; and the edition without date or place in BL 1608/734(2), which STC 813 dates as probably 1530. There is a further, undated edition in BL 717.e.34, although this is scarcely to be dated 1520, as in STC 813, for most of its contents and titlepage seem to indicate a date closer to BL 1608/734(2), that is, around or after 1530.

70   *Practica ausgezogen von Sybilla* (1521), fols. Aiii v, Bi r. See Peuckert 1948: 157–64 for the Cologne prophecy.

71   *Sant Hildegardten Weissagung, uber die Papisten, und genanten Geystlichen, welcher erfullung zu unser zeytten hat angefangen und vol gezogen sol werden. Eyn Vorred durch Andrean Osiander im MDXXVII Jar.* (n.p., 1527).

72   *Ibid.*, fol. Aii r.

73   *Ibid.*, fol. Bii r.

74   Largely through use of their coats of arms, such as those of the Medici or Farnese, see ills. 32, 60, 128; there was also physical resemblance, the pope in Cranach's *Passional* resembling Leo X, or in the *Abbildung des Papstums* Paul III.

75   For these identifications, see Schmidt 1962: 105, 108, 111.

76   *Ibid.*: 216.

77   *Ibid.*: 192.

78   WA *Deutsche Bibel*, vol. 7, 422–77 *passim* and notes 51–2 above.

79   Preuss 1906: 175–6.

7 Teaching the Gospel: propaganda as instruction

1   This also appeared without text, see Röttinger 1927: 58.

2   On this type of crucifix, related to Christ in the winepress, see Preuss 1926: 106–9; Thomas 1936: 15–16.

3   On the biblical basis of the vineyard image, see Kirschbaum 1968: vol. 4, 486.

4   T. Stör, *Von dem Christlichen Weingarten* (J. Gastel, Zwickau, 1524).

5   J. Grunpeck, *Spiegel der naturlichen himlischen und prophetischen Sehungen* (W. Stöckel, Leipzig, 1522), with earlier editions in German and Latin from 1508; see STC 373.

6   Buchholz 1928: 40 dates this as 1569. The painting is now in too poor a condition to reproduce, but is depicted in Thulin 1958.

7   Pascal 1968.

8   In at least one version, with text by Hans Sachs, see Stuhlfauth 1919, although the dating 1524 seems incorrect; Röttinger 1927: 57 suggests 1531.

9   As often remarked, see Buchholz 1928: 72 and Preuss 1926: 173, this contrast replaces that between the Church and the Synagogue, common during the middle ages.

10   J. Eberlein, *Ain fraintlich vermanung an alle frummen Christen zu Augspurg* [P. Ulhart, Augsburg, 1522].

11   On the significance of informal, open-air preaching, Scribner 1980: 107–8.

12   H. Schedel, *Buch der Chroniken* (A. Koberger, Nuremberg, 1493).

13   Buchholz 1928: 14–16 points out that this is not a new emphasis in evangelical art, but an extension of trends from the late fifteenth century.

14   Drews 1905: ill. 33.

15   A similar iconographic idea is found in the illustration to Hosea 13.14 in Luther's 1534 Bible; see Schmidt 1962: 201, no. 138. This shows a preacher expounding evangelical doctrine to a group of interested believers. The content of the sermon is indicated by background scenes of the crucifixion and the risen Christ overcoming death and the Devil, in explanation of Hosea: 'Shall I redeem them from death?' Inexplicably, this is reproduced in Laube *et al.* 1974: 330 and Jäckel 1975: 40 as a depiction of an Anabaptist preacher, yet omitting the background scenes which show how it is to be read.

16   On the *Rufer*, see Zschelletzschky 1975: 288.

17   For the first, L. Culman, *Confabulatio ... evangelici & papistici de verae religionis articulis* (1545); the second is reproduced from an original block by Derschau 1808: vol. 2, no. D10. Stuhlfauth 1918: 243–4 called attention to the relationship between the three items.

18   Geisberg 1923: no. 654–5 dated the work as *c.* 1545, overlooking the reference to Johann Friedrich; Strauss 1975: no. 619 follows this dating.

19   See above, ill. 100.

20   Taken over from the *Fox-brush Shop*, Geisberg 1923: no. 1165.

21   On the Elector Johann Friedrich's 'martyrdom' for the Gospel, see Mentz 1908: vol. 3, 278, 342; also WA Tischreden, vol. 6, no. 6961.

22   A similar depiction of Luther preaching, but with the crucified Christ in the centre of the picture, is found in the predella of the altarpiece of the Wittenberg city church; see Thulin 1955: ill. 27, facing 24.

23   Preuss 1933: 69 sees this as another example of the Christ parallel applied to Luther.

24   See Kirschbaum 1968: vol. 4, 247, 493; Schiller 1966: vol. 4/i, 63–5.

25   This interpretation is far from unambiguous. Dahlem Catalogue 1967: 128, no. 206 interprets it merely as Luther discussing with John Frederick, and indeed it certainly is not as explicit as the depiction of Bugenhagen exercising the power of the keys in the altarpiece of the city church in Wittenberg; see Thulin 1955: 22. That a mere discussion is intended scarcely seems to fit in with the carefully constructed programme of the rest of the picture.

26   The theme can also be traced in Cranach's numerous depictions of Christ blessing the children; see Kibisch 1950.

27   Schiller 1971: vol. 2, 40.

28   This work has rarely been commented upon, and seems to have been last published by Derschau 1808: vol. 2, no. C24 from the original blocks, then in his possession, and now in the Derschau Sammlung Berlin. Apart from Derschau, only Nagler 1864: vol. 4, 749, no. 2401 seems to have mentioned it.

29   See, for example, WA vol. 36, 687–9; vol. 40, 260–2.

30   WA vol. 36, 366–7.

31   WA vol. 51, 136, line 31.

32   WA vol. 40/ii, 66–7.

33   See WA vol. 36, 687–8.

34   Buchholz 1928: 73; Preuss 1926: 184, 200 for examples.

35   On *Bänkelsinger* in general, see Burke 1978: 95–9, and also Praschinger 1950: 18, who cites a 1552 Austrian statute prohibiting the spread of ideas by singing and ballads.

36   The pamphlet is *Ein gesprech auff das kurtzt zwuschen eynem Christen und Juden ... den Eckstein Christum betreffend* [M. Buchführer, Jena], (1524), BL 1226.b.14 and 4372.e.29 (1), published in Clemen 1907: vol. 1, 375–422; for the woodcut, see Geisberg 1923: no. 926; Strauss 1974: vol. 3, 860. The connection between the two has not been previously remarked.

37   Clemen 1907: vol. 1, 400–1.

38   *Ibid.*: 413–14.

39   *Ibid.*: 406–7, 418.

40   *Ibid.*: 410.

41   *Ibid.*: 408.

42   Thus, the pamphlet discusses first the central figure: *ibid.*: 400–1; then numbers 3 and 5 (403); 2 and 3 (406); 7 and 11 (408); 6 (410); the six figures around the square (413–15) and the figure on the white horse (418).

43   See Yates 1969: ch. 4 especially.

44   Schiller 1971: vol. 2, 12.

45   Cranach's Law and Grace allegory, and its variants, has been commented upon frequently; see especially Foerster 1909; Meier 1909. Its content has not always been closely analysed, but see Schiller 1971: vol. 2, 161–3; Thulin 1955: 126–48.

46   This feature has been discussed by Ehresmann 1966.

47   WA vol. 40, 260–2; see also Luther's *Kirchenpostillen*, WA vol. 10/iii, 205–6.

48   Ehresmann 1966: 41 calls it 'a sort of visual breviary'. On the *biblia pauperum*, see Schmitt 1937: vol. 1, 1072–84; the version issued during the Reformation had no polemical tendencies; see *Leien Bibel* (Wendel Rihel, Strassburg, 1540), BL 555.a.10, and STC 123 for other editions. Numerous versions of the Law and Grace depictions were supplied with scriptural quotations; see Foerster 1909: 124–7, 137; Ehresmann 1966: 37 n. 20.

49   It appears in the following altarpieces or panels, some of which were workshop pieces: Gotha, Landesmuseum (dated 1529); Prague, Rudolphinum; former Stadtgeschichtliches Museum, Königsberg; Weimar, Schlossmuseum; Nuremberg, GNM; Schneeberg, Wolfgangskirche; a fragment in Munich, Alte Pinakothek; a privately owned panel in New York; and a fresco in Pirna, Stadtkirche. See Buchholz 1928: 48, 72; Preuss 1926: 184; Schiller 1971: vol. 2, 161–2; Ehresmann 1966: 38 n. 21.

50   For Gottland, see Bartsch 1808: vol. 11, 234: no. 2 (dated 1552); for Melchior

Sachs, see titlepage to *Das Evangelion von der grausamen, erschrecklichen Zerstörung Jerusalem. Ausgelegt durch Magister Johan. Sutel* (Wittenberg 1539), Munich, no. 158767 (Monogrammist MS), also in BL 698.e.22(4); for Hans Brosamer, titlepage to M. Luther, *Auslegung der Evangelien an den furnemsten Festen von Ostern bis auffs Advent* (Wittenberg, 1545), BM Brosamer 1895-1-22-163, Dodgson 1911: 389, no. 4. The influence of the theme in the later sixteenth and the seventeenth centuries is traced by Meier 1909 and Thulin 1955: 139–48.

51   *Biblia Deudsch* (H. Lufft, Wittenberg, 1541), BL 679.i.15; a slightly different version is found in Bugenhagen's Low German Bible of 1533, *Die Biblie uth der uthlegginge Doctors Martini Luthers* (L. Dietz, Lübeck, 1533), BL 2.d.11.

52   *Dat Nye Testament. Vordüdeschet dorch D. Martinum Lutherum* (Wittenberg, 1541); see Dodgson 1911: 341, no. 8.

53   See Luther 1909: vol. 2, nos. 52–3, who lists Georg Rhau, Peter Seitz, Joseph Klug and Hans Weiss as Wittenberg printers who used the schema as a title border. The version reproduced here corresponds to no. 52; for that corresponding to no. 53, see J. Sutel, *Das Evangelion von der grausamen Zerstörung Ierusalem* (H. Weiss, Wittenberg, 1539), BL 698.e.22(4).

54   Schiller 1971: vol. 2, 40.

55   A broadsheet in the Wickiana, PAS II/13/20, commemorating Hus as a divinely inspired martyr, mentions the legend that on the pyre Hus foretold that although the goose was burned (Hus meaning 'goose' in Czech), a swan would come who could not be burned, a prophecy of Luther's appearance. Luther applied the prophecy to himself; see WA vol. 30, 387.

56   On the role of Johann Frederick, see WA Tischreden, vol. 6, no. 6961; also *Corpus Reformatorum* 1834: vol. 7, 1083.

57   Besides the version in Dahlem, there was a version by the Master MS in Coburg, see Strauss 1975: vol. 3, 1283, no. 6; another by the Master AF was used in Luther's *Hauspostille* (Hans Lufft, Wittenberg, 1562). The etching by Balthasar Jenichen is in Dahlem, dated 1568, see Dahlem Catalogue 1967: 132, no. 215. A variant was also used in the titlepage of Luther's works, vol. 2, published in Wittenberg in 1546; see Koepplin and Falk 1974: vol. 1, 411, no. 283.

58   The continuity with Catholic church art in Protestant works which include the donors as 'confessors' is stressed by Gertz 1936: 65.

59   For these identifications, see H. Zimmermann in Geisberg 1930: vol. 1/iv, 11. Copies of this work are located in Berlin YA 283; in Coburg Schlossmuseum XIII 419, 391; and in the Herzog August Bibliothek in Wolfenbüttel.

60   There was also an oil painting on the theme, attributed to Lucas Cranach the Younger; see Dahlem Catalogue 1967: 145, no. 90.

61   Geisberg 1923: no. 899, attributed to Jacob Lucius, located in Coburg Schlossmuseum I 44, 81. This also appeared as a book illustration to J. Vuillebrochius, *Historia baptizati Christi*, which also stressed the devotional purpose; see Röttinger 1921: 85, no. 4, who gives Vienna Albertina as location.

62   There are two extant copies: Berlin YA 408, and Munich 95497 a-e.

63   Erasmus appears among the Reformers, for example, in the epitaph panel for Bürgermeister Meienberg of Nordhausen, by Cranach the Younger, dated early in the second half of the sixteenth century; see Thulin 1955: 88.

64   See, for example, Melanchthon's growing appreciation of Erasmus after Luther's death; Flitner 1952: 14–17,

65   Forster, for example, was Provost in Nuremberg in 1540; Eber was educated in Nuremberg and married a Nuremberg woman and Major was born there.
66   The woodcut, GNM HB 12091, Kaps. 1247; for the painting, see note 60 above.
67   Preuss 1926: 177.
68   Dahlem Catalogue 1967: 145.
69   Geisberg 1923: no. 650; Strauss 1974: vol. 1, no. 615. This is doubtless the result of it being printed from three blocks, but the use of three rather than two blocks seems dictated by the triptych form.
70   Thulin 1955: 75–6, 96–8; Buchholz 1928: 68, who mentions the Rheinsberg altar, dated 1574.

8 The rhetoric of the image

1   On image-to-print culture, see Stone 1969: 78; on Reformation hostility to popular culture, see Burke 1978: ch. 9; however, see Roos 1972: 23 on the ways in which the Reformation furthered popular superstition.
2   Bächthold-Stäubli 1927: vol. 2, 541–4.
3   Berlin YA 108. For depictions of Luther as *Junker Jörg*, see appendix nos. 49–52.
4   B. Lutzenburg, *Catalogus haereticorum* [E. Cervicornus, Cologne, 1522], fol. Bii r, BL 272.g.23. Also in the 1523 edition, BL 11900.a.49, fol. B6v.
5   P. Sylvius, *Luthers und Lutzbers eintrachtige vereinigung* (1535), BL T2205 (13). The pamphlet gives twenty-two points of comparison between Luther and Lucifer, and comparisons between their two Churches.
6   On the pact with the Devil, see Roos 1972: 43–51.
7   J. Cochleus, *Sieben Kopffe Mertini Luthers* (V. Schumann, Leipzig, 1529), BL 3905.f.81 (1); another edition by W. Stöckel, Dresden, 1529, BL 3905.f.81 (2); the Latin edition, *Septiceps Lutherus* (V. Schumann, Leipzig, 1529), BL 3905.e.109.
8   There are interpretations of the seven heads, which I have used for this description, in Cochleus, *Sieben Kopffe*, fol. Aii r.
9   J. Cochleus, *Dialogus de bello contra Turkas, in Antilogias Lutheri* (V. Schumann, Leipzig, 1529), BL 697.b.25 (2). Palinodus is one of the characters in the dialogue, but see Sleumer 1926: 587 on the palinode. It can also be a recantation, so an ironic play on Luther's refusal to recant.
10   Schreckenbach and Neubert 1916: 100.
11   GNM HB 25914.
12   For this depiction, see Geisberg 1923: no. 1511; Strauss 1974: vol. 4, 1473.
13   Berlin YA 875 m (3), which contains two other versions.
14   T. Murner, *Von dem grossen Lutherischen Narren wie im Doctor Murner beschworen hat* (I. Grienninger, 1522), [Strassburg], BL 11517.c.33, published in Merker 1918.
15   On the *Funfzehn Bundgenossen*, see Ozment 1975: 91–2.
16   On *Landsknechte*, accounted with peasants, vagrants, beggars and dishonourable professions as part of the 'common man', see Radbruch 1961: 9; for some of their more unpleasant practices, see Franz 1953: 90–1.
17   Merker 1918: 182, lines 2265–7; see also the ills. on 220, 222 of Luther's *Landsknechte* allies storming a church and a town.
18   Merker 1918: 165, lines 1800–3.
19   See above, p. 74.

20   Merker 1918: 40–3.
21   On the Cranachs and their school, see Koepplin and Falk 1974: vol. 1, 34 on the workshop; vol. 2, 498–522 on Reformation themes in their painting.
22   Röttinger 1927 lists comprehensively Sachs' broadsheet works.
23   On the Cranachs as court painters, see Lüdecke 1953: 33–8.
24   See Zschelletzschky 1975: chaps. 1–4.
25   For all these artists, I have used the biographical material in Strauss 1974 and 1975, and Thieme and Becker 1907.
26   On Gerung, see Wagner 1896; on Lorch, see Harbeck 1911: esp. 103.
27   See Albig 1956: 80–1 on these two stages.
28   See Balzer 1973: 27 on such stereotypes, which he calls auto- and hetero-stereotypes.
29   Ellul 1973: 10.
30   *Ibid.*: 31 on propaganda as creator of myth.
31   Cohen 1969: 337.
32   *Ibid.*: 349–50.
33   Ellul 1973: 11–14; on symbolic communication, see Douglas 1973: 73; this is close to Barthes 1972: 109 notion of myth as a type of speech.
34   Barthes 1967: 89–94.
35   *Ibid.*: 90, and 1972: 114–15.
36   Elaborated and restricted codes are not used in the sense of Douglas 1973: 44.
37   Barthes 1977: 39.
38   On anchorage and relay, see *ibid.*: 39.
39   *Ibid.*: 18, and in more detail 46–51.
40   *Ibid.*: 46–7.
41   WA vol. 18, 409.
42   WA vol. 10/ii, 458.
43   Ozment 1975: 9; and see the comment by Brady 1978: 9.
44   Stirm 1977: 79, 85.
45   Ellul 1973: 187.
46   See Preuss 1906: 175–6 who mentions the alleviation of anxiety, but not the intensification.
47   Roos 1972: 21.
48   On exorcism, see Bächthold-Stäubli 1927: vol. 1, 1109–10, 1113–16, 1118–22; and Oesterreich 1966: 92–108.
49   Stirm 1977: 35.
50   *Ibid.*: 35–6.
51   See WA vol. 18, 409.
52   This model is suggested by Ellul 1973: 162–6, and by other studies which emphasise psychological effects such as 'displacement' (Doob 1948: 70–7) or 'cognitive dissonance' (Lane and Sears 1964: 45). See also Balzer 1973: 113.
53   See Ellul 1973: 62–4, what he calls 'sociological propaganda'.
54   *Ibid.*: 34–6, 116.
55   Uhrig 1936.
56   Balzer 1973: 129–36 emphasises this change in Hans Sachs' work, locating it in 1524.
57   Moeller 1962.
58   Ellul 1973: 70–1, 180.
59   For example, in Göttingen or Hannover, see Lubecus 1967: 15–30; Bahrdt 1908: 32–44. In both cases there seems to have been a handful of committed supporters of the Reformation, and a genuine desire to know more about the

new teaching by the general populace; however, the actual advance of reform was rather the result of action enabling the appointment of a Reformation preacher.

60   From the very beginning of the Reformation, the Edict of Worms included in its condemnations both printed works and *Schandgemele*, a reflection of Charles V's anger in 1521, who commented that when he got his mandate he would have hanged from his window the very first person caught with a work or image of Luther; see Kalkoff 1886: 174.

61   Strauss 1978.

62   Brückner 1975: 267–8.

63   Strauss 1978: 299.

64   WA, vol. 37, 63.

BIBLIOGRAPHY

Early printed works

Note: in alphabetical order of first substantive.

Absag, oder vhed schrifft Des Hellischen Fürstenn Lucifers, Doctor Martin Luther ietzt zu gesandt [J. Gastel, Zwickau, 1524].

Acta et res gestae . . . in comitis principum Wormatiae (J. Schott, Strassburg, 1521).

Eyn kurtze anred zu allen missgunstigen Doctor Luthers und der Christenlichen freyheit (1522).

Ain anzaigung wie D. Martinus Luther zu Wurms auff dem Reichstag eingefaren (M. Ramminger, Augsburg, 1521).

Eyn Ausstzug etlicher Practica und Propheceyen auff vergangne und tzukunfftige Jar Sybille, Brigitte, Cirili, Joachim des Abttes, Methodii und bruder Reynharts, wird meren bis auff das MDlxxxi Jar (s.d. & l.).

Des Bapsts und der Pfaffen Badstub (J. Cammerlander, Strassburg, 1546).

Die Biblie uth der uthlegginge Doctors Martini Luthers (L. Dietz, Lübeck, 1533).

Diss biechlin zaygt an die weyssagung von zukunfftiger betrubnuss . . . Sant Birgitta, Sannt Sybilla, Sant Gregorius, Sant Hilgart, Sant Joachim. Und wirt genant die Burde der Welt (H. Schönsperger, Augsburg, 1522).

Bruder Claus [P. Wagner, Nuremberg, 1490].

S. Brant, *Narrenschiff* (I.B. [J. Bergman], Basel, 1499).

J. Cochleus, *Dialogus de bello contra Turcas, in Antilogias Lutheri* (V. Schumann, Leipzig, 1529).

Septiceps Lutherus (V. Schumann, Leipzig, 1529).

Sieben Kopffe Martini Luthers vom hochwirdigen Sacrament des Altars (V. Schumann, Leipzig, 1529).

J. Cochleus, *Sieben kopffe Martin Luthers von sieben sachen des Christlichen glaubens* (W. Stöckel, Dresden, 1529).

Ein frischer Combisst vom Bapst [J. Cammerlander, Strassburg, 1535].

Compendium de vita antichristi, in *Dialogus inter clericum et milites super dignitate papali et regia* [J. Froschauer, Augsburg, 1505?].

J. Copp, *Was auff diss dreyundtzweyntzigist und tzum teyl vierundtzweyntzigist jer des hymmels lauff kunfftig sein aussweyss Doctoris Joannis Copp urteyl* (W. Stöckel, Leipzig), [1523].

L. Culman, *Confabulatio seu disputatio pia hominis Evangelici & Papistici de verae religionis articulis* (1545).

Das hond zwen schweytzer bauren gemacht. Furwar sy hond es wol betracht [M. Ramminger, Augsburg, 1521].

Ain schöner dialogus von zwayen gutten gesellen genant Hanns Tholl unnd Claus Lamp, sagendt vom Antichrist und seynen jungern.

Dialogus zwischen Petro und eynem Bawrn (M. Bachfürer, Erfurt, 1523).

J. Eberlin von Günzburg, *Ain fraintlich trostliche vermanung an alle frummen Christen zu Augsburg am Leech* [P. Ulhart, Augsburg, 1522?].

Ain dümietige ermanung an ain gantze gemayne Christenheit, von Eckhart zu Drübel (Strassburg), [1523].

281

Die heilig frauw Sant Interim [M. Apiarius] (Bern, 1552).

J. Geiler von Kaisersberg, *Das Schiff des Heils, Auff das aller kürtzest hie uss geleget, Nach der figur die doctor Johannes von Eck gemacht hat zu Ingolstadt* (J. Grüninger, Strassburg, 1512).

Laux Gemigger, *Zu lob dem Luther und eren der gantzen Christenhait* [J. Preuss, Strassburg, 1520?].

P. Gengenbach, *Diss ist ein jemerlich clag uber die Todtenfresser* [Augsburg, 1522].

Wie der Haillig Vatter Bapst Adrianus eingeritten ist (M. Ramminger, Augsburg, 1522).

Ein gesichte Bruder Clausen ynn Schweytz und seine deutunge (N. Schirlentz, Wittenberg, 1528).

Ein gesprech auff das kurtzt zwuschen eynem Christen und Juden, auch eynem Wyrthe sampt seynem Haussknecht, den Eckstein Christum betreffendt [M. Buchführer, Jena] (1524).

Eyn gesprech zwyschen vyer Personen, wie sie eyn getzengk haben, von der Walfart ym Grimmetal [W. Sturmer, Erfurt, 1526].

Gesprech büchlein, von eynem Bawern, Belial, Erasmo Roterodam, und doctor Johann Fabri [J. Fabri, Speyer, 1524].

M. Gnidius, *Defensio Christianorum de cruce id est Lutheranorum* [J. Schott, Strassburg, 1521].

J. Grunpeck, *Speculum naturalis coelestis et propheticae visionis* (G. Stuchs, Nuremberg, 1508).

Spiegel der naturlichen himlischen und prophetischen sehungen (G. Stuchs, Nuremberg, 1508).

Spiegel der naturlichen himlischen und prophetischen sehungen (W. Stöckel, Leipzig, 1522).

Sant Hildegardten Weissagung, uber die Papisten, und genanten Geystlichen, welcher erfullung zu unser zeytten hat angefangen und vol gezogen sol werden. Eyn Vorred durch Andrean Osiander im MDxxvii Jar [H. Andreas Formschneider, Nuremberg], (1527).

U. von Hutten, *Gesprech buchlein* [J. Schott, Strassburg, 1521].

Joachimi abbatis Vaticinia circa Apostolicos vivos per Hieronymum Benedictum (Bononiae, 1515).

H. von Kettenbach, *Eyn gesprech Brüder Hainrich von Kettenbach mit aim frommen alte mütterlein von Ulm* [G. Stuchs, Nuremberg], (1523).

H. von Kettenbach, *Ein Practica practiciert, auss der heylgen Bibel, uff vil zukunfftig jar* [G. Erlinger, Bamberg], (1523).

Klag und antwort von Lutherischen und Bebstischenn pfaffen uber die Reformacion so neulich zu Regenspurg der priester halben aussgangen ist im Jar MDxxiiii.

Kögel spil gebracttiziert auss yeczigen zwytracht des glaubens [M. Ramminger, Augsburg, 1522].

Leien Bibel in deren fleissig zu samen bracht sind Die furnemere Historien beder Testament, mit iren uber gesetzten Summarien (W. Rihel, Strassburg, 1540).

M. Luther, *Abbildung des Bapstums* [Wittenberg], (1545).

Auslegung der Evangelien an den furnemesten Festen von Ostern bis auffs Advent (Wittenberg, 1545).

Biblia, trans. M. Luther (H. Lufft, Wittenberg, 1534).

Biblia Deudsch, trans M. Luther (H. Lufft, Wittenberg, 1541).

Das Hauptstuck des ewigen und newen Testaments (J. Nadler, Augsburg, 1522).

De captivitate Babylonica Ecclesiae [Augsburg, 1520].

Grund und Ursach aller Artickel (J. Nadler, Augsburg, 1520).

Hauspostille (H. Lufft, Wittenberg, 1562).

Das Newe Testament Deutzsch, trans. M. Luther (M. Lotter, Wittenberg, September 1522).

Das Newe Testament Deutzsch, trans. M. Luther (M. Lotter, Wittenberg, December 1522).

Dat Nye Testament. Vordüdeschet dorch D. Martin Lutherum (M. Lotter, Wittenberg, 1541).

Ain Sermon von der beschneyden am newen Jarstag [H. Steiner, Augsburg, 1524].

Ein Sermon geprediget tzu Leipssgk uffm Schloss am tag Petri und pauli im xviii Jar (W. Stöckel, Leipzig, 1519).

Doctor Martini Luthers offentliche verhör zu Worms imm Reychstag [S. Grimm & M. Wirsing, Augsburg, 1521].

Doctor Mar. Luthers Passio, durch Marcellum beschrieben [S. Grimm, Augsburg, 1521].

B. Lutzenburg, *Catalogus haereticorum* [E. Cervicornus, Cologne], (1523).

C. Lycosthenes, *Prodigiorum ac ostentorum chronicon* (H. Petri, Basel, 1557).

Wunderwerck oder Gottes unergrundtliches vorbilden (H. Petri, Basel, 1557).

H. Marschalck, *Ain Spiegel der Blinden* [H. Petri, Basel].

Von dem weyt erschollen Namen Luther: Was er bedeut und wie er wirt missbraucht [S. Otmar, Augsburg], (1523).

P. Melanchthon, *Der Bapstesel durch Philippum Melanchthon gedeutet und gebessert. Mit D. Mart. Luth. Amen.* (N. Schirlentz, Wittenberg, 1535).

T. Murner, *Von dem grossen Lutherischen Narren wie in Doctor Murner beschworen hat* (I. Grienninger, 1522), [Strassburg].

Murnarus Leviathan [J. Schott, Strassburg, 1521].

J. Nazarei, *Vom alten und nüen Gott, Glauben und ler* [A. Petri, Basel], (1521).

Ain schöner newer Passion [M. Ramminger, Augsburg, 1521].

Passional Christi und Antichristi (J. Grunenberg, Wittenberg, 1521).

Practica ausgezogen von Sybilla, Brigitta, Cirilli, Joachim Methodii und Bruder Reinharts (Speyer), [1520].

(J. Fabri, Speyer, 1521).

(1527).

Ain grosser Preiss so der Furst der hellen genant Lucifer yetzt den geystlichen . . . zu weysst (M. Ramminger, Augsburg, 1521).

Ratschlag von der kirchen, eins ausschus etlicher Cardinal Bapst Pauls des namens dem dritten, auff seinen befelh geschrieben und uberantwortet [1538].

Philadelphus Regius, *Von Lutherischen wunderzaychenn mit angehencktem bericht, Wye mann gotlich und teuffelisch mirackel vor ain ander erkennen unnd urtaylen soll* [M. Ramminger, Augsburg, 1524].

L. Reynmann, *Practica uber die grossen manigfaltigen Conjunction der Planeten* (H. Höltzel, Nuremberg, 1523).

Urbanus Rhegius, *Wie man die falschen propheten erkennen ja grieffen mag* (A. Goldbeck, Brunswick, 1539).

H. Schedel, *Buch der Chroniken* (A. Koberger, Nuremberg, 1493).

M. Schrott, *Von der Erschrocklichen Zurstorung und Niderlag dess gantzen Bapstums* (s.l. & a.).

Schutzred und christenlich antwort . . . ains erbern liebhabers gottlicher warheit [S. Otmar, Augsburg], (1520).

M. Stiefel, *Von der Christfermigen leer M. Luthers* [P. Ulhart, Augsburg, 1522?].

[J. Schott, Strassburg, 1522?].

[J. Schott, Strassburg, 1525?].

T. Stör, *Von dem Christlichen Weingarten* (J. Gastel, Zwickau, 1524).

Die Luterisch Strebkatz [P. Schöffer, Worms, 1524?].

J. Sutel, *Das Evangelion von der grausamen, Erschrecklichen Zerstörung Jerusalem* (Wittenberg, 1539).

P. Sylvius, *Luthers und Lutzbers eintrechtige vereinigung* (1535).

Eyn schöns tractetlein von dem Gotlichen und romischen Ablass [J. Schmidt, Speyer, 1525].

Triumphus Capnionis, in Eleutherius Bizenius, *Joannes Reuchlin encomium* [T. Anshelm, Hagenau, 1515].

Triumphus veritatis. Sick der warheyt (1521).

Ein underred des bapsts und seiner cardinelen wie im zu thun sey, und das wort Gottes under zu trucken [1524?].

Verhor und Acta vor dem Byschoff von Meyssen kegen dem Byschoff tzu der Lochau [J. Grunenberg, Wittenberg, 1522].

H. Virdung, *Practica von dem Entchrist und dem jungsten tag auch was geschehen sal vor dem Ende der Welt* (s.l. & a.).

H. Wallser, *Ain Bericht Wie Doctor Martini Luther von ersten hinder sollichen schwären handel kummen say und was in dar zu geursacht und bewegt hat* (1521).

Eyn wunderliche Weyssagung von dem Bapstum (H. Guldenmundt, Nuremberg, 1527).

Das Wolffgesang [P. Ulhart, Augsburg, 1522?].

Other references

Aichele, K. 1974. *Das Antichristdrama des Mittelalters und der Gegenreformation.* The Hague.

Albig, W. 1956. *Modern Public Opinion.* New York.

Andreas, W. 1959. *Deutschland vor der Reformation*, 16th ed. Stuttgart.

Andresen, A. 1864–78. *Der deutsche Peintre-Graveur*, 5 vols. Leipzig.

Aston, M. 1977. Lollardy and literacy. *History* 62, 347–71.

Auerbach, E. 1953. *Typologische Motive in der mittelalterlichen Literatur.* Krefeld.

Babcock, B. (ed.) 1978. *The Reversible World. Symbolic Inversion in Art and Society.* Ithaca & London.

Bächtold-Stäubli, H. (ed.) 1927–42. *Handwörterbuch des deutschen Aberglaubens*, 12 vols. Berlin & Leipzig.

Bahrdt, A. 1908. Die Einführung der Reformation in Hannover. *Hannoversche Geschichtsblätter* 11, 32–44.

Bainton, R.H. 1963. *Studies on the Reformation.* Boston.

Bakhtin, M. 1968. *Rabelais and his World.* Cambridge, Mass.

Ball, B.W. 1975. *A Great Expectation. Eschatological Thought in English Protestantism to 1660.* Leiden.

Balzer, B. 1973. *Bürgerliche Reformationspropaganda. Die Flugschriften des Hans Sachs in den Jahren 1523–1525.* Stuttgart.

Barbu, Z. 1976. Popular culture. A sociological approach. In *Approaches to Popular Culture*, ed. C.W.E. Bigsby, London.

Barthes, R. 1967. *Elements of Semiology.* London.

1972. *Mythologies.* St Albans, Herts.

1977. *Image, Music, Text.* London.

Bartsch, A. 1808–23. *Le Peintre-Graveur*, vols. 6–11. Vienna.

1866. *Le Peintre-Graveur*, vol. 8. Leipzig.

Bartsch, F. 1854. *Die Kupferstichsammlung der k.k. Hofbibliothek in Wien.* Vienna.

Bataillon, M. 1937. *Erasme et l'Espagne.* Paris.

Baticle, Y. 1973. *Clés et codes du cinéma.* Paris.

Bauckham, R. 1978. *Tudor Apocalypse: Sixteenth Century Apocalyptism, Millenarianism and the English Reformation*. Oxford.

Baumgarten, F. 1904. Hans Baldungs Stellung zur Reformation. *Zeitschrift zur Geschichte des Oberrheins*, Neue Folge 19, 245–62.

Beitz, E. 1921. Allegorien der Reformationszeit. *Zeitschrift für christliche Kunst* 34, 165–9.

Berger, P. and Luckmann, T. 1971. *The Social Construction of Reality*. London.

Beringer, L. 1946. Das Zeitalter des Humanismus und der Reformation. In *Deutsche Literaturgeschichte in Grundzügen*, ed. B. Boersch. Bern.

Berliner, R. 1955. Arma christi. *Münchner Jahrbuch der bildenden Kunst* 6, 35–116.

Bernheimer, R. 1952. *Wild Men in the Middle Ages*. Cambridge, Mass.

Bezold, F. von 1892. Astrologische Geschichtskonstruktion im Mittelalter. *Deutsche Zeitschrift für Geschichtswissenschaft* 8, 29–72.

Boase, T.S.R. 1972. *Death in the Middle Ages*. London.

Böckmann, P. 1944. Der gemeine Mann in den Flugschriften der Reformationszeit. *Deutsche Vierteljahrschrift für Literaturwissenschaft und Geistesgeschichte* 22, 186–230.

Borchardt, F.L. 1971. *German Antiquity in Renaissance Myth*. London.

Bousset, W. 1896. *The Antichrist Legend*. London.

Brady, T.A. 1978. *Ruling Class, Regime and Reformation at Strasbourg 1520–1555*. Leiden.

Brückner, W. 1966. *Bildnis und Brauch. Studien zur Bildfunktion des Effigies*. Berlin.
    1969. *Populäre Druckgraphik Europas vom 15. bis 20. Jht*. Munich.

Brückner, W. (ed.) 1975. *Volkserzählung und Reformation*. Munich.

Buchberger, M. (ed.) 1930–8. *Lexikon fur Theologie und Kirche*, 10 vols. Freiburg.

Buchholz, F. 1928. *Protestantismus und Kunst im 16. Jht*. Leipzig.

Burckhardt-Biedemann, T. 1905. Über Zeit und Ablass des Flugblatts: Luther als *Hercules Germanicus. Basler Zeitschrift fur Geschichte und Altertum* 4, 38–44.

Burke, P. 1976. Oblique approaches to the history of popular culture. In *Approaches to Popular Culture*, ed. C.W.E. Bigsby. London.
    1978. *Popular Culture in Early Modern Europe*. London.

Caillois, J. 1967. *Les jeux et les hommes*. Paris.

Christensen, C.C. 1979. *Art and the Reformation in Germany*. Athens, Ohio.

Clemen, O. 1900–3. *Beiträge zur Reformationsgeschichte*, 3 vols. Berlin.
    1904. Die lutherische Strebkatz. *Archiv für Reformationsgeschichte* 2, 78–93.
    1907–11. *Flugschriften aus den ersten Jahren der Reformation*, 4 vols. Leipzig.

Cohen, P.S. 1969. Theories of myth. *Man* 4, 337–53.

Corpus Reformatorum 1834–1914. 101 vols. Leipzig.

Coupe, W.A. 1966–7. *The German Illustrated Broadsheet in the Seventeenth Century*, 2 vols. Baden-Baden.

Curtius, E.R. 1953. *European Literature and the Latin Middle Ages*. London.

Dahiem Catalogue 1967. *Von der Freiheit eines Christenmenschen. Kunstwerke und Dokumente aus dem Jahrhundert der Reformation*. Berlin.

Davis, N.Z. 1973. The rites of violence: religious riot in sixteenth century France. *Past & Present* 59.

Davis, N.Z. 1974. Some tasks and themes in the study of popular religion. In *The Pursuit of Holiness in Late Medieval and Renaissance Religion*, ed. C. Trinkaus & H.A. Oberman. Leiden.

Delumeau, J. 1977. *Catholicism between Luther and Voltaire*. London.

Deppermann, K. 1979. *Melchior Hoffman. Soziale Unruhen und apokalyptische Visionen im Zeitalter der Reformation*. Göttingen.

Derschau, H.A. von 1808–16. *Holzschnitte alter deutscher Meister*, 3 vols. Gotha.

Dickens, A.G. 1974. *The German Nation and Martin Luther*. London.

Diehl, A. 1912. Die Zeit der Scholastik. In *Geschichte des humanistischen Schulwesens in Württemberg bis 1559*. Stuttgart.

Dodgson, C. 1902, 1911. *Catalogue of Early German and Flemish Woodcuts preserved in the Department of Prints and Drawings, B.M. London*, 2 vols. London.

  1908. Eine Holzschnittfolge Matthias Gerungs. *Jahrbuch der königl. preuss. Kunstsammlung* 29, 195–216.

Dörfliche Fasnacht 1966. *Dörfliche Fasnacht zwischen Neckar und Bodensse. Beiträge des Tübinger Arbeitskreises für Fasnachtsforschung*. Tübingen.

Dommer, A. von 1888. *Lutherdrucke auf dem Hamburger Stadtbibliothek 1516–1523*. Leipzig.

Doob, L.W. 1948. *Public Opinion and Propaganda*. New York.

Doren, A. 1922. Fortuna im Mittelalter und in der Renaissance. *Vorträge der Bibliothek Warburg* 2, 80–92.

Douglas, M. 1973. *Natural Symbols*. Harmondsworth.

Drescher, K. 1908. *Das Nürnbergische Schönbartbuch. Nach der Hamburger Handschrift herausgegeben*. Weimar.

Drews, P. 1905. *Der evangelische Geistliche in der deutschen Gergangenheit*. Jena.

Edgerton, S.Y. 1972. *Maniera* and the *Mannaia*: decorum and decapitation in the sixteenth century. In *The Meaning of Mannerism*, ed. F.W. Robinson and S.G. Nichols. Hanover, New Hampshire.

Ehresmann, D.L. 1966. The brazen serpent: a Reformation motif in the works of Lucas Cranach the elder and his workshop. *Marsyas* 13, 32–47.

Ehrmann, J. 1968. Homo Ludens revisited. *Yale French Studies* 41, 31–57.

Eisenstein, E.L. 1968. Some conjectures about the impact of printing on western society and thought: a preliminary report. *Journal of Modern History* 40, 1–56.

  1971. L'avènement de l'imprimerie et la Réforme. *Annales ESC* 26, 1355–82.

  1979. *The Printing Press as an Agent of Change*, 2 vols. Cambridge.

Ellul, J. 1973. *Propaganda. The Formation of Men's Attitudes*. New York.

Engelsing, R. 1973. *Analphabetentum und Lektüre. Zur Sozialgeschichte der Lesens* in *Deutschland zwischen feudaler und industrieller Gesellschaft*. Stuttgart.

Erk, L. and Böhme, F. 1893–4. *Deutscher Leiderhort*, 3 vols. Leipzig.

Falk, R. 1923. Zwickauer Chroniken aus dem 16. Jht. *Alt-Zwickau*.

Fasnacht 1964. *Fasnacht. Beiträge des Tübinger Arbeitskreises für Fasnachtsforschung*. Tübingen.

Febvre, L. 1947. *Le problème de l'incroyance au xvie. siècle*. Paris.

Febvre, L. and Martin, H.-J. 1976. *The Coming of the Book*. London.

Ficker, J. 1920. *Älteste Bildnisse Luthers*. Magdeburg.

  1924. Die frühen Lutherbildnisse Cranachs. *Zeitschrift des Vereins für Kirchengeschichte des Provinz Sachsens* 20, Beilage.

  1934. Die Bildnisse Luthers aus der Zeit seines Lebens. *Luther Jahrbuch* 16, 103–69.

Finucane, R.C. 1977. *Miracles and Pilgrims. Popular Beliefs in Medieval England*. London.

Firth, K.R. 1979. *The Apocalyptic Tradition in Reformation Britain 1530–1645*. Oxford.

Fleming, G. 1973. On the origins of the Passional Christi und Antichristi. *Gutenberg Jahrbuch*, 351–68.

Flitner, A. 1952. *Erasmus im Urteil seiner Nachwelt*. Tübingen.

Foerster, R. 1909. Die Bildnisse vom Johann Hess und Cranachs 'Gesetz und Gnad'.

Jahrbuch des schlesischen Museums für Kunstgewerbe und Altertümer, Neue Folge 5, 117–63.

Fraenger, W. 1955. Der Teppich von Michelfeld. *Deutsche Jahrbuch für Volkskunde* 1, 183–211.

Franz, G. 1953. Von Ursprung und Brauchtum der Landsknechte. *Mitteilungen des Instituts für österreichische Geschichtsforschung* 61, 90–105.

Franz, G. and Rössler, H. 1958. *Sachwörterbuch zur deutschen Geschichte*. Munich.

Friedrich, J. 1864. *Astrologie und Reformation*. Munich.

Fuchs, E. 1902. *Die Karikatur der europäischen Völker*. Berlin.

Funck, H. 1934. Zur Komponistenfrage und Überlieferung des einzigen mehrstimmigen Spottgesanges auf das Augsburger Interim. *Zeitschrift für Musikwissenschaft* 16, 92–7.

Gaignebet, C. 1972. Le combat de carnaval et de carême de P. Breugel (1559). *Annales ESC* 27, 313–45.

Galling, K. (ed.) 1957–62. *Religion in Geschichte und Gegenwart*, 3rd edn, 7 vols. Tübingen.

Geertz, H. 1975. An anthropology of religion and magic. *Journal of Interdisciplinary History* 6, 71–89.

Geisberg, M. 1923–30. *Der deutsche Einblatt-Holzschnitt in der ersten Hälfte des 16. Jhts.*, 40 parts. Munich.

1930–1. *Die deutsche Buchillustration in der ersten Hälfte des 16. Jhts.*, 2 vols. Munich.

Gertz, U. 1936. *Die Bedeutung der Malerei für die Evangeliumsverkündigung in der evangelischen Kirchen des 16. Jhts.* Berlin.

Götze, A. 1902. Lutherisch. *Zeitschrift für Wortforschung* 3, 183–98.

Götzinger, E. 1865. *Zwei Kalender vom Jahre 1527. D. Johannes Copp evangelischer Kalender und D. Thomas Murner Kirchendieb und Ketzerkalender*. Schaffenhausen.

Gombrich. E. 1960. *Art and Illusion*. London.

Goody, J.R. (ed.) 1968. *Literacy in Traditional Societies*. Cambridge.

Goody, J. and Watt, I. 1968. The consequences of literacy. In Goody, J. (ed.) *Literacy in Traditional Societies*. Cambridge.

Gravier, M. 1942. *Luther et l'opinion publique*. Paris.

Grimm, J. and W. 1854–1954. *Deutsches Wörterbuch*, 16 vols. Leipzig.

Grisar, H. and Heege, F. 1921–3. *Luthers Kampfbilder*, 4 vols. Freiburg.

Hagelstange, A. 1907. Die Wandlungen eines Lutherbildnisses in der Buchillustration des xvi. Jhts. *Zeitschrift für Bücherfreunde* 11, 97–107.

Hamburg Catalogue 1967. *Die Wilden Leute des Mittelalters. Ausstellungskatalog des Museums für Kunst und Gewerbe*. Hamburg.

Hampe, T. 1904. *Nürnberger Ratsverlässe über Kunst und Künstler im Zeitalter der Spätgotik und Renaissance*, 2 vols. Vienna & Leipzig.

Harbeck, H. 1911. *Melchior Lorichs*. Hamburg.

Harms, W. 1972. Reinhart Fuchs als Papst und Antichrist auf dem Rad der Fortuna. *Frühmittelalterliche Studien* 6, 418–40.

Hegg, P. 1954. Die Drucke der 'Göttliche Mühle' um 1521. *Schweizerisches Gutenberg Museum* 40, 135–50.

Hellmann, G. 1914. *Aus der Blütezeit der Astrometeorologie. J. Stoefflers Prognose für das Jahr 1524*. Berlin.

Henkel, A. and Schöne, A. 1967. *Emblemata. Handbuch zur Sinnbildkunst des xvi. und xvii. Jhts.* Stuttgart.

Henze, H. 1912. *Die Allegorie bei Hans Sachs*. Halle.

Herrmann, J. 1962. *Augsburg-Leipzig-Passau. Das Leipziger Interim nach Akten des Landeshauptarchivs Dresden 1547–52*. Leipzig.

Hess, W. 1911. *Himmels- und Naturerscheinungen in Einblattdrucke des xv.–xvii. Jhts.* Leipzig.

Hillerbrand, H. 1964. *The Reformation in its Own Words.* London.

1967. *Brennpunkte der Reformation.* Göttingen.

Hind, A.M. 1963. *An Introduction to the History of Woodcut.* New York.

Höllander, E. 1921. *Wunder, Wundergeburt und Wundergestalt in Einblattdrucken des 15.–16. Jhts.* Stuttgart.

Hoffmann, K. 1978. Typologische Exemplarik in reformatorischer Bildsatire. In *Kontinuität und Umbruch. Theologie und Frömmigkeit in Flugschriften und Kleinliteratur an der Wende vom 15. bis 16. Jht.*, ed. J. Nolte *et al.* Stuttgart.

Holborn, L. 1942. Printing and the growth of a Protestant movement in Germany from 1517 to 1524. *Church History* 11, 123–37.

Holtschmidt, W. 1907. Kölner Ratsverfassung vom Sturz der Geschlechterherrschaft bis zum Ausgang des Mittelalters. *Beiträge zur Geschichte des Niederrheins* 21, 81–96.

Hoyer, S. and Rudiger, B. 1975. *An die versammlung gemeiner bauernschaft. Eine revolutionäre Flugschrift aus dem deutschen Bauernkrieg (1525).* Leipzig.

Huizinga, J. 1955. *The Waning of the Middle Ages.* London.

1970. *Homo Ludens. A Study of the Play Element in Culture.* London.

Hupp, O. 1930. *Scheltbriefe und Schandbilder.* Munich.

Ivins, W.M. 1969. *Prints and Visual Communication.* Cambridge, Mass.

Jäckel, G. (ed.) 1975. *Kaiser, Gott und Bauer. Die Zeit der deutschen Bauernkrieg im Spiegel der Literatur.* Berlin.

Kalkoff, P. 1886. *Die Depeschen des Nuntius Aleander vom Wormser Reichstag.* Berlin.

1898. *Briefe, Depeschen und Berichte über Luther vom Wormser Reichstag 1521.* Halle.

Kawerau, G. (ed.) 1895. *Passional Christi und Antichristi. Lucas Cranach's Holzschnitte mit dem Texte von Melanchthon.* Berlin.

Kawerau, W. 1894. Johann Fritzehans. *Geschichtsblätter für Stadt und Land Magdeburg* 29,

Kelchner, E. (ed.) 1891. *Der Enndkrist der Stadt-Bibliothek zu Frankfurt am Main.* Frankfurt.

Kibisch, C.G. 1950. Lucas Cranach's Christ blessing the children. A problem of Lutheran iconography. *Art Bulletin* 37, 196–203.

Kieckhefer, R. 1976. *European Witch Trials. Their Foundations in Popular and Learned Culture, 1300–1500.* London.

Kirschbaum, E. 1968–76. *Lexikon der christlichen Ikonographie*, 8 vols. Freiburg.

Klersch, J. 1961. *Die kölnische Fastnacht von ihren Anfängen bis zur Gegenwart.* Cologne.

Klingner, E. 1912. *Luther und der deutsche Volksaberglaube.* Berlin.

Koegler, H. 1907. Das Mönchskalb vor Papst Hadrian und das Wiener Prognostikon. Zwei wiedergefundene Flugblätter aus dem Presse des Pamphilus Gegenbach in Basel. *Zeitschrift für Bücherfreunde* 11, 411–16.

Koepplin, D. and Falk, T. 1974–6. *Lucas Cranach. Gemälde, Zeichnungen, Druckgraphik*, 2 vols. Basel.

Kolve, V.A. 1966. *The Play called Corpus Christi.* London.

Korsgen-Wiedeburg, A. 1976. Das Bild Martin Luthers in den Flugschriften der frühen Reformationszeit. In *Festgabe für Ernst Walter Zeeden*, ed. H. Rabe *et al.* Münster.

Kretzenbacher, L. 1958. *Die Seelenwaage.* Klagenfurt.

Kriss-Rettenbach, L. 1963. *Bilder und Zeichen religiösen Volksglaubens.* Munich.

Kuck, E. (ed.) 1896. *Judas Nazarei, Von altem und neuen Gott, Glauben und Lehre.* Halle.

Künstle, K. 1926–8. *Ikonographie der christlichen Kunst*, 2 vols. Freiburg.

Kunzle, D. 1978. World upside-down. The iconography of a European broadsheet type. In *The Reversible World. Symbolic Inversion in Art and Society*, ed. B. Babcock, Ithaca and London.

Kürth, W. 1927. *Albrecht Dürer. Samtliche Holzschnitte.* Munich.

Lane, R.E. and Sears, D.O. 1964. *Public Opinion.* Engelwood Cliffs.

Lange, K. 1891. *Der Papstesel. Ein Beitrag zur Kultur- und Kunstgeschichte des Reformationszeitalters.* Göttingen.

Lascault, G. 1973. *Le monstre dans l'art occidental.* Paris.

Latendorf, F. 1876. *Sebastian Francks erste namenlose Sprichwörtersammlung vom Jahre 1532.* Poesneck.

Laube, A. *et al.* 1974. *Illustrierte Geschichte der deutschen frühbürgerliche Revolution.* Berlin.

Lefebvre, J. 1968. *Les fols et la folie.* Paris.

Leger, A. 1959. *Der gute Hirt.* Düsseldorf.

Lepp, F. 1908. *Schlagwörter der Reformation.* Leipzig.

Lienhard, M. 1978. Held oder Ungeheuer? Luthers Gestalt und Tat im Lichte der zeitgenossischen Flugschriftenliteratur. *Luther Jahrbuch* 45, 56–79.

Loescher, F.H. 1925. *Schule, Kirche und Obrigkeit im Reformationsjahrhundert.* Leipzig.

Lubecus, F. 1967. *Bericht über die Einführung der Reformation in Göttingen.* Göttingen.

Lüdecke, H. 1953. *Lukas Cranach der Ältere im Spiegel seiner Zeit.* Berlin.

Luther, J. 1909–13. *Die Titeleinfassung der Reformation-Zeit*, 3 vols. Leipzig.

Luther, M. 1883–1978. *D. Martin Luthers Werke. Kritische Gesamtausgabe.* Weimar.

McGinn, B. 1979. *Visions of the End. Apocalyptic Traditions in the Middle Ages.* New York.

McLuhan, M. 1973. *Understanding Media.* London.

Mandrou, R. 1975. *Introduction to Modern France 1500–1640.* London.

Masken 1967. Masken zwischen Spiel und Ernst. Beiträge des Tübinger Arbeitskreises fur Fasnachtsforschung. Tübingen.

Meier, K.E. 1909. Fortleben der religiös-dogmatischen Komposition Cranachs in der Kunst des Protestantismus. *Repertorium für Kunstwissenschaft* 32, 415–35.

Mentz, G. 1908. *Johann Friedrich der Grossmütige.* Jena.

Merker, P. (ed.) 1918. *Thomas Murner, Deutsch Schriften*, vol. 9: *Von dem grossen Lutherischen Narren.* Leipzig.

Meuche, H. (ed.) 1976. *Flugblätter der Reformation und des Bauernkrieges.* Leipzig.

Meyer, A.L. 1938. Die heilbringende Schau in Sitte und Kult. In *Heilige Überlieferung. Festschrift für I. Herwegen.* Münster.

Moeller, B. 1962. *Reichsstadt und Reformation.* Gütersloh.

1979. Stadt und Buch. In *Stadtbürgertum und Adel in der Reformation*, ed. W.J. Mommsen *et al.* Stuttgart.

Moser, H. 1955. Archivalisches zu Jahreslaufbräuchen der Oberpfalz, *Bayerisches Jahrbuch für Volkskunde.*

1964. Die Geschichte der Fasnacht im Spiegel von Archivforschungen. In *Fasnacht* 1964.

1967. Städtische Fasnacht des Mittelalters. In *Masken* 1967.

Mühlmann, W.E. 1961. *Chiliasmus und Nativismus.* Berlin.

Müller, G. (ed.) 1975. *Andreas Osiander d. Ältere. Gesamtausgabe*, vol. 1. Gütersloh.

Musper, H.T. 1970. *Der Antichrist und die fünfzehen Zeichen.* Munich.

Nagler, G.K. 1864. *Die Monogrammisten*, vol. 4. Munich.

Obelkevich, J. 1979. *Religion and the People 800–1700*. Chapel Hill.

Oesterreich, T.K. 1966. *Possession, Demonical and Other*. New York.

Ozment, S.E. 1975. *The Reformation in the Cities*. New Haven.

Panofsky, E. 1930. *Hercules am Scheideweg*. Leipzig.

1970. *Meaning in the Visual Arts*. London.

Pascal, P. (trans.) 1968. *The 'Julius Exclusus' of Erasmus*. London.

Passavant, J.D. 1860–4. *Le peintre-graveur*. Leipzig.

Perlbach, M. *et al.* (eds.) 1875. *Simon Grunaus preussische Chronik*, vol. 2. Leipzig.

Peuckert, W. 1948. *Die grosse Wende. Das apokalyptische Saeculum und Luther*. Hamburg.

Pfeiffer, G. (ed.) 1968. *Quellen zur Nürnberger Reformationsgeschichte*. Nuremberg.

Phythian-Adams, C. 1972. Ceremony and the citizen: the communal year in Coventry 1450–1550. In *Crisis and Order in English Towns 1500–1700*, ed. P. Clark & P. Slack. London.

Praschinger, I. 1950. *Beiträge zur Flugschriftenliteratur der Reformation und Gegenreformation in Wien und dem Lande Oesterreich unter der Enns*, Ph.D. thesis, typescript. Vienna.

Preuss, H. 1906. *Die Vorstellung vom Antichrist im späteren Mittelalter, bei Luther und in der konfessionellen Polemik.*

1926. *Die deutsch Frömmigkeit im Spiegel der bildenden Kunst*. Berlin.

1933. *Martin Luther der Prophet*. Gütersloh.

Radbruch, R.M. 1961. *Der deutsche Bauernstand zwischen Mittelalter und Neuzeit*. Göttingen.

Radice, B. (trans.) 1971. *D. Erasmus. Praise of Folly*. London.

Rauh, H.D. 1973. *Das Bild des Antichrist im Mittelalter*. Münster.

Réau, L. 1956–9. *Iconographie de l'art chrétien*, 3 vols. Paris.

Reeves, M. 1969. *The Influence of Prophecy in the Later Middle Ages*. Oxford.

Ritter, A. 1923. *Collectio Vaticiniorum, das ist, Propheceien und Weissagungen*. Berlin.

Roller, H.-U. 1965. *Der Nürnberger Schembartlauf*. Tübingen.

Roos, K.L. 1972. *The Devil in 16th Century German Literature: the Teufelsbücher*. Bern & Frankfurt.

Rosenberg, J. 1960. *Die Zeichnungen Lucas Cranachs des Älteren*. Berlin.

Röttinger, H. 1916. *Peter Flettners Holzschnitte*. Strassburg.

1921. *Beiträge zur Geschichte des sächsischen Holzschnittes*. Strassburg.

1925. *Erhard Schön und Niklas Stör, der Pseudo-Schön*. Strassburg.

1927. *Die Bilderbogen des Hans Sachs*. Strassburg.

Sach, A. 1891. *Deutsches Leben in der Vergangenheit*, vol. 2. Halle.

Saussure, F. de 1966. *General Course in Linguistics*. New York.

Saxl, F. 1957. *Lectures*, vol. 1. London.

Schade, O. 1856–8. *Satiren und Pasquillen aus der Reformationszeit*, 3 vols. Hannover.

Scharfe, S. 1951. 'Religiöse Bildpropaganda der Reformationszeit', typescript. Göttingen.

Schiller, G. 1966–74. *Ikonographie der christlichen Kunst*, 4 vols. Gütersloh.

1971–2. *Iconography of Christian Art*, 2 vols. London.

Schmidt, H. 1929. *Bilder-Katalog zu Max Geisberg 'Der deutsche Einblatt-Holzschnitt'*. Munich.

Schmidt, P. 1962. *Die Illustration der Lutherbibel 1522 bis 1700*. Basel.

Schmidtke, D. 1968. *Geistliche Tierinterpretation in der deutschsprachigen Literatur des Mittelalters*. Berlin.

Schmitt, O. (ed.) 1937–73. *Reallexikon fur deutsche Kunstgeschichte*, 6 vols. Stuttgart.

Schofield, R. 1968. The measurement of literacy in pre-industrial England. In Goody, J. (ed.). *Literacy in Traditional Societies*. Cambridge.

Schönherr, D. (ed.) 1867. *Franz Schweygers Chronik der Stadt Hall (in Tyrol) 1303–1572*. Innsbruck.

Short-title Catalogue 1962. *Short-title Catalogue of Books Printed in the German-speaking Countries . . . from 1455 to 1600 now in the British Museum*. London.

Schottenloher, K. 1912. Denkwürdige Reformationsdrucke mit dem Bilde Luthers. *Zeitschrift für Bücherfreunde* 4, 221–31.

1922. *Flugblatt und Zeitung*. Berlin.

Schramm, A. 1923. *Die Illustration der Lutherbibel*. Leipzig.

Schreckenbach, P. and Neubert, F. 1916. *Martin Luther. Ein Bild seines Lebens und Werkens*. Leipzig.

Schütte, J. 1973. *'Schympffred'. Frühformen bürgerlicher Agitation in Thomas Murners 'Grossen Lutherischen Narren' (1522)*. Stuttgart.

Scribner, R. 1978. Reformation, carnival and the world turned upside-down. *Social History* 3, 303–29.

1980. Practice and principle in the German towns: preachers and people. In *Reformation Principle and Practice – Essays presented to A.G. Dickens*, ed. P.N. Brooks. London.

Sleumer, A. 1926. *Kirchenlateinisches Wörterbuch*. Limburg/Lahn.

Spamer, A. 1930. *Das kleine Andachtsbild vom 14.–20. Jht.* Munich.

Stirm, M. 1977. *Die Bilderfrage in der Reformation*. Gütersloh.

Stone, L. 1969. Literacy and education in England 1640–1900. *Past & Present* 42, 69–139.

Strauss, G. 1978. *Luther's House of Learning. The Indoctrination of the Young in the German Reformation*. Baltimore & London.

Strauss, H.A. 1926. *Der astrologische Gedanke in der deutschen Vergangenheit*. Munich.

Strauss, W.L. 1974. *The German Illustrated Broadsheet 1500–1550*, 4 vols. New York.

1975. *The German Single-leaf Woodcut 1550–1600*, 3 vols. New York.

Stuhlfauth, G. 1918. Drei zeitgeschichtliche Flugblätter des Hans Sachs mit Holzschnitten des Georg Pencz. *Zeitschrift für Bücherfreunde*, Neue Folge 10, 237–48.

1919. Das Haus des weisen und das Haus des unweisen Mannes, Math. 7. *Zeitschrift für Bücherfreunde*, Neue Folge 11, 1–9.

1920. Neue Beiträge zur sächsischen Holzschnitte. *Zeitschrift für Bücherfreunde*, Neue Folge 11/ii, 200–2.

1921a. Die beiden Holzschnitte der Flugschrift 'Triumphis veritatis' von H.H. Feiermut. *Zeitschrift für Bücherfreunde*, Neue Folge 13, 49–56.

1921b. Älteste Bildnisse Luthers. *Die christliche Welt* 35, 129–31.

1940. Neuschöpfung christlicher Sinnbilder. In *Brauch und Sinnbild. Eugen Fehrle zum 60. Geburtstag*. Karlsruhe.

Sumberg, S.L. 1941. *The Nuremberg Schembart Carnival*. New York.

Theobald, L. 1936. *Reformationsgeschichte der Reichsstadt Regensburg*. Nuremberg.

Thieme, U. and Becker, F. 1907–50. *Allgemeines Lexikon der bildenen Kunstler*, 37 vols. Leipzig.

Thomas, A. 1936. *Die Darstellung Christi im Kelter. Eine theologische und kultur-historische Studie*. Düsseldorf.

Thomas, K. 1973. *Religion and the Decline of Magic*. Harmondsworth.

Thompson. C.R. (trans.) 1965. *The Colloquies of Erasmus*. Chicago.

Thompson, E.P. 1973. Patrician society, plebeian culture. *Journal of Social History* 7, 382–405.

Thorndike, L. 1934, 1941. *A History of Magic and Experimental Science*, vols. 4–5. New York.

Thulin, O. 1955. *Cranach-Altäre der Reformation*. Berlin.

1958. Die Reformatoren im Weinberg des Herrn. Ein Gemälde Lucas Cranachs des Jungeren. *Luther Jahrbuch* 25, 141–5.

Tompert, H. 1978. Die Flugschrift als Medium religiöser Publizistik. In *Kontinuität und Umbruch. Theologie und Frömmigkeit in Flugschriften und Kleinliteratur an der Wende vom 15. bis 16. Jht.*, ed. J. Nolte *et al.* Stuttgart.

Toussaert, J. 1963. *Le sentiment religieux en Flandre a la fin du moyen age*. Paris.

Träger, J. 1970. *Der reitende Papst*. Munich.

Trexler, R.C. 1972. Florentine religious experience: the sacred image. *Studies in the Renaissance* 19, 7–41.

1974. Ritual in Florence: adolescence and salvation in the Renaissance. In *The Pursuit of Holiness in Late Medieval and Renaissance Religion*, ed. C. Trinkaus & H.A. Oberman. Leiden.

Turner, V. 1978. *Image and Pilgrimage in Christian Culture*. Oxford.

Uhrig, K. 1936. Der Bauer in der Publizistik der Reformation bis zum Ausgang des Bauernkrieges. *Archiv für Reformationsgeschichte* 33, 70–125, 165–225.

Vetter, E.M. 1969. 'Sant peters schifflin'. *Kunst in Hessen und am Mittelrhein* 9, 7–23.

1971. Das allegorische Relief Peter Dells d. Ä. im Germanischen Nationalmuseum. In *Festschrift H. Ladendorf*. Cologne & Graz.

Völker, K. 1977. *Papstin Johanna*. Berlin.

Wackernagel, W. 1872. *Kleinere Schriften*, vol. 1. Leipzig.

Wadstein, E. 1896. *Die eschatologische Ideengruppe. Antichrist–Weltsabbat–Weltende und Weltgericht*. Leipzig.

Wäscher, H. 1955. *Das deutsche illustrierte Flugblatt*. Dresden.

Wagner, A. 1896. Mathias Gerung. Eine kunstgeschichtliche Studie. *Jahrbuch des historischen Vereins zu Dillingen* 9, 69–106.

Walzer, A. 1967. Tierkopfmasken in Bild und Brauch. In *Masken* 1967.

Wander, K.F.W. 1867–80. *Deutsches Sprichwörter-Lexikon*, 5 vols. Leipzig.

Warburg, A. 1919. Heidnisch-antike Weissagung in Wort und Bild zu Luthers Zeit. *Sitzungsberichte der Heidelberger Akademie der Wissenschaften*. Heidelberg.

Weber, M. 1964. *The Theory of Social and Economic Organisation*. London.

1965. *The Sociology of Religion*. London.

Weckwerth, A. 1960. Christus in der Kelter. Ursprung und Wandlung eines Bildmotives. In *Beiträge zur Kunstgeschichte. Festschrift fur H.R. Rosemann*. Munich.

Weinhold. K. 1892. Glücksrad und Lebensrad. *Abhandlungen der Berliner Akademie der Wissenschaften*. Berlin.

Weinstein, D. 1970. *Savanarola and Florence*. Princeton.

Weller, E. 1862. Die Lieder gegen das Interim. *Serapeum* 23, 289–97.

Wickiana 1975. *Die Wickiana. Johann Jakob Wicks Nachrichtensammlung aus dem 16. Jht.* Zurich.

Wirth, K.A. 1963. Imperator pedes papae deosculator. In *Festschrift für Harald Keller*. Darmstadt.

Wolf, J. 1925. Ein bisher unbekannter Spottdruck auf das Augsburger Interim. *Zentralblatt für Bibliothekswesen* 42.

Wollen, P. 1974. *Signs and Meaning in the Cinema*. London.

Worsley, P. 1968. *The Trumpet Shall Sound*. London.

Wuttke, D. 1974. Sebastian Brants Verhältnis zu Wunderdeutung und Astrologie. In *Studien zur deutschen Literatur und Sprache des Mittelalters. Festschrift für Hugo Moser*, ed. W. Besch. Berlin.

Wuttke, D. 1976a. Wunderdeutung und Politik. Zu den Auslegungen der sog. Wormser Zwillinge des Jahres 1495. In *Landesgeschichte und Geistesgeschichte. Festschrift für Otto Herding*. Stuttgart.

     1976b. Sebastian Brant and Maximilian I. Eine Studie zu Brants Donnerstein-Flugblatt des Jahres 1492. In *Die Humanisten in ihrer politischen und sozialen Umwelt*, ed. O. Herding and R. Stupperich. Boppard.

Yates, F.A. 1969. *The Art of Memory*. Harmondsworth.

Zimmermann, H. 1927. Holzschnitte und Plattenstempel mit dem Bilde Luthers und ihre Beziehung zur Werkstatt Cranachs. *Jahrbuch der Einbandkunst* 1, 112–21.

Zink, F. 1968. *Die deutschen Handzeichnungen des Germanischen Nationalmuseum*. Nuremberg.

Zschelletzschky, H. 1975. *Die 'drei gottlose Maler' von Nürnberg*. Leipzig.

INDEX